3 pounds each!

by Cathy Guisewite

Selected Cartoons from
A HAND TO HOLD, AN OPINION TO REJECT
Volume 2

FAWCETT CREST • NEW YORK

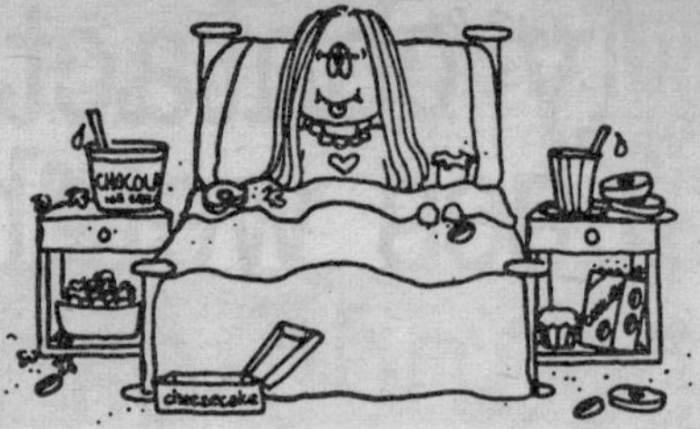
cheesecake

Cathy ® is syndicated internationally by Universal Press Syndicate.

A Fawcett Crest Book
Published by Ballantine Books

Library of Congress Catalog Card Number: 88-92987

ISBN 0-449-21635-7

This book comprises a portion of A HAND TO HOLD, AN OPINION TO REJECT and is reprinted by arrangement with Andrews and McMeel, Inc., a Universal Press Syndicate Affiliate.

Manufactured in the United States of America

First Ballantine Books Edition: May 1989

flight. The women and children and old men jeered the survivors and mourned the dead with a great and depressing noise. All the villages of that region suffered hunger, for the fishing and hunting had been long neglected.

Scarcely had they settled in their lodges again, humbled and sad, before Wise-as-a-she-wolf appeared among them, and unseated the remaining chiefs and set others in authority. After which, seeing that their vanity was broken, he drove a herd of caribou close to their village, that they might have food with which to support their lives while they mended their ways. He made medicines for the sick among the women and children and old men, and gave healing salves to some of the wounded warriors. Then he left them, and flew upon his magic moccasins to quell other clans and still the fighting in every quarter of the island. In some cases he punished and in others he showed mercy, always reading the hearts of the people. So, in a few days, he had brought the island to peace again and struck all the evil counsellors, save Bright Robe, with his wrath.

But Bright Robe he could not find, though he heard from many that he had been in the country,

urging the clans to warfare and flying through the air like a bird.

So he knew that the red feathers were in the possession of his rival again, and vowed to his heart that he would seek him over the length and breadth of the world.

CHAPTER XXVI

BRIGHT ROBE'S DISCRETION

WHILE Bright Robe was yet a little brown owl, watching the pine tree in which he had hidden the red feathers, far away in the Land of Giants, old Whispering Grass had gathered her herbs and roots together, and gone down into a valley where some families of her own kin had built themselves a village. Little Heron, the chief of this village, was her grandson. He was a quiet man, of a good heart and contented mind, and he received the old medicine-woman with warmth and respect, and gave her a fine lodge in which to brew her doses and dream her ancient dreams.

"I am an old woman now," Whispering Grass had told him, on the day of her arrival, "and my blood has so little of glow in it that the winds on the mountain shake me with the fear of death. Also, it is hard for me to travel in the forests and gather the leaves and roots, and the very cooking of food has become a weariness. So I have

crawled from my lonely house, with much labour and pain, to this warm valley, that I may teach my knowledge of curing human ills to some one who will live many years. And I want to die warm, with women of my own clan beside me, and a bright fire before the doorway of the lodge."

Little Heron and his people treated the old woman with kindness and respect. Her lodge was warm with the pelts of animals, and all her food was cooked for her by the wife of the chief. Little children came about her, to hear the wonderful stories that were half of memory and half of invention. And to several of the young women of the village she taught all that she knew of the science of medicine. One day she told Little Heron the story of the battle between Wise-as-a-she-wolf and Bright Robe, and of how Bright Robe had been stripped of his powers for five seasons, and turned into the shape of a little owl, by the good magician. She told of Bright Robe's hate of her, and of her fear that he should seek her and kill her when his evil power was returned to him.

For a winter and a summer she lived in peace and comfort with her kinsfolk; and before she died she warned Little Heron once more against

Bright Robe, and gave to Star Flower, the chief's little daughter, a whistle made of willow, small and wrinkled; and with her last breath she told the child the virtue of the whistle.

When the clans were rising on every side, the strong to raid, and the weaker to defend their homes, Little Heron remained quietly in his valley and told his people that warfare was more dangerous than any form of labour and utterly without profit to the greatest warriors. His people listened and nodded their heads, for they believed Little Heron to be one of the wisest men in the world. Later, when a fugitive from some distant battle staggered into their valley and told them of the bloodshed and ruin, and of the evil advice of Bright Robe, they were doubly convinced of their chief's wisdom. And the women who had learned the science of medicine from Whispering Grass, cured the stranger of his hurts; and he, poor warrior, was so charmed with the treatment and the quiet, that he married one of his doctors and became a member of Little Heron's village. That was wise of him, for even while he lay sick of his wounds the lodges of his own people were blazing like a hundred torches.

Though the horrors of war passed by the village

in the secluded valley, Bright Robe found his way to it. And this was the manner of his coming and his going. As soon as the fighting was well commenced and every man slaying or being slain, robbing or being robbed, in a satisfactory manner, the evil magician retired to secluded places, and desisted from flying above the tree-tops, except at night, for fear of Wise-as-a-she-wolf, of whose whereabouts he knew nothing. While he skulked about, trying to decide upon some plan of action, he remembered his old grudge against Whispering Grass. So he made his way straight to the little clearing on the mountain, the scene of his ignoble defeat five seasons before. But he found nothing but an empty lodge with tattered sides and rotted poles. Moss was creeping over the floor of beaten earth, and the thousand little fires at which the old woman had brewed her medicines were covered with forest growth.

" Death has cheated me of my revenge," reflected Bright Robe.

Wandering aimlessly about, he happened upon the valley in which dwelt the peace-loving Little Heron and his contented people. Here, perhaps, he could rest for awhile in safety and make trouble before stealing away. It looked, to his wicked

eye, like a place sadly in need of trouble. He descended into the valley and the cluster of lodges, and was met by the chief.

" I am a poor hunter, who lived alone beside the River of the Beavers," he said. " Six nights ago I was attacked by a party of fighting men, and fled for my life. Ever since then I have wandered, homeless. My lodge is flat on the ground and my stores and furs are stolen."

Little Heron gazed at the evil black eyes of the stranger, and, remembering Whispering Grass's descriptions of Bright Robe, knew him for the evil magician. He showed nothing of this in face or manner, but invited the stranger into his lodge and called for food of the best to be brought, and a little of the liquor of crushed berries. Bright Robe ate and drank with zest, and in his heart chuckled at the simplicity of Little Heron. He glanced about him with his keen eyes, noting every sign of peace and prosperity with delight.

" What a change shall be here, in the space of a few days," he thought, and forcing a smile, congratulated the chief on his good food and comfortable condition.

" The war has not touched you," he said. " You are fortunate, chief; for here am I, a lover of

peace and honesty, ruined and a fugitive. The gods are blind when the strong clans go forth with their war-shields. If one does not kill, then must he be killed, or else run away."

" You speak truth," replied Little Heron, as he removed a broiled snipe from the fire and placed it before his guest. " When the clans go to war, urged on by the lust in their blood and the evil tongues of wicked magicians, then 'tis a sad time for the peaceful and honest. But this is a small village, well hidden, and far from the great chief's, and my people are a quiet, home-staying folk. And having escaped for so long, I have nothing to fear, for Wise-as-a-she-wolf, the good magician, who visited me seven nights ago, and promised to come again in eight days' time, which will be to-morrow, will soon quiet the fighting. He is also in quest of a magician called Bright Robe."

The stranger glanced furtively at his imaginative host; but in the face of Little Heron there was nothing to be read but simplicity and contentment.

" I have heard of that great magician, Wise-as-a-she-wolf, and shall remain with you, if you will keep me, to enjoy the honour of seeing him," replied Bright Robe. But his appetite was gone,

and he ate very little of the snipe. In spite of his power of dissembling, he showed considerable uneasiness during the afternoon; and Little Heron was quick to note it. When the men gathered together, in the evening, to tell stories of past adventures, Bright Robe had little to say. Pleading weariness, he retired early to a lodge courteously placed at his disposal by the chief. In the morning, much to the wonder of the villagers, the lodge was empty. But when they ran to Little Heron with the news, that great chief smiled knowingly.

"The stranger was Bright Robe, the evil magician," he said, calmly. "I knew him; so I had to warn him to pass on."

Bright Robe flew from the village in the secluded valley as soon as every one had retired and the lodges were quiet, and raced westward at his best speed. The island of his birth was no place for him while Wise-as-a-she-wolf was stirring about. He knew that another meeting with his powerful rival could mean nothing but five seasons more of undignified retirement for him, to say nothing of the painful wounds which he would be sure to receive before he was reduced to submission. Without his silver robe, he knew that he

could not hide for long from the keen-eyed, invisible Wise-as-a-she-wolf. So he flew westward across the darkness, determined to remain in the far places of the earth until he had acquired sufficient strength to return and overthrow his rival. He crossed the Narrow Sea, and before dawn was at the edge of a village of the mountaineers.

CHAPTER XXVII

THE DIPLOMACY OF BRIGHT ROBE

BRIGHT ROBE was well aware that, until his power should be as great as his rival's, or the quest of the red feathers should be forgotten, he must practise every precaution to avoid attracting that magician's attention afresh, must move artfully, and play a part in life for which, by nature, he was but ill-suited. His old, arrogant tactics must be forsworn, or at least amended, for with Wise-as-a-she-wolf on his trail he must needs have a following of loyal men who would give no information concerning him. He knew that his enemy would seek him everywhere; so he sat down in the woods, at the edge of the village of mountaineers, and devoted several hours to thought. He decided that the mountaineers, a strong, clannish nation, should be honoured by his patronage and used like tools, to his purpose. He had never had much to do with these people, and if they knew anything of his true nature, it

was only by hearsay. He would use all his magic
to the advancement of their prosperity, even as
his enemy did for the islanders. And he dreamed
that the time was not far off (as time is calculated
by magicians) when he should use these mountaineers as a weapon against his enemy.

He did not appear immediately to the people
whom he had chosen to shape to the fulfilment of
his plans, but waited until nightfall, and then
flew northward, hundreds of miles beyond the
knowledge of the mountaineers, and descended
upon a village of the fat folk who eat raw flesh.
He increased his stature to seven times that of
the human body, and thus struck terror into the
hearts of the blubber-eaters. They offered him
their wealth of ivory and furs if he would but
leave them in peace.

" My name is Bright Robe," said he, in reply
to their abject cries. " I do not want your ivory
or walrus tusks, nor yet all your furs. But bring
me your best robes, for I am going to my great lodge
of ice, seven suns' journey to the northward,
where the cold is so sharp that no animal can live
save the great white wolves."

From their stores he selected a score of robes
of the finest black fox skins, and a few great pelts

of musk-ox, and white bear. Then, having the
furs which he had chosen placed in a heap, he
reduced them to within a portable compass with
his magic, lifted them to the hollow of his arm,
and sprang into the air. He flew due north; and
the blubber-eaters stared after him, in silence
and sorrow, until he vanished from their sight.

Beyond the range of vision of the blubber-
eaters, Bright Robe altered his course. This
talk of his lodge of ice, and this northward flight,
were but moves in his new game. By sunrise
of the next morning he was in the largest village
of the mountaineers, standing before the tent of
the head chief. This chief was no other than
Black Eagle, from whom Wise-as-a-she-wolf had
once asked for information concerning the flight
of Spotted Seal, the warrior who had stolen the
red feathers from the lodge of Run-all-day. The
dogs advanced upon Bright Robe even as they
had upon his rival, on a former occasion; but they
soon fell back, and slunk away, before the glance
of his eyes. He threw the little bundle, which he
had brought from the north, to the ground in front
of Black Eagle's lodge. He passed his hand above
it, and muttered a few swift words, and there
lay the twenty robes of fox skin and the other

pelts. Then he called upon the chief, by name.

Black Eagle looked cautiously from his lodge, and stared in wonder at the stranger and the great pile of furs.

" I am Bright Robe," said the magician, " and behold I have brought you a gift of great price, to show my friendship for you and your people."

At that, Black Eagle eyed him suspiciously.

" Why do you make me such a gift? " he asked. " I have done you no service. What is it you want of me? For I know that it is not for nothing that you lay all these skins of the black fox in front of my door."

" I shall be honest with you, chief," replied Bright Robe. " I could not deceive so shrewd a man as you, even if it were in my heart to do so. I bring you this gift of furs, all stitched into broad robes, and shall make you other gifts, hoping that you will do me a favour. Let me enter your lodge and talk with you, and you will be glad of my coming."

" That may be as it proves," replied Black Eagle, drily. " The proof of the good hunt is in the cooking-pot. The best magician who honoured me with a visit, nearly broke the head

of one of my strongest warriors. And he — he was known, far and wide, as a gentle magician."

" And what was his name? " inquired Bright Robe.

" Wise-as-a-she-wolf," replied the chief. He noted the look of surprise on the other's face, and added the information that the warrior had angered the magician by hurling a spear at him. But by then Bright Robe was shaking his head mournfully.

" He is bloodthirsty at heart," he said. " I have known it for a long time. But let me into your lodge, chief, for I have a long story to tell you."

Black Eagle hesitated, and eyed his visitor uneasily, for he did not relish the thought of a private interview with him.

" My chiefs will be offended if they are not called to hear your talk. They are like children, in such matters," he said.

" You do not trust me," said Bright Robe, sadly. " But I trust you," he added, " so you may call your leading warriors to hear what I have to say."

Black Eagle lost no time in summoning the more important men of the village to his lodge.

They gathered swiftly, armed with spears and clubs and looking even more savage than their dogs.

Bright Robe, pretending to be quite unnerved by the sight of their weapons, pointed to the heap of furs, and then, very modestly, told the story of his fear of Wise-as-a-she-wolf, and of his wish to take shelter with the strong warriors of the mountains. He explained that he did not ask them to defend him with their weapons, or run any risk on his behalf, but only to hide all knowledge of him from Wise-as-a-she-wolf, or any stranger; and in return for this service he promised to supply their chief village with all the food and fur required by its people.

The mountaineers considered the matter with wise and lengthy deliberation. They examined the furs which lay before the lodge, and questioned the magician as to where he had obtained them. He told them how he had robbed the blubber-eaters, miles and miles to the northward, only a few hours before.

" I tell you the truth because I trust you, because you are my friends," he said. " But the day will surely come, and perhaps it will be very soon, when Wise-as-a-she-wolf will see these skins

and ask you the same question which you have asked me. Then you must say that they are of your own killing."

"But he would not believe us," said Black Eagle, "for the great white bear and the musk-ox are not of this country. In the old days we sometimes obtained such skins, in small numbers, from the fat people. But now we have no dealings with them. And Wise-as-a-she-wolf knows all these things as I know the taste of deer-meat."

"Say you so," cried Bright Robe. "Then behold, they are all the skins of little foxes." And so they were, in the flash of an eye.

"We hear you, and we see," said an old warrior. "The ears of questioners shall be filled with lies, according to your wish. But why do you fear this other magician, you who are such a great magic-maker, and can travel so fast and so far? Could you not change him into a fox skin, as you have just done to these pelts of bear and musk-ox?"

"He is stronger than I, and his speed is even greater than mine. Also, he can make himself invisible as the wind," replied Bright Robe, truthfully.

"We know that. He did it before our eyes," said Black Eagle. And all the others nodded their

heads in agreement. At last it was decided that
Bright Robe should be given a home in the tribe,
and such protection as lies and pretended igno-
rance could furnish, in return for a generous
supply of food and furs. They led him up the
mountain-side, and showed him a cave, the mouth
of which was hidden by climbing bushes. The
magician examined it, and thankfully accepted
it as his home, until such time as he should be in
a position to choose a better. The chief was
about to order a man to bring robes and food to
the cave, but the magician laughed and shook
his head.

" I mean to fly abroad to-night, to gather six
days' food for the village, so I shall furnish this
place at the same time," he explained. " Now
I must rest," he added, anxious to get the warriors away from the mouth of the cave; for a chill-
ing fear that his great enemy might be somewhere
near, alert to note anything unusual, was on his
heart. So Black Eagle returned to the village
with his followers, and Bright Robe crawled
deep into his cave and began a minute ex-
amination of it. He was not entirely satisfied
with the result of the investigation, for the cave
was nothing but a tunnel, nowhere of more

than half the height of a man, and of a width scarcely more generous. It sloped gently downward, and ended in a natural wall of the mountain's rib.

"A very fine trap," remarked the magician, "and I am playing too unproved a part to risk living in a trap. There might be disagreements," he continued. "Then a good fire at the mouth of the cave would make it very uncomfortable, even for me — if I happened to be at home."

He found bones scattered about, and decided that many wolves had denned there in the past. He lay down on his back, placed his feet against the end of the tunnel, and anchored himself to the rocky sides, by the grip of his hands. Then, with a word, his strength was increased twentyfold, though his stature remained normal. He thrust tentatively with his feet. He pushed harder; and harder yet; and at the third effort he felt the rock shift a little. At that, he rested from his work long enough to test the roof and walls, to make sure that they, also, were not giving way. Lying flat again, he applied his feet to what he now knew to be an unattached mass of rock, and pushed slowly but steadily, and a shower of earth and small stones rattled down upon his

feet and legs. He drew himself forward, took a fresh grip with his hands on the sides of the tunnel, and unbent all his strength in a last, sudden thrust. Outward flew the mass of earth-bound rock, bigger than the lodge of Black Eagle, and rolled downward for a short distance, leaving behind it a jagged hole through which entered a glow of shaded daylight.

Bright Robe cleared the earth from his person and looked cautiously out from the hole which he had just kicked in the mountain. Already his magic strength had faded out of his muscles and bones, for he had not the power to command it for long at a time. He saw before him a deep, narrow valley of the mountains, and steep, wooded slopes rising on all sides. A few yards below him lay the great mass of rock which he had dislodged from its resting-place of centuries. No living thing was in sight, except a hawk perched in a tree-top half-way up the western slope of the valley. Black Eagle's village lay to the eastward, on the other side of the ridge through which Bright Robe had crawled, by way of the cave. The magician viewed the result of his labour with grim satisfaction.

" I like a lodge with two doorways," he said.

" But it is as well that my friends should have a knowledge of one only."

He saw that the rock which he had rolled into the valley might attract attention of any chance wanderer on the mountain sides, or, worse still, of any one flying in the air. Fresh earth still clung to it, in patches, and it had cut a deep gash in the moss and soil of the valley. It was altogether too evident for his liking. So he crawled from the back-door of the cave, worked such magic on the great boulder as to reduce it to the dimensions of a pebble, and hurled it over the western wall. Then he repaired the damages suffered by the moss and young trees, bent a few spruces from their places so that they hid the unnatural hole in the mountain, and retired.

Bright Robe spent the early part of the night in spying upon his allies. He lay hidden in a clump of bushes close to their evening fire, and listened to their talk; but, though he heard many things that made his ears tingle, they were planning no treachery against him. At last he crawled away, and flew westward and northward, beyond the giant's country, and robbed a camp of fishermen of all the fruits of their toil. He found some pemmican and a few furs, which he kept for him-

self.   When the mountaineers awoke next morning and discovered the great store of fish, they were well pleased with the bargain they had made.

CHAPTER XXVIII

THE QUEST

HAVING restored peace to his beloved islanders, Wise-as-a-she-wolf allowed Featherfoot to return to his father, and devoted himself to the search for the red feathers. He questioned every inhabitant of every village in the island, and beat every grove for his cunning enemy. He investigated the mountains and the rocky coasts, and scanned every foot of the barrens; but not a sign of Bright Robe rewarded him. But from Little Heron, he learned of the fugitive's visit to the secluded valley, and of his furtive departure in the night. Assured that he was no longer in the island, he crossed the Narrow Sea, and repeated the question which he had put to Black Eagle once before, when on the trail of Spotted Seal. And Black Eagle made the same answer. " I saw a man flying over the mountains, ten days ago, toward the land of the giants," he said.

" Have you not yet caught the warrior who stole the magic feathers? " he asked.

But the good magician had no time to spend in replying to foolish and impertinent questions. In a second he was high above the village again, speeding toward the black places where the giants lived their sullen and stupid lives. He found Stone Hand squatting before the entrance of his mound-like lodge, and questioned him from a distance. But it happened that the chief of the giants was in even a worse temper than usual, for he had but just eaten too largely of bear meat that was not very fresh.

" Who asks me questions," he cried, " disturbing me when I am in pain? Show yourself, whoever you are."

The good magician showed himself at a safe distance from the disgruntled giant. " I am Wise-as-a-she-wolf," he said, and again asked if anything had been seen of Bright Robe, or of a man flying in the air.

" I know nothing of such things, save that Crack Bone once thought he could fly like a little bird," growled the giant. " And it did him no good," he added, with a grunt of laughter.

The magician could read nothing in that hairy,

dirty, lowering face. The skull was too thick to allow the workings of the little brain to affect the glassy eyes. But his suspicions were aroused. " You are encased in stupidity like a seal in blubber," said he, and vanished from the giant's indifferent sight. But he did not go away. For three days he continued in the vicinity of the giants' village, listened to their infrequent talk without learning anything, and examined at one time or another, the interior of every lodge. This led to nothing, however, and he was forced to confess to himself that he had mistaken the giant's stupidity and ill-temper for an intelligent and preconceived attempt to evade his questions.

So he left the giants and travelled northward. In the Land of Little Sticks he searched the camps of lonely hunters, but found no trace of Bright Robe. Passing on, he reached the land of the blubber-eaters, where the streams and lakes were already frozen. At last he happened upon the village which his enemy had so recently visited, and from which he had taken the furs. On learning what these people had to tell him, he set out for the land of eternal winter, and for Bright Robe's lodge of ice.

For the time of two days and nights (though

the sky changed not) Wise-as-a-she-wolf ran straight on the frozen air, between the white fields and the ruddy north-lights. He was clothed in many garments of fur, for well did he know the cold of those regions, where only the great white wolves, that are the care of the northern gods, can live. He had brought food, and he ate as he ran. The north-lights shook and clashed before him and above him, blew like flame to right and left and came crackling back again. He heard the hunting-cries of the white wolves, as they ran on a mad, age-old trail, the scent of which was nowhere but in their own blind souls. And when they passed beneath him, white as frost and death, he sprang upward between the curtains of the north-lights.

He came to the wall of ice, beyond which live the four gods of the north; and yet he had seen nothing of Bright Robe or his lodge. He did not cross the wall, for he felt that his enemy was in no position to court the attention of the gods; and the cold gnawed him, and was like the hand of death against his heart, so he turned and sped southward. Again he hunted through the lands of the little fat men with smoky faces, and among the lonely hunters, and westward even to the

tribes who wear crests of feathers that hang down their backs as far as their belts, and whose numbers are as a thousand times the numbers of the islanders. Then his suspicions of the giants awoke again, and he returned to their country and watched them narrowly. For three days he studied them, and though he learned much of their savage natures and huge appetites, he saw no signs of Bright Robe and nothing to indicate that they knew anything of that vanished magician.

Again Wise-as-a-she-wolf visited Black Eagle; and now he sat in the big lodge, and had the warriors brought together, to hear his talk. And while he sat among the great men of the tribe, a lad stole up to the cave and warned Bright Robe that his enemy was in the village. So Bright Robe, from well within the cave, lightened a great rock that lay without with his magic, and then told the lad to place it in the entrance, so that the cave would be hidden. The boy did as he was told, and lifted the great stone into the mouth of the cave, much to his own amazement. Then he went back to the village, thinking himself a great magician. From within, Bright Robe returned its weight to the stone, and it filled the mouth of

the cave as if it were a part of the everlasting foundation of the mountain. Then he retired by the back way, flew over the western cliff, and hid himself among tumbled granite boulders and clumps of spruce-tuck.

Wise-as-a-she-wolf, seated at his ease in the chief's lodge, with the savage warriors around him, took note of many things.

" Those are fine robes of fox-skins," said he, with his glance on one of the articles of the fugitive magician's gift.

" My people are great hunters," replied Black Eagle, calmly.

" And how is it that you are not hunting to-day? " he asked, having seen all the warriors lolling about the village.

" The mighty Wise One is interested in his humble servants," remarked Black Eagle, staring haughtily at his unwelcome visitor.

Wise-as-a-she-wolf nodded, and met the other's gaze with severe eyes.

" Then it will grieve the Wise One to hear that our storehouses are well supplied with food of other people's killing and curing," said the chief. " The good magician is a lover of peace; but we are fighting-men. And we make war when we

please, and when the hunting is poor we take what we want from lesser tribes."

He spoke threateningly, and all his warriors glared at the quiet youth in their midst, and laid their hands on their weapons. But Wise-as-a-she-wolf lost nothing of his habitual composure.

"As you are not of my people," he said, "it is no affair of mine how you fight, or how you fill your storehouses, so long as you do not slay or rob the clans of the island. In this matter of answering harmless questions, however, I must beg you to assume a gentler manner. Though I am a hater of bloodshed and quick to forgive injury, yet I am sometimes moved to sudden wrath."

"My manners were never of the best, great chief," replied Black Eagle, cowed by the other's hinted threat. "I am sorry that you are displeased with me and my people, for I am ignorant of neither your power nor virtue."

"You speak fairly," replied the good magician; "and I ask no more of the chief of a savage and deceitful race. I have given my life's work to my own people, and still the blood-thirst and greed are strong in many of their hearts. I could do

nothing inside the space of an hundred seasons to mend your ways save by slaying you, and I am not a god, to judge if you are worthy to live or not."

"You speak rashly, even for a mighty magician," said one of the warriors. "Here we sit around you, with our hands on our weapons, and yet you insult us at your pleasure."

"I fear your weapons no more than twigs in the hands of children," replied Wise-as-a-she-wolf, calmly. "But throw a club, or draw a knife, and your doom is upon you."

The warriors glanced at one another, impressed by their visitor's manner and voice, and yet doubtful of the truth of his words. Magic was a great thing, but muscles and clubs and weight of numbers were also great things. Black Eagle looked at them, and shook his head.

"He speaks the truth," he murmured. Then, turning to the magician, "What do you want of us, great chief?" he asked.

"I want you to tell me if you have seen anything of Bright Robe, who runs upon the air," said Wise-as-a-she-wolf.

"We saw the figure of a warrior flying north-ward, many days ago, as I told you before," re-

plied the chief. " Did you hear nothing of him, among the blubber-eaters? "

" I heard of him from a village which he robbed," answered the magician.

Then he arose, passed out of the lodge, and vanished in the sunlight.

CHAPTER XXIX

PEACE

THE brief but sanguinary uprising of the clans was followed by nine years of peace. Feather-foot spent a great deal of his time with his own people, and the rest of it in Wise-as-a-she-wolf's service. He travelled about the island, visiting the camps and villages, watchful for any signs of uneasiness among the people. He continued to grow, both mentally and physically, as he had begun in the magic lodge; and though he was still without the red feathers, he had the silver robe which had once belonged to the evil magician, which his master had given him. He was of a kind and merry disposition, and wonderfully modest for one so young and yet so powerful. The good magician had purged him of the selfish vanity of youth, without despoiling him of anything of the glory, romance, and faith of that brave season. So his wisdom sat easily upon him, and he made friends at every fire. He per-

fected himself in wood-craft and all manly sports,
entering in friendly contest in the same, with the
young men, on an equal footing with them; for
he considered his magic a thing to use only on
needful occasions, and not to display boastfully
in the eyes of his friends. His natural strength,
and size of limb and bone, were already equal
to those of a hardened and well-grown youth of
sixteen years. He was a great story-teller, a
weaver of narratives that held his listeners en-
tranced; and he had learned a great deal of the
master's skill in painting, and could mix pigments
as bright as sunshine. With these pigments he
drew the portraits of his friends, and pictures of
their deeds in the chase, on the dressed skins of
caribou and seal. His pleasant fame grew through-
out the island until it came near to rivalling that
of the good magician, Wise-as-a-she-wolf.

During the nine years that followed the fighting
among the clans, Run-all-day grew steadily in
power, thanks to his honesty and energy, his
wife's sane counsel, and the especial friendship
of Wise-as-a-she-wolf. People gathered to him
from the smaller villages, and strong chiefs and
warriors took service with him, until his clan
was the largest and strongest in the island. His

people were soon so numerous that he had to establish a dozen villages, scattered over a great region; and these villages were strongly situated, and each commanded by a chief whom he trusted. He made laws, by which thieves and murderers were to be dealt with, and these were proclaimed in every village of his clan, after they had received the sanction of the good magician. The chief of each village was judge of petty offences among his own people; and if one man stole from another, the chief saw that he either made good the amount of the theft by double its value, either in skins, provisions, or service, or left the village in disgrace. In cases of murder, Run-all-day delivered judgment, after hearing what the prisoner, and every one else concerned, had to say. There had been laws before, in the history of the island; but never before the same laws in force over so large a territory, nor half the conscientiousness shown in their observance.

There were many who objected to this new order of things, maintaining that every warrior had a right to settle his private affairs (even if they included the braining of a fellow-villager or the stealing of a few robes) without the interference of the chiefs. It was for the injured parties

themselves to retaliate, in the second case, and for their relatives, in the first, they said. What business the village chiefs, and Run-all-day, had to thrust their hands in such small matters they could not see, at least for some time. But after a few of these exponents of the Rights of Man had suffered death for slaying people against whom they nursed private grudges, the complaints ceased, and the laws were respected.

Wise-as-a-she-wolf during this time was much abroad, searching the far places of the earth for his old enemy. Sometimes he felt that he was close upon the flying heels of his quarry; for Bright Robe had made a long journey southward, travelling always under cover of darkness, and had proclaimed himself among many foreign people. Then he had returned to his friends the mountaineers, and continued quietly about his affairs.

The very nearness of Black Eagle's village to Wise-as-a-she-wolf's own country was in its favour as a hiding-place. And now he did less plundering than of old, in spite of the complaints of the mountaineers, for he wanted the tales of his depredations to fade from men's talk. When he did hunt, it was always far a-field, distant many nights' flight from Black Eagle's village. And

thus, by taking toll of the distant tribes, flashing his name here and there in far countries, and letting the nearer people rest in peace and security, he set false trails for his enemy to follow. His longest journey had extended even to the sea islands where it is always summer, and where tribes of strange little people, with long tails and furred bodies, and the faces of old men, chatter in the tree-tops. There, also, are men of duskier complexions than the blubber-eaters, and hair as straight and black as the mountaineers, who shape canoes out of great tree-trunks and make voyages of several days' duration between island and island. To these people he showed his magic, and told his name and a fine tale of how he intended to build a great lodge in some southern forest; and then he returned, under cover of night, to his cave above Black Eagle's village.

While the silent struggle of cunning went on between the two magicians, with the whole world for their battleground, and in the ninth summer of peace among the islanders, young Featherfoot came to the village of Little Heron, in the secluded valley. When he told his name, he was welcomed as a great chief, for his fame had travelled before him. Little Heron led him to

his own lodge, set the best of food before him,
and afterward begged him to tell one of his de-
lightful stories. So the youth told the story of
the Crimson Wigwam, as he had heard it in his
own heart, and it sang with the adventures and
happy emotions of a young warrior and a maiden.
As he talked, he felt the grave, bright eyes of Star
Flower, the chief's daughter, upon him, and his
glance met hers, and lo, they both looked downward and the trend of Featherfoot's narrative
wavered for the space of a heart-beat.

The tale was well received by the chief and his
wife and his old mother. Star Flower alone of
the company did not lift her voice in praise;
but her eyes again met those of the young chief,
and were hidden again as swiftly by the dark
lashes. After the evening meal, the entire village
gathered about a great fire, and Featherfoot told
the stories of the Wallet of Plenty, and the Magic
of the Red Arrow; and though he was but vaguely
conscious of the acclamations of the hunters, his
eyes glanced frequently, yet furtively, toward
Star Flower, reading the shy signs of her approval
with inward delight.

Featherfoot spent ten days in the village of
Little Heron, and told stories, and painted won-

derful pictures, and dreamed a glorious dream
in his heart. Star Flower told him the magic
of the whistle that had been given her by old
Whispering Grass; how Wise-as-a-she-wolf had
given it to the medicine-maker, and how its
possessor, if in peril, had but to sound a note on
it and the good magician would hear, though he
were at the world's end, and would hasten to the
rescue.

" I, too, would hear the sound, if you were in
danger," replied the youth.

He knew this was so, for his heart said it and
his heart was never mistaken; but he believed
that it was so because of his love for the girl, and
that it had nothing to do with the magic he had
been taught by Wise-as-a-she-wolf. He told her
how old Whispering Grass had saved his life with
her medicines, when he was a very little baby;
and how his father, Run-all-day, had made the
journey to the old woman's lodge and home
again on the red feathers, — all of which he had
heard from his mother. In return, she told him
of her childhood; and the old people were quick
to remark all this whispering, and meeting and
beaming of eyes, and nodded their heads wisely
at one another. On the tenth day after his ar-

rival, Featherfoot left the village, to continue the work that the master had given him to do.

" I shall return, when I have proved myself a strong warrior," he said to Little Heron.

But to Star Flower he whispered that he would return before the coming of another summer, whether men called him a strong warrior or no. And she blushed, and replied that indeed it would matter little what men said of him who was already the greatest chief, and warrior, and magician in the world.

The summer waned, and again the berries ripened on the barrens, the birds took wing and the caribou moved to sheltered pastures; and Wise-as-a-she-wolf, in whose heart a restless aching for new sights and adventures was ever present, left the island again and flew on the long trails of the plover and snipe and honking geese. He had no fear for Featherfoot's safety or for the welfare of the people in general, for he knew that Run-all-day's clans would maintain order while he was away, and he did not think that Bright Robe was within thousands of miles of his native place. In truth, he was beginning to hope that his enemy had either given up all thought of revenge, or suffered some new re-

verse of fortune. And yet, if such were the case, what had become of the red feathers? Perhaps he had met and been vanquished by some foreign magician. If so, the feathers should be easily found, for the new owner would make use of them openly; and if he were not too strong — but the good magician would follow the vague suppositions no further. The world held what he desired to know, and he was keen to read; and when the secret was disclosed would be the time to act.

Wise-as-a-she-wolf visited the islands of the southern seas, where frosts and seasons of unfruitlessness are unknown, and there, for the second time, found the false trail of Bright Robe. He journeyed westward and southward, into a land of vast and tangled forests. In those dark and stagnant places, lit only by the blooms of poisoned vines, and inscrutable as the heart of a god, a fugitive might well find a secret dwelling. So thought the good magician; and after a day's flight above those millions and millions of crowded tree-tops, he felt that here, if anywhere, was his enemy hidden. He descended through the roof of vivid, tangled green, and looked about him, somewhat daunted at the gloom, the netted vegetation on all sides, and the strange noises over-

head. " A thousand thieves might hide securely for a thousand years in this jungle," he exclaimed, and felt a pang of hopelessness. He stood motionless for a little while, staring about him. Then, drawing his axe of magic workmanship, he began to cut his way through the vines and creepers and smaller growth that surrounded him. Intent on his labour, he relaxed that effort of will by which he made and maintained his invisibility. He struck lustily, to right and left, advancing steadily after every stroke. Already he felt in better spirits, reflecting that here would be found some great, new things to learn and unfamiliar aspects of truth, even if Bright Robe should continue to slip through his fingers. The fire of the explorer burned within him.

For never before, in all his wanderings, had he descended into these forests. He would pierce to the heart of this vivid, inscrutable country, and lay bare all its secrets.

CHAPTER XXX

THE POISONED DART

HE felt a sudden pang, as of the touch of flame, in his arm. He reeled backward, and at a glance discovered a tiny arrow of strange form, and no longer than a man's finger, embedded in the muscles below his shoulder. He plucked it out; and in the same instant of time made himself invisible. Already a horrible madness was upon him, tearing at limbs, and brain, and heart. The walls of living green billowed and span around him.

" I am struck by magic," he cried; " but I, too, am a magician."

His voice sounded like the voice of a stranger. He saw grinning faces on every side — green, grinning masks that mouthed and vanished and returned. He sprang at them, striking with his magic axe, wrenching them apart with hands that contained the strength of giants and the madness of the poison in his blood. Something

strangely familiar got within his reach, something human of body, and armed with a long stick, and he snatched it, and broke it, and hurled it away among the reeling masks of green. Here was another. And here they ran like ants in a forest of moss, darting this way and that. He leaped upon them in his madness, and crushed them. Again the faces swayed in upon him, and he tore at them with all the strength of his magic and the blindness of his agony. He beat them back. He tore them, and struck them down. Then he turned and ran through a tide of leaping, bubbling green that washed about him, and over him, with a pleasant music of waves. And so he drowned, and yet resolved to fight on. And he looked up through the fathoms of green tide and had not the strength, nor the thought, to close his eye-lids. But his brave spirit, armed with all the magic he had ever known, fought on, unbidden, to save the quiet body against the poison of the dart.

Of a sudden, after what may have been an age of death or only a night of sleep, he sobbed his lungs full of air again like one who wins to the surface of the water after a long dive. The blackness that had weighed upon him rolled

away; and behold, the green tide was gone, and he saw the open sky and felt a ruffling of wind on his face. " I have tasted death," he murmured, " and found it bitter in my soul, for all my power of magic."

He moved a little, turning on his left side, and his body was full of darting pain. The dew of sweat broke out on him, streaming on brow and limbs and breast. He saw that he had struggled from the jungle and now lay on a grassy hummock; but on all sides stood the hideous, green forest, as if waiting to engulf him again. He glanced at his right arm, and saw a tiny ring of purple, hot and puckered, on the sunburned skin. Then he knew that it was poison, and not magic, that had leaped upon him, and filled him with madness and the pangs of death. Yet is not poison a kind of magic, after all, compounded by the gods of hate, in the beginning of the world, such hidden death as Bright Robe would make, if he were wise enough?

Wise-as-a-she-wolf touched the grass near him in a dozen places, with his left hand, starting a dozen little fires that weaved a tent of smoke for protection from the sun. He took a leather bottle from his belt and drank his fill of cool

water; and no sooner had he withdrawn the vessel from his lips than it was full again. But as he did not possess the Wallet of Plenty, he drew his magic hunger-belt tight. So he lay until night, with the little fires burning around him, yet consuming nothing, and the smoke of them shutting him in as with walls and roof. Strange and terrible sounds rang from the forest, but he gave small heed to them, knowing that neither weapon nor living body could pass the thin boundaries of his circle of fires. His body ached and his brain felt like a withered leaf in his skull. At last he sank into a troubled sleep. Again the green faces mouthed at him; and he struggled with sleep — or was it death? — and threw the monster off. After that he lay awake until sunrise, drinking frequently of the cool water.

When the sun came up, throwing level shafts of gold across the walls of the forest, a cool wind arose with it, bending the frailer tree-tops and washing the stagnant night from where he lay. There was a tang of salt in the wind, and the good magician breathed it with thankfulness. " I must get down to the sea," he murmured, " and wash in the strong, salt waters, and forget

these tides of poisoned leaves." But when he tried to raise himself on his elbow, the pain of every bone and muscle was so keen that he had to sink flat again. All that day, and for two days afterward, he fasted. But he drank the water from the magic bottle, without denying his thirst, and felt the poison weakening. On the fourth morning he stood upright and sniffed the wind that swooped and baffled over the eastern wall of the forest. Though his head span dizzily, and horrible pains gripped him, he fastened the magic bottle to his belt, took up his weapons, and jumped feebly into the air. He arose like a wounded bird, struggled crookedly and at last topped the barrier of living, threatening green. In front, beyond miles of jungle, he saw a thin line of crested, wind-bent palms, and further out, the haze and glint of the sea. The clean, salt wind blew against him, and he set his feet upon it and staggered forward. Sometimes he dropped so low that his moccasins touched the massed foliage of the forest, that seemed to look upward, with smeared, uncertain faces, waiting for him; but he arose again and again, with desperate efforts, and held on his course. At last he won to the fringe of palms, and fell to

the white sand beside the crystal lip of the tide.

The good magician dwelt in the shade of the wind-bent palms for many days, at first lying inactive, but soon going down to the water each morning and evening to bathe. It was not a great while before he was strong enough to kill a few of the fish that swam in those clear waters, using one of his magic arrows for a spear. Between the beach of white sand and the outer sea-ways, lay a still lagoon, fenced by a reef that stood gleaming in the sun at the time of low water, and broke white and green with surf when the tide was high. In this sheltered water Wise-as-a-she-wolf bathed without fear of treacherous currents and prowling monsters of the deep. Day by day the poison left him, the pains became milder and less frequent in their attacks, and muscle and flesh regained a little of their old strength.

" It is midwinter in my island now, and Feather-foot is telling stories at his father's fire, and my lodge is empty," said the good magician, one morning. His heart was sore with homesickness; and his eyes were weary of the everlasting sun-shine, the white surf and the green water; his

ears were tired of the continual rattling of the wind in the harsh leaves of the palms and his body was tired of its feebleness. Far to seaward, like a shadow of cloud on the horizon, lay an island, and he resolved to fly to it, as soon as the heat of the day was spent, thereby to test his strength. By this time his head was steady, and he could use all the joints of his body without more pain than a man would wince at. Also, he could walk quite briskly, for a short distance, without the aid of the magic moccasins.

When the sun was touching the westward forests, Wise-as-a-she-wolf tightened the thongs of the moccasins of the wind, ran forward for a few steps and sprang into the air. He crossed the lagoon, and the naked reef where the crabs scuttled heavily in the red light, and rose a little when he saw the outer waters heaving beneath him.

" It is a long flight," he said. " I must save my strength." And so he ran cautiously, measuring every well-considered stride. Sometimes he touched the smooth back of a billow, and not until then would he put forth fresh effort and rise a few yards in the air. He flew visibly, so as to have all his mind and energy in the flight. The island

grew on the darkling sea-rim. He glanced backward and saw the long coast of the mainland flat
under the red sky. Beneath him swam a great
shark, like a shadow in the deep. He looked
down on the dim shape of the fish, and knew why
it cruised there, patient yet expectant.

" It is but a short flight after all," he said,
and laughed a little to feel so much of the old
strength in his heart and legs. So he ran faster,
and saw that the wavering shape below also
gathered speed. " We are all hunters or hunted,"
he mused. " The shark follows me, because of
the poor flesh on my bones; and I follow Bright
Robe because of the red feathers on his feet.
Yes, and because he has injured my people and
struck at my power. But if it were not for the
feathers, I think I should forsake this dreary
quest."

He reached the island safely, just at the fall
of the sudden night. Here, too, he found a white
beach, the sand of which was still pleasantly
warm from the day-long heat of the sun. He
was tired, so lit his circle of magic fires immediately, and lay down. For three nights he
dreamed that his people needed him. " It is
foolishness," he assured himself. " What can

they want of me, now that they are at peace with each other, and ruled by wise heads and strong hands? The poison is filling my brain with ugly dreams, in its last efforts to injure me." And on the second morning he told himself the same thing; but on the third, his argument rang falsely to his heart. He went down to the sea, just at the rising of the sun, and splashed about in the crystal water; but he could not clear his mind of his dream. He fished, cooked, and ate his breakfast, and retired into his tent of smoke; but still the dream whispered within him. When the heat of the day was spent, he started northward, over the rocking sea.

Wise-as-a-she-wolf's homeward journey proved to be both slow and painful. He was forced to rest many times, in many strange lands.

CHAPTER XXXI

THE FREEZING OF THE NARROW SEA

EVENTS had moved swiftly in the great northern island during Wise-as-a-she-wolf's absence.

As autumn stole over the forests and barrens, ripening, searing, and slaying, old men predicted a winter of more than usual severity. They read the signs in the moss, in the flight of certain fowl, in the fur and intestines of animals. Then came the frost, and gripped the island in an aching, relentless vise for ten days before the sky thickened to snow. The snow fell steadily, for two days and two nights; and with the passing of the frozen clouds came pitiless winds from the north, sweeping between the blue and the white. The snow, dry as dust, was blown into long ridges, and beaten to the firmness of packed sand, and banked high against the lodges of men and the lairs of beasts.

Beyond the Narrow Sea the mountaineers were called together, from their several villages,

by Black Eagle. Bright Robe was summoned from his hiding-place, and took his seat on the chief's right hand.

" This will be a hungry winter," said the chief. " Hunting will be difficult, for the caribou have travelled far. Bright Robe will not be able to feed us all, for his heart has so softened of late, that he will rob no village unless it be distant a three days' journey."

The warriors grunted agreement to the chief's words, but the magician held his peace and wondered what was in the other's mind.

" The Narrow Sea is frozen," continued Black Eagle. " A safe way leads to the island, where the warriors are feeble as old women and the storehouses are full. We shall march across the frozen water and take the richness of that old island."

The warriors shouted approval, for they loved easy fighting and full meals.

" I do not advise it," said Bright Robe. " Wise-as-a-she-wolf would scatter and slay you with his magic."

Black Eagle looked at him with an evil smile.

" With you on our side, why need we fear the magic of Wise-as-a-she-wolf? " he said. " You

are the greatest magician in the world. You are too modest, my friend, and have hidden so long in the mountains that you have forgotten your strength."

" I will not fight the men of the great island," said Bright Robe.

" You have the heart of a mouse," returned Black Eagle, with a smile on his lips, but a gleam of rage in his eyes. " If you do not help us against the people of the island, then shall we sit peacefully here, while our swiftest runner carries word of you to Wise-as-a-she-wolf."

" Unless he is fleeter than the red feathers, he will not run very far," said Bright Robe, dangerously calm.

The chief glanced at him again. " So you have a little courage, after all," he cried, in feigned amazement. " No messenger will be sent," he added, " but when next Wise-as-a-she-wolf comes to the village, he will be told of how you have made such a fool of him."

Bright Robe moved uneasily, and his sinister eyes flashed over the company of squatting warriors. They were all armed with bows, clubs, and spears; but he knew that, by the help of his magic, he could scatter and slay them at but

small risk to himself. What would the routing of these people avail him, however? Word of the fight would travel swiftly to the ears of his powerful enemy; and who would then hide him from that awful meeting with lies and cunning? He realized that the time was not yet ripe for him to disagree too violently with Black Eagle and his people.

" Let us not talk any longer like enemies and fools," he said. " It would be useless for me to deny my fear of Wise-as-a-she-wolf, for you know what is in my heart concerning that blood-thirsty magician. But I will first cross to the island, to spy upon my enemy. It may be that he is far away, hunting for me at the other end of the earth."

Black Eagle did not answer for a long time. At last he said, " A swift runner can go, and inquire of the villages on the coast as to the where-abouts of the one you fear. Each way is but a half-day's journey for a seasoned runner."

" I think, chief, that the villagers are more likely to kill your messenger than to answer his questions," replied Bright Robe, sneeringly.

Black Eagle realized that it was now his turn to practise diplomacy. He knew that his only

hold on the other was that evil magician's fear of Wise-as-a-she-wolf. He did not think that Bright Robe would desert him, and all claim on future services, except in an extreme case; and he was sure that he would not try to make peace with his enemy by carrying word to him of the intended invasion, for Wise-as-a-she-wolf would not forget past injuries for so small a favour.

"Go, then," said the chief. "We will await your return."

"It will be dark in a few hours, and then I will go," replied Bright Robe, with dignity.

When he set out, through the starlight, for the land of his enemy, his heart was torn with un-certainty as to how he should act in this unfore-seen dilemma which the freezing of the Narrow Sea had forced upon him. To openly assist the mountaineers against Wise-as-a-she-wolf's own people, would be madness; to desert the men who had helped him deceive his enemy for the past nine years would be as fatal in the end. His only hope lay in the chance that the good magi-cian might be far from home, in which case he would help the mountaineers, unobtrusively, until they had fully committed themselves, and then flee under cover of night. He reflected that,

while Wise-as-a-she-wolf was busily engaged in punishing the men from beyond the Narrow Sea, he would have ample time to find a new hiding-place, far, far away from the scenes of his failures. Then he would get rid of the feathers in some way, and live quietly, relinquishing all hope of future greatness.

When Bright Robe reached the coast of the island, he was still struggling with the problem. The temptation to turn southward and continue his flight was almost too strong to resist; but the thought of how the mountaineers would explain to his enemy all his nine-year scheme of evasion, making similar practices useless in the future, daunted him afresh. For a moment his brain turned, in brief consideration, on surrender. He would seek the just and angry magician (whose people he had so often despoiled and slain) and give him the feathers, and confess his sins, and — and? Neither brain nor heart had courage to answer the unasked question. His enemy was just — and what was he to gain by surrendering himself to justice?

Bright Robe went dully about his work. He discovered a cluster of lodges, drifted deep in snow. He approached them, and raised a feeble

voice. " I am cold, I am hungry," he cried. " I
have been lost in a storm."

A figure crawled from the nearest lodge.
Bright Robe staggered forward and fell. Strong
arms lifted him and carried him to warmth and
shelter. He was fed, and soft furs were laid over
him, and all the while he played the part of one
brought close to death by cold and exhaustion.
He spent several hours in the lodge, and learned
from the honest fellow whom he questioned that
Wise-as-a-she-wolf had not been seen in the western villages since autumn. After learning this,
he pretended to sleep; but he soon crawled from
the lodge, leaving the hospitable, unsuspecting
hunter snoring peacefully. He flew eastward and
inland, now with some assurance of spirit. The
night had clouded, though it was still bitterly
cold. He found several villages in the darkness
and, by using the same tactics as before, learned
again that the good magician had not been seen
for two moons. Then he faced westward again
and ran at his best speed.

CHAPTER XXXII

THE INVASION OF THE ISLAND

THE westward villages made but slight resistance to the mountaineers. They were taken unawares, scattered blindly and many were slain. Some of the fugitives hid, and others ran to warn the nearer settlements. The invaders travelled slowly, in spite of Bright Robe's efforts to hurry them, stopping to rest and feast in every village and encumbering themselves with booty and prisoners. Their only prisoners were women. Bright Robe did his share of the fighting, but was careful to make it no more than a man's share. He fought on the ground, like his fellows, and though he served as guide to the hidden encampments, he played an inconspicuous part. And so they raided, fought and feasted for three days, hearing nothing in all that time of Wise-as-a-she-wolf. The main body held straight to the eastward, and small companies branched off to the north and south.

On the fourth day of the invasion the mountaineers reached a large village of deserted lodges. Even the storehouses were empty. The disappointment angered them, and they pushed forward with more haste. For three days they travelled, without finding anything of the islanders except tracks of their snow-shoes and their empty lodges. By this time, Bright Robe had decided that he had mixed as deeply in the invasion as was wise, and that nightfall should be the signal for his southward flight; for his old enemy, wherever he was wandering, would surely take a hand in the game before long. But he said no word of this to Black Eagle.

" Let the fool suffer for his foolishness," he muttered.

The mountaineers were careless soldiers, and sent no scouts ahead of their army. " What have we to fear from these men with the hearts of mice and the muscles of women? " sneered Black Eagle. " They run before us, even before they see our spears. In a few days we will drive them into the great salt water in the east."

Shortly after noon they reached another empty village. They rushed into the lodges, shouted

angrily, and fought among themselves for what little the departed inhabitants had left behind. The five hundred warriors crowded into the open space, overturning the lodges, and reviling the islanders. Arrows leaped from the woods on every side. Two flights sprang forth and tasted blood before the mountaineers realized what had happened. Then they rallied and dashed for the hidden enemy. Black Eagle turned furiously upon Bright Robe.

" You have brought us to this trap," he cried, and struck at him with his club. The blow fell harmlessly on the magician's shield; and in a second in the crush and tumult of the battle they were separated.

Many of the mountaineers who advanced into the woods, to close with the surrounding enemy, were swiftly forced back to the clearing. Blood melted the snow, and contending warriors, with their racquets slipped or broken from their feet, struggled deep in the drifts, stabbing blindly. Shouts and cries of dismay rang up to the frozen sky. Men fought hand to hand, even breast to breast, — yes, and tooth to flesh. The lodges were torn and overturned, and as more men continued to pour into the clearing the snow was

trampled hard as earth and crusted with frozen blood.

Bright Robe dared not fly openly from the scene and yet he was eager to get away, fearing always the arrival of Wise-as-a-she-wolf. At last he broke from the thick of the fight, hurling friend and foe alike from his path by means of his magic strength. Many sturdy strokes were aimed at him, but his magic turned them all aside, and he won to the shelter of the forest without hurt. It was his intention to run to a safe distance from the battle, hide until dark, and then take flight. He ran straight through the woods, beating down the occasional warriors who tried to bar his way. He had travelled nearly a mile, and was clear of the outskirts of the battle, when, in pausing for breath, he heard the springing of parted branches close behind him. He turned with ready club, but saw nothing.

I must turn back a little, and look at the fight from the islanders' side of it.

From the fugitives from the western villages word of the invasion travelled quickly to the ears of Run-all-day. Swift runners were sent in every direction, to warn the clans of the danger and bid

them prepare to fight. The people of the villages which lay in Black Eagle's course were told to fall back, with all their possessions, upon Run-all-day's country. Then Run-all-day divided his own warriors and the men who joined him from the other clans, into three bodies of about four hundred men each. One of these armies, under Jumping Wolf, was sent forward immediately to encounter the mountaineers on their probable course. Another was hurried forward in the same direction, but several miles to the southward. The third was held in readiness near the villages where the women and children and stores of the fugitives were sheltered.

Jumping Wolf sent scouts in advance of the little army, to scour the country for miles. These scouts were not long in finding the invaders, and for a whole day before the attack the commander was constantly in receipt of information concerning the approach of the enemy. He did not rush his men, but advanced at an easy pace, ever on the look-out for a suitable position in which to stand and strike. When night fell, his men ate the cooked food that they had brought, dug great trenches in the snow, and slept without fires. Shortly before noon he arrived at a large, deserted

village, and halted his men. A scout came running to him.

" They are close at hand," he said, " and one who guides them is pointing the way to this village."

So Jumping Wolf placed his eager warriors in the edge of the woods that surrounded the clearing in which stood the empty lodges.

" Now is the time for you to put your magic to good use," he said, to Featherfoot.

But the youth shook his head. " Unless they have a magician among them, I shall not use my magic," he replied, placing a common arrow on the string of his bow.

The islanders waited patiently, crouching on their thong-woven racquets, peering eagerly into the clearing. Their bows were strung and the arrows were loose in their belts, and their hearts were hot for the battle. At last the invaders appeared, dashing into the clearing and among the lodges in noisy disorder; and at the sight a thrill of joy and rage ran through the waiting islanders. The notches of arrows met the taut strings; and still the chiefs crouched motionless, giving no sign. The place fairly squirmed with the shouting, dark-skinned mountaineers. Jump-

ing Wolf raised his hand above his head; up went the hands of the other chiefs; out leaped the arrows upon the crowding, struggling invaders. Again the bows were bent and released; and then the islanders sprang to meet the rallying mountaineers, and struck with clubs and spears.

It was soon quite evident to Featherfoot that the Beothics had the upper hand in the engagement, though the invaders were the more numerous. So he fell back from the struggle for a moment's rest. In surveying the struggle from a vantage point at the edge of the clearing, his attention was attracted by a big stranger who fought for the mountaineers and yet was lighter of skin. He saw this warrior suddenly make his way out of the thick of the fight, dashing friend and foe from his way with a strength that was more than human. He saw him win, unhurt, to the edge of the clearing, and dart from sight among the trees. " He fights with strong magic, and shields himself with magic," said Featherfoot, and immediately gave chase. As he ran among the snatching, buffeting branches, he drew his most powerful arrow from his belt, and pulled the silver robe above his head.

Featherfoot soon came in sight of the stranger.

At the sound of his approach the other turned; but the youth, knowing himself to be invisible by virtue of the silver robe, halted and unhurriedly set the magic arrow to the string of the magic bow. So great was the magic of that arrow, that its weight became as the weight of a small mountain the moment it hit its mark. There was no pity in Featherfoot's heart, for he had seen the strange magician slay both friend and foe, with weapons from which they had no chance of escape; so he drew the bow calmly and loosed the shaft. The stranger fell, staggered to his feet, struck the arrow from his breast and leaped high above the tree-tops. There he hung for a little, struggling desperately; but when another arrow found him he dropped back to earth, turning over and over in his fall. Featherfoot was upon him as soon as he touched the snow. Knowing now that the stranger was Bright Robe, he bound the nerveless limbs with magic thongs that no giant could break. Then, undoing the moccasins from the unresisting feet, he found the red feathers. Quick as thinking, they were transferred to his own moccasins, and his snow-shoes were cast aside.

No sooner were the magic feathers in place against the soles of his feet, than the shrill note

of the whistle which old Whispering Grass had given to Star Flower sounded faintly but terrifically in Featherfoot's ears. He sprang into the air and ran swiftly in the direction of Little Heron's village, leaving the evil magician bound and unconscious on the snow.

He caught a blurred glimpse of the battle below, now scattered and abating in fury, but so dazed and breathless was he with the frightful speed at which he rushed through the air, his eyes could not distinguish friend from foe. But whatever the outcome of the battle, he had heard the whistle and must answer the call. So he ran on, though his brain reeled, and his eyes ached, and his breath was like ice and smoke in his throat. Presently, as he became accustomed to the new manner and rate of travelling, the sensations grew less painful. Soon he was able to see clearly, and run steadily, and draw his breath with comparative ease.

Suddenly, as he raced along between the fading sky and the dimming wastes of the earth, he heard the whispering of flight beside him. Then he found that the silver robe had slipped from his head, and he snatched at it with his left hand, to draw it into place.

"Hold," cried the voice of Wise-as-a-she-wolf, close at his elbow.

"It is I, Featherfoot," cried the youth in answer, desisting from his efforts to hide himself beneath the robe and at the same time returning his club to his belt. At that, the good magician appeared close beside, and threw his arm about his neck.

"I had my axe raised to strike you, lad," he whispered. "I thought my old enemy was in my power at last."

"I have wounded him and bound him, master," replied Featherfoot, breathlessly. "He lies near Diving Beaver's village, where the warriors are still fighting. But I have heard the call of the whistle, master, and must hasten to answer it. Star Flower is in need of me."

"Go, my son. I, too, have heard the whistle. But now I will hasten to my warriors," said the good magician. And so they parted, between the shadowy wilderness and the darkling sky, with no questions of the months of separation. Wise-as-a-she-wolf turned in the direction of Diving Beaver's encampment, and ran slowly on the icy currents of the wind. He was still weak with the poison of the little arrow, and felt the weari-

ness of the long flight which he had just made. He wondered to feel so little elation of spirit at the knowledge of Bright Robe's capture. His thoughts were all of Featherfoot, who was as dear as a son to him. " Star Flower, Star Flower," he repeated, and smiled pensively. " Whoever this Star Flower is, and however she came to possess the whistle, I think she will teach the lad a magic of which I have no mastery," he reflected. " He will build a lodge of bark and skins, and it will be more beautiful to his eyes than my great house in the pine wood, with its smokeless lamps and magic walls. He is young, and Youth is the greatest magician. He loves a woman, and that is the strongest magic." Thus, with mingled tenderness and distress, he considered the case of Featherfoot as he flew to the succour of his warriors.

CHAPTER XXXIII

THE RESCUE OF STAR FLOWER

THE note of the whistle was not repeated; but Featherfoot ran straight toward the village of Little Heron. The last red light of the short winter day was fading below the west, when he reached the valley that he knew and loved so well. He descended among the lodges. All was quiet. There was no light of cooking-fires, or sound of contented voices. He glanced at the trampled snow under his feet, and beheld a war-club with a splintered haft. And there, a step beyond, lay an arrow, and there a dark stain melted into the snow. With a low cry of consternation, he ran to the chief's lodge and peered within. It was empty, and even the furs were gone from the couches. He started to run to the next lodge, but the dusk of night was deepening, and his foot tripped in something and he fell heavily. He recovered himself quickly, and found that the thing over which he had stumbled was the life-

less body of Little Heron. Then he knew that it would be useless to look in the other lodges. He arose on the magic feathers and circled close about the village. He found the corpses of warriors and old men and boys, and even of old women. He flew in a wider circle, and yet a wider, swooping low to every open glade. Here and there lay the cold bodies, now of a mountaineer, now of a villager whom he had known, showing how in the unequal struggle they had scattered and how the fugitives had been overtaken. Still he widened the circle of his flight. At last, away to the westward, he caught the glint of fire at the base of a dark hill, and even as he swerved in his course, the little fire spark leaped to the flame of a comfortable fire. He swooped nearer, and peered out upon the scene from the cover of the tree-tops. There were more than a dozen mountaineers, a few busy preparing food at the newly kindled fire, the others lolling nearby on out-spread furs. In the background a group of women were huddled, and their half-stifled sobbing came piteously to his ears. Featherfoot drew his club from his belt, pulled the hood of the silver robe over his head, and soared noiselessly from the tree-tops.

" Have no fear, Star Flower," he cried, and descended, like a hawk upon its prey. The first mountaineer to receive a blow of the club fell across the fire, and lay there. Two more went down, with broken skulls, before any of them realized the danger. Ten of them reached the cover of the woods, which proved no protection at all. Six gained a distance of several hundred yards from the fire, before the invisible death overtook them. Three won half-way up the hill, but none reached the top. Then Featherfoot returned to the camping-place, plucked the body from the fire and threw it into the bushes, loosed the thongs that bound the women and clasped Star Flower in his arms. She made frantic efforts to free herself from his embrace, and the other women and girls screamed and gazed wildly around.

" It is I, Featherfoot," whispered the bewildered youth, still holding her firmly.

" I cannot see you," she cried. " It is the voice of Featherfoot, but — "

The youth dropped his arms from her slender body, tore the silver robe from his head and shoulders and tossed it on the snow. Then he turned back to Star Flower, smiling. The other

women drew nearer, and ceased their screaming.

"Yes, it is the young chief who drew the beautiful pictures," said one. "It is the great story-teller," said another.

Star Flower stepped close to him, clasped her little hands behind his neck and hid her face in the furs on his breast.

"Oh, I was not sure," she whispered. "It was your voice; but I heard the rushing of winged feet, and saw the savage warriors run and fall before no visible danger. I thought the good magician had answered the call of the whistle."

Then Featherfoot laughed softly, and held her close, and in his heart he pitied his friend and master, the greatest magician in the world. And as for the good red feathers, he forgot all about them.

"Fear nothing," he said, tenderly and joyfully. "Your lover answered the call, and love winged his feet."

Hail, Youth, speaking such truth through very inexactness and the vagueness of dreams. Hail, Love, who sees so far and so clearly through glory-blinded eyes.

CHAPTER XXXIV

REST

THE good magician found his old enemy bleeding in the snow, and bound by thongs magic-strengthened, which he was powerless to break in his weakened condition. Having seen that the enemy was broken and scattered, and that every mountaineer ran, inspired by no purpose except the saving of his own life, he lifted Bright Robe in his arms and carried him into one of the few lodges that remained standing. He loosened the thongs and poured water between the swollen lips.

" What now? " asked Bright Robe, with the courage of despair.

For a little while the good magician sat silent, in the darkness, as if he had not heard.

" Though I defeated you before, and loosed you in the wilderness in the shape of a little owl," he said, at last, " yet you outwitted me at the end of the five years. And though your magic possessed but half its former strength when you

regained your old shape, yet you managed to hide from me for nine years and have led invaders into my country. Now, even were I to let you go away without punishment, your strength would be no more than that of the least of the magicians, for magic is a thing that weakens under defeat. It is a vanity, failing in adversity, but growing ever stronger and more vain with success. By it, one may win fear, and if he uses it for the protection of his people, it brings him respect and friendship; but the greatest magician cannot win love by his magic."

Bright Robe lay very still, listening and wondering. " I have no fear of you," continued Wise-as-a-she-wolf, " and, seeing you bleeding there, overthrown in your evil doing by a lad whom I love, I find but little hate of you in my heart. You must live for ever, in weakness or in strength, in wickedness or in virtue, even as I, and that is punishment beyond any man's deserving."

" Yes, chief. If the water of everlasting life were held to my lips again, how gladly would I spill it on the ground," said Bright Robe.

" And yet we fought and bled, suffered weariness and cold and loneliness, to win that drink," replied the good magician.

" I left a woman and child — a child of my blood — to starve in an empty lodge, that I might drink of that accursed water," whispered Bright Robe. " Strike me, old enemy," he cried. " Beat me to nothingness. I would go, even now, and make my peace with those two."

" Your spirit would still be bound to this old earth," replied Wise-as-a-she-wolf, " though I should strike with all my magic and scatter your body to the winds."

For a long time they sat silent in the darkness of the lodges. It was Bright Robe who spoke first.

" I, too, have lost fear," he said, " though I have been a coward at heart since my mother bore me. For nine years I have been no better than a slave of Black Eagle's, because of fear. Fear of you, and fear of the shadow in my heart, have driven me so hard that even the thirst for blood is dead in me and I have no more desire for evil power. I care not what you do with me."

" When you recover from your wounds," said Wise-as-a-she-wolf, " I fear you will thirst again for power and blood and mischief. But I pity you, Bright Robe, for the age of sleeping and waking and remembrance that are before you.

So I will deal with you as mercifully as I may."

"There is no more lust of life in me. You cannot give me death. Then what do I care how you deal with me?" said Bright Robe.

For two days the hunting and slaying of the mountaineers by the islanders continued, and not one of those savage invaders returned to his own country. But as the cold continued as intense as ever, and it was thought that the ice would remain in the Narrow Sea until spring, Jumping Wolf marched his men westward and encamped them on the coast. Wise-as-a-she-wolf took word of the victory to Run-all-day, and was so cordially received by that honest chief and his family that his heart lightened. He had brought the wounded Bright Robe with him, and he told Run-all-day of Featherfoot's encounter with, and overthrow of, that magician. Also, he narrated his own adventures in the south; and the chief growled with rage when he heard of the little arrow tipped with poison.

"Now you may rest, master, since your enemy is delivered into your hands," said Run-all-day. "Our people are strong now, and live under the laws, and even the southward clans are at peace

with their neighbours. So surely the time has come for you to rest, master."

" I have one more journey to make," replied the good magician. " One more long journey to the southward, and then I will lay aside the moccasins of the wind, and sit at home and help you in your wise government of the people."

The chief looked at him in wonder.

" Help me! " he exclaimed. " Why, master, I am your servant, though the strongest chief in the island. Whatever I have done for the good of the people has been through your friendship and guidance. Yes, and in little matters, Red Willow has given good counsel."

Wise-as-a-she-wolf looked at the woman, who sat nearby, with downcast eyes.

" Your magic is greater than mine," he said.

She raised her eyes and looked at him — at the strongest of magicians, with something of motherly tenderness.

" To fill a heart, even one heart, with love and trust, is a greater matter than flying through the air," he said.

" You are loved. You are called the good magician," replied Red Willow.

" And I am feared," said Wise-as-a-she-wolf.

" Yes, I am feared, even by those who think of me most kindly. But the time was when — "

They waited, gazing upon their guest.

" We are listening, master," said the chief.

" I have forgotten it," answered the other. " It was nothing. But I, too, was once young and the chief of a village."

When Bright Robe had nearly recovered from his wounds, Wise-as-a-she-wolf bound him with thongs, lifted him in his arms, and flew southward. Night and day, the good magician ran above the sea, and many lands glimmered into his vision and faded again. At last he descended to the beach of an island, where mountains towered high, robed in green to their summits. Between the white beaches and the climbing slopes stood hundreds of cocoanut trees, their long stems bent and their crests for ever shaken by the wind. The music of the surf drummed around the island, day and night, night and day. Birds of bright plumage and harsh voices flew above the hillside forests. No other land was to be seen from any point of this island, but everywhere the uneasy ocean and the straight horizon.

Wise-as-a-she-wolf broke the thongs from Bright Robe's limbs. " Here you will find food

and drink and shelter," he said, " and somewhere on the mountain is a small stream that flows with the water of forgetfulness."

" Have you drunk of that stream? " asked Bright Robe.

" No. There are things that I do not wish to forget," replied the other.

Bright Robe looked at the sea, and the windy palms, and the towering mountains. A shadow stole across his keen eyes.

" And this — for ever," he whispered.

" If you drink often enough of the water of forgetfulness," said the good magician, " then life will stretch no farther than from day to day."

He turned, hesitated, then faced the motionless Bright Robe again.

" There is a village beyond the mountain. Be wise, for I do not forget."

Then he sprang high into the blustering wind.

.THE END.

SELECTED NEW CANADIAN LIBRARY TITLES

Asterisks (*) denote titles of New Canadian Library Classics

n 1. OVER PRAIRIE TRAILS / Frederick Philip Grove
n 2. SUCH IS MY BELOVED / Morley Callaghan*
n 3. LITERARY LAPSES / Stephen Leacock
n 4. AS FOR ME AND MY HOUSE / Sinclair Ross*
n 5. THE TIN FLUTE / Gabrielle Roy*
n 6. THE CLOCKMAKER / Thomas Chandler Haliburton
n 7. THE LAST BARRIER AND OTHER STORIES / Charles G. D. Roberts
n 8. BAROMETER RISING / Hugh MacLennan*
n 9. AT THE TIDE'S TURN AND OTHER STORIES / Thomas H. Raddall
n10. ARCADIAN ADVENTURES WITH THE IDLE RICH / Stephen Leacock
n11. HABITANT POEMS / William Henry Drummond
n12. THIRTY ACRES / Ringuet
n13. EARTH AND HIGH HEAVEN / Gwethalyn Graham
n14. THE MAN FROM GLENGARRY / Ralph Connor
n15. SUNSHINE SKETCHES OF A LITTLE TOWN / Stephen Leacock*
n16. THE STEPSURE LETTERS / Thomas McCulloch
n17. MORE JOY IN HEAVEN / Morley Callaghan
n18. WILD GEESE / Martha Ostenso
n19. THE MASTER OF THE MILL / Frederick Philip Grove
n20. THE IMPERIALIST / Sara Jeannette Duncan
n21. DELIGHT / Mazo de la Roche
n22. THE SECOND SCROLL / A. M. Klein*
n23. THE MOUNTAIN AND THE VALLEY / Ernest Buckler*
n24. THE RICH MAN / Henry Kreisel
n25. WHERE NESTS THE WATER HEN / Gabrielle Roy
n26. THE TOWN BELOW / Roger Lemelin
n27. THE HISTORY OF EMILY MONTAGUE / Frances Brooke
n28. MY DISCOVERY OF ENGLAND / Stephen Leacock
n29. SWAMP ANGEL / Ethel Wilson*
n30. EACH MAN'S SON / Hugh MacLennan
n31. ROUGHING IT IN THE BUSH / Susanna Moodie
n32. WHITE NARCISSUS / Raymond Knister
n33. THEY SHALL INHERIT THE EARTH / Morley Callaghan
n34. TURVEY / Earle Birney
n35. NONSENSE NOVELS / Stephen Leacock
n36. GRAIN / R. J. C. Stead
n37. LAST OF THE CURLEWS / Fred Bodsworth*
n38. THE NYMPH AND THE LAMP / Thomas H. Raddall
n39. JUDITH HEARNE / Brian Moore
n40. THE CASHIER / Gabrielle Roy
n41. UNDER THE RIBS OF DEATH / John Marlyn
n42. WOODSMEN OF THE WEST / M. Allerdale Grainger
n43. MOONBEAMS FROM THE LARGER LUNACY / Stephen Leacock
n44. SARAH BINKS / Paul Hiebert
n45. SON OF A SMALLER HERO / Mordecai Richler
n46. WINTER STUDIES AND SUMMER RAMBLES IN CANADA / Anna Brownell Jameson

n47. REMEMBER ME / Edward Meade
n48. FRENZIED FICTION / Stephen Leacock
n49. FRUITS OF THE EARTH / Frederick Philip Grove
n50. SETTLERS OF THE MARSH / Frederick Philip Grove
n51. THE BACKWOODS OF CANADA / Catharine Parr Traill
n52. MUSIC AT THE CLOSE / Edward McCourt
n53. MY REMARKABLE UNCLE / Stephen Leacock
n54. THE DOUBLE HOOK / Sheila Watson
n55. TIGER DUNLOP'S UPPER CANADA / William Dunlop
n56. STREET OF RICHES / Gabrielle Roy
n57. SHORT CIRCUITS / Stephen Leacock
n58. WACOUSTA / John Richardson
n59. THE STONE ANGEL / Margaret Laurence*
n60. FURTHER FOOLISHNESS / Stephen Leacock
n61. SAMUEL MARCHBANKS' ALMANACK / Robertson Davies
n62. THE LAMP AT NOON AND OTHER STORIES / Sinclair Ross
n63. THE HARBOR MASTER / Theodore Goodridge Roberts
n64. THE CANADIAN SETTLER'S GUIDE / Catharine Parr Traill
n65. THE GOLDEN DOG / William Kirby
n66. THE APPRENTICESHIP OF DUDDY KRAVITZ / Mordecai Richler*
n67. BEHIND THE BEYOND / Stephen Leacock
n68. A STRANGE MANUSCRIPT FOUND IN A COPPER CYLINDER / James De Mille
n69. LAST LEAVES / Stephen Leacock
n70. THE TOMORROW-TAMER / Margaret Laurence
n71. ODYSSEUS EVER RETURNING / George Woodcock
n72. THE CURE OF ST. PHILIPPE / Francis William Grey
n73. THE FAVOURITE GAME / Leonard Cohen
n74. WINNOWED WISDOM / Stephen Leacock
n75. THE SEATS OF THE MIGHTY / Gilbert Parker
n76. A SEARCH FOR AMERICA / FrederickPhilip Grove
n77. THE BETRAYAL / Henry Kreisel
n78. MAD SHADOWS / Marie-Claire Blais
n79. THE INCOMPARABLE ATUK / Mordecai Richler
n80. THE LUCK OF GINGER COFFEY / Brian Moore
n81. JOHN SUTHERLAND: ESSAYS, CONTROVERSIES AND POEMS / Miriam Waddington
n82. PEACE SHALL DESTROY MANY / Rudy Henry Wiebe
n83. A VOICE FROM THE ATTIC / Robertson Davies
n84. PROCHAIN EPISODE / Hubert Aquin
n85. ROGER SUDDEN / Thomas H. Raddall
n86. MIST ON THE RIVER / Hubert Evans
n87. THE FIRE-DWELLERS / Margaret Laurence
n88. THE DESERTER / Douglas LePan
n89. ANTOINETTE DE MIRECOURT / Rosanna Leprohon
n90. ALLEGRO / Felix Leclerc
n91. THE END OF THE WORLD AND OTHER STORIES / Mavis Gallant
n92. IN THE VILLAGE OF VIGER AND OTHER STORIES / Duncan Campbell Scott
n93. THE EDIBLE WOMAN / Margaret Atwood
n94. IN SEARCH OF MYSELF / Frederick Philip Grove
n95. FEAST OF STEPHEN / Robertson Davies
n96. A BIRD IN THE HOUSE / Margaret Laurence
n97. THE WOODEN SWORD / Edward McCourt

n98. PRIDE'S FANCY / Thomas Raddall
n99. OX BELLS AND FIREFLIES / Ernest Buckler
n100. ABOVE GROUND / Jack Ludwig
n101. NEW PRIEST IN CONCEPTION BAY / Robert Traill Spence Lowell
n102. THE FLYING YEARS / Frederick Niven
n103. WIND WITHOUT RAIN / Selwyn Dewdney
n104. TETE BLANCHE / Marie-Claire Blais
n105. TAY JOHN / Howard O'Hagan
n106. CANADIANS OF OLD / Philippe Aubert de Gaspé. Translated by Sir Charles G. D. Roberts
n107. HEADWATERS OF CANADIAN LITERATURE / Archibald MacMechan
n108. THE BLUE MOUNTAINS OF CHINA / Rudy Wiebe
n109. THE HIDDEN MOUNTAIN / Gabrielle Roy
n110. THE HEART OF THE ANCIENT WOOD / Charles G. D. Roberts
n111. A JEST OF GOD / Margaret Laurence
n112. SELF CONDEMNED / Wyndham Lewis
n113. DUST OVER THE CITY / André Langevin
n114. OUR DAILY BREAD / Frederick Philip Grove
n115. THE CANADIAN NOVEL IN THE TWENTIETH CENTURY / edited by George Woodcock
n116. THE VIKING HEART / Laura Goodman Salverson
n117. DOWN THE LONG TABLE / Earle Birney
n118. GLENGARRY SCHOOL DAYS / Ralph Connor
n119. THE PLOUFFE FAMILY / Roger Lemelin
n120. WINDFLOWER / Gabrielle Roy
n121. THE DISINHERITED / Matt Cohen
n122. THE TEMPTATIONS OF BIG BEAR / Rudy Wiebe
n123. PANDORA / Sylvia Fraser
n124. HOUSE OF HATE / Percy Janes
n125. A CANDLE TO LIGHT THE SUN / Patricia Blondal
n126. THIS SIDE JORDAN / Margaret Laurence
n127. THE RED FEATHERS / T. G. Roberts
n128. I AM MARY DUNNE / Brian Moore
n129. THE ROAD PAST ALTAMONT / Gabrielle Roy
n130. KNIFE ON THE TABLE / Jacques Godbout
n131. THE MANAWAKA WORLD OF MARGARET LAURENCE / Clara Thomas
n132. CONSIDER HER WAYS / Frederick Philip Grove
n133. HIS MAJESTY'S YANKEES / Thomas Raddall
n134. JEAN RIVARD / Antoine Gérin-Lajoie
n135. BOGLE CORBET / John Galt
n136. A CHOICE OF ENEMIES / Mordecai Richler
n137. RESPONSES AND EVALUATIONS: ESSAYS ON CANADA / E. K. Brown
n138. THE MASTER'S WIFE / Sir Andrew Macphail
n139. THE CRUELEST MONTH / Ernest Buckler
n140. THE ATONEMENT OF ASHLEY MORDEN / Fred Bodsworth
n141. WILD ANIMALS I HAVE KNOWN / Ernest Thompson Seton
n142. SCANN / Robert Harlow
n143. ON POETRY AND POETS / A. J. M. Smith
n144. CRACKPOT / Adele Wiseman

McCLELLAND AND STEWART LIMITED
publishers of The New Canadian Library
would like to keep you informed about
new additions to this unique series.

For a complete listing of titles and
current prices – or if you wish to be added
to our mailing list to receive future catalogues
and other new book information – write:

BOOKNEWS
McClelland and Stewart Limited
25 Hollinger Road
Toronto, Canada M4B 3G2

McClelland and Stewart books are
available at all good bookstores.

Booksellers should be happy to order from our catalogues
any titles which they do not regularly stock.

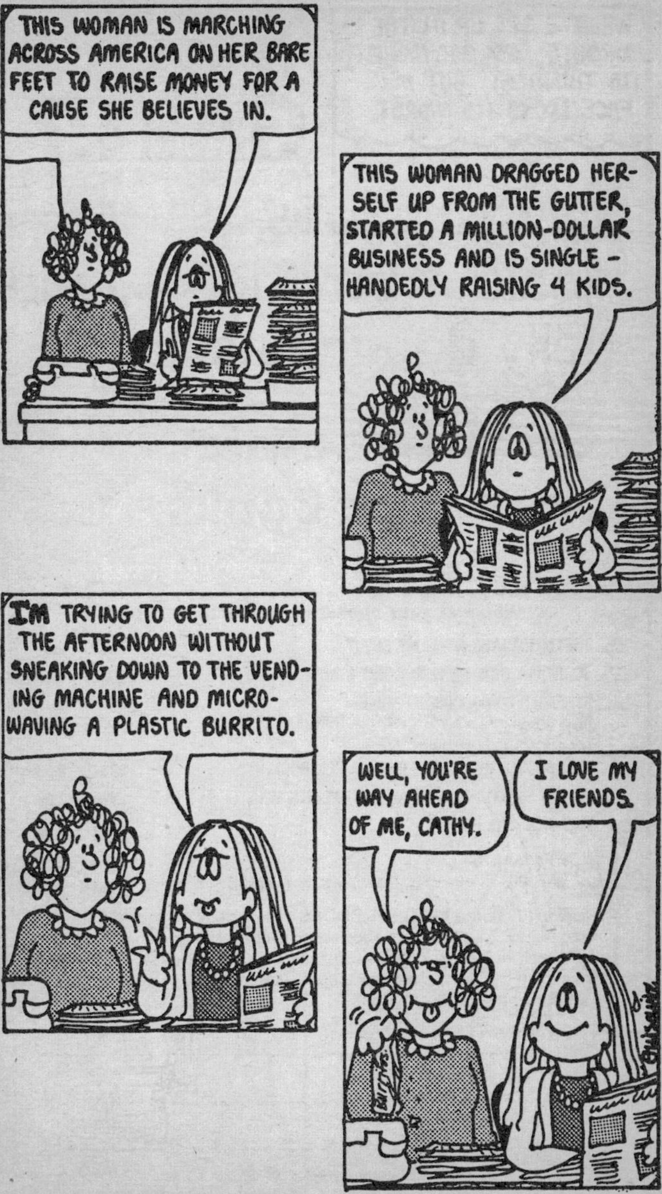
THIS WOMAN IS MARCHING ACROSS AMERICA ON HER BARE FEET TO RAISE MONEY FOR A CAUSE SHE BELIEVES IN.
THIS WOMAN DRAGGED HER-SELF UP FROM THE GUTTER, STARTED A MILLION-DOLLAR BUSINESS AND IS SINGLE-HANDEDLY RAISING 4 KIDS.
I'M TRYING TO GET THROUGH THE AFTERNOON WITHOUT SNEAKING DOWN TO THE VEND-ING MACHINE AND MICRO-WAVING A PLASTIC BURRITO.
WELL, YOU'RE WAY AHEAD OF ME, CATHY.
I LOVE MY FRIENDS.

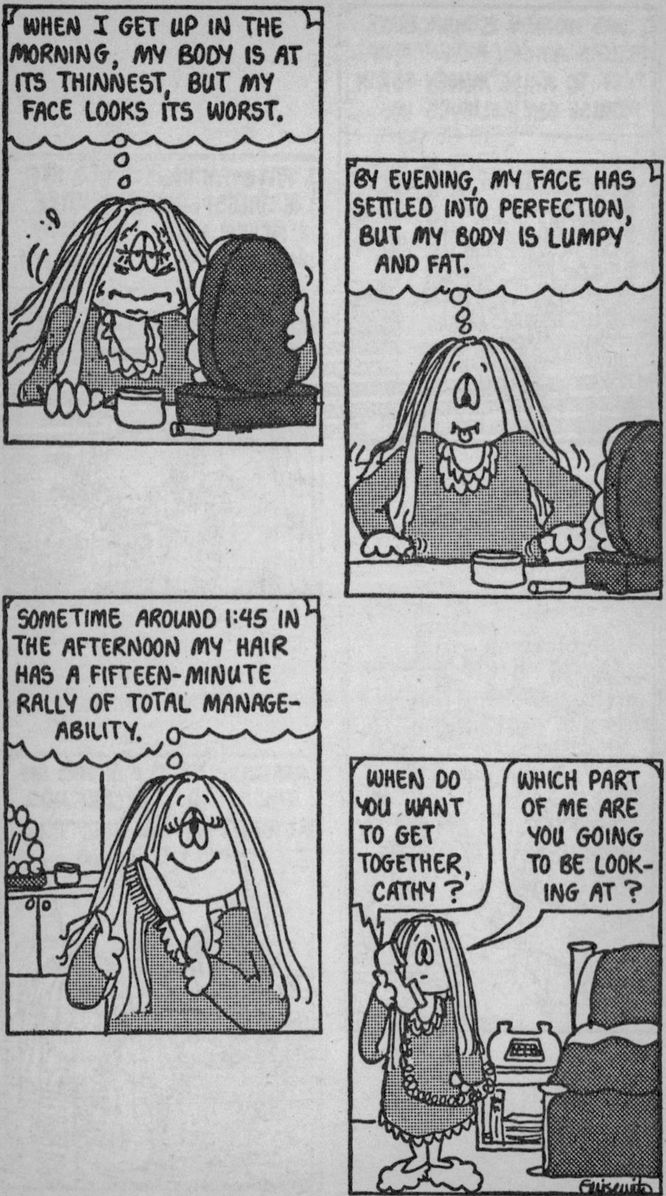
WHEN I GET UP IN THE MORNING, MY BODY IS AT ITS THINNEST, BUT MY FACE LOOKS ITS WORST.
BY EVENING, MY FACE HAS SETTLED INTO PERFECTION, BUT MY BODY IS LUMPY AND FAT.
SOMETIME AROUND 1:45 IN THE AFTERNOON MY HAIR HAS A FIFTEEN-MINUTE RALLY OF TOTAL MANAGE-ABILITY.
WHEN DO YOU WANT TO GET TOGETHER, CATHY?
WHICH PART OF ME ARE YOU GOING TO BE LOOK-ING AT?
Guisewite

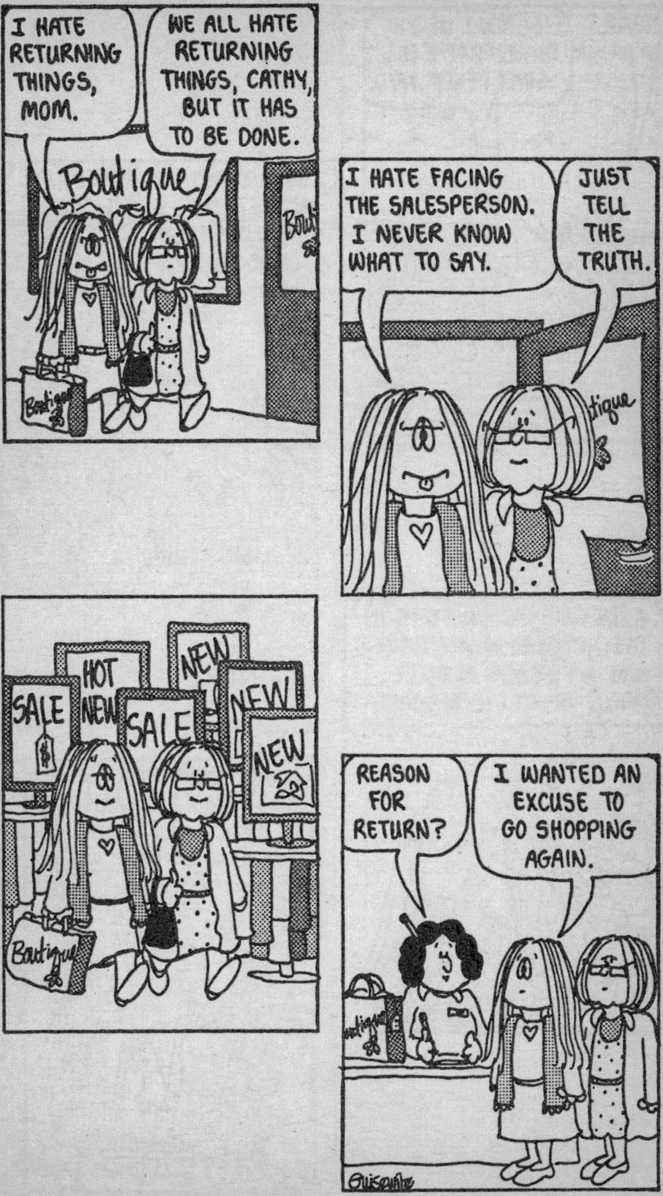
I HATE RETURNING THINGS, MOM.
WE ALL HATE RETURNING THINGS, CATHY, BUT IT HAS TO BE DONE.
Boutique
I HATE FACING THE SALESPERSON. I NEVER KNOW WHAT TO SAY.
JUST TELL THE TRUTH.
HOT NEW
NEW
SALE
SALE
NEW
NEW
Boutique
REASON FOR RETURN?
I WANTED AN EXCUSE TO GO SHOPPING AGAIN.
Guisewite

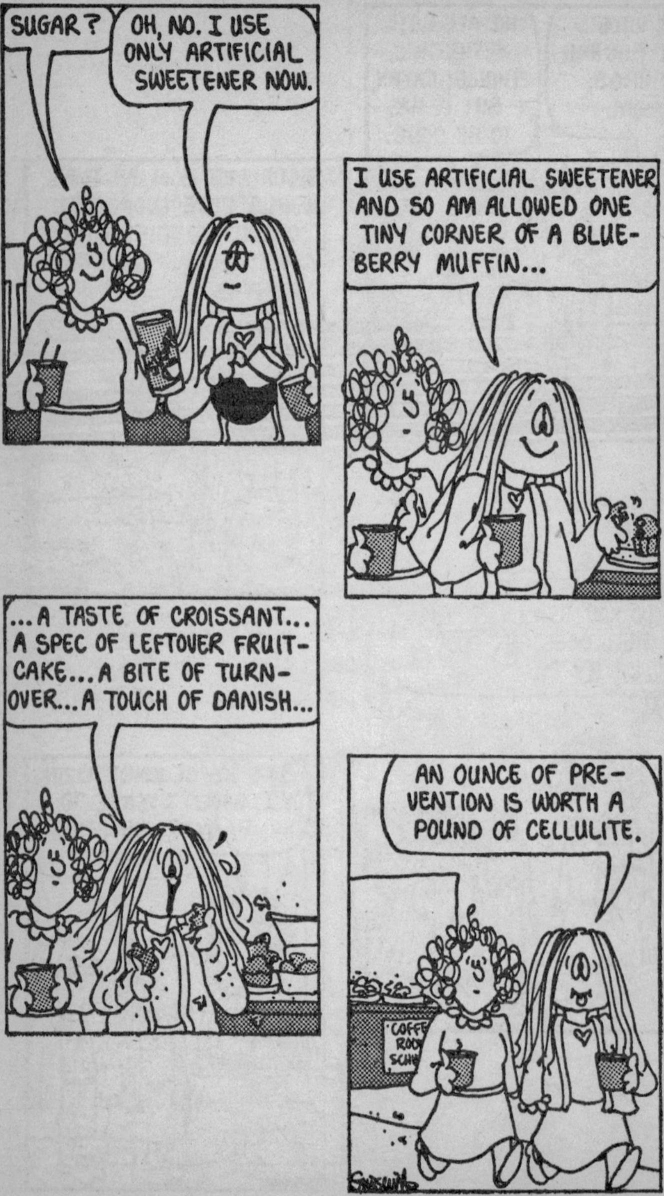
SUGAR?
OH, NO. I USE ONLY ARTIFICIAL SWEETENER NOW.
I USE ARTIFICIAL SWEETENER, AND SO AM ALLOWED ONE TINY CORNER OF A BLUE-BERRY MUFFIN...
...A TASTE OF CROISSANT... A SPEC OF LEFTOVER FRUIT-CAKE...A BITE OF TURN-OVER...A TOUCH OF DANISH...
AN OUNCE OF PRE-VENTION IS WORTH A POUND OF CELLULITE.

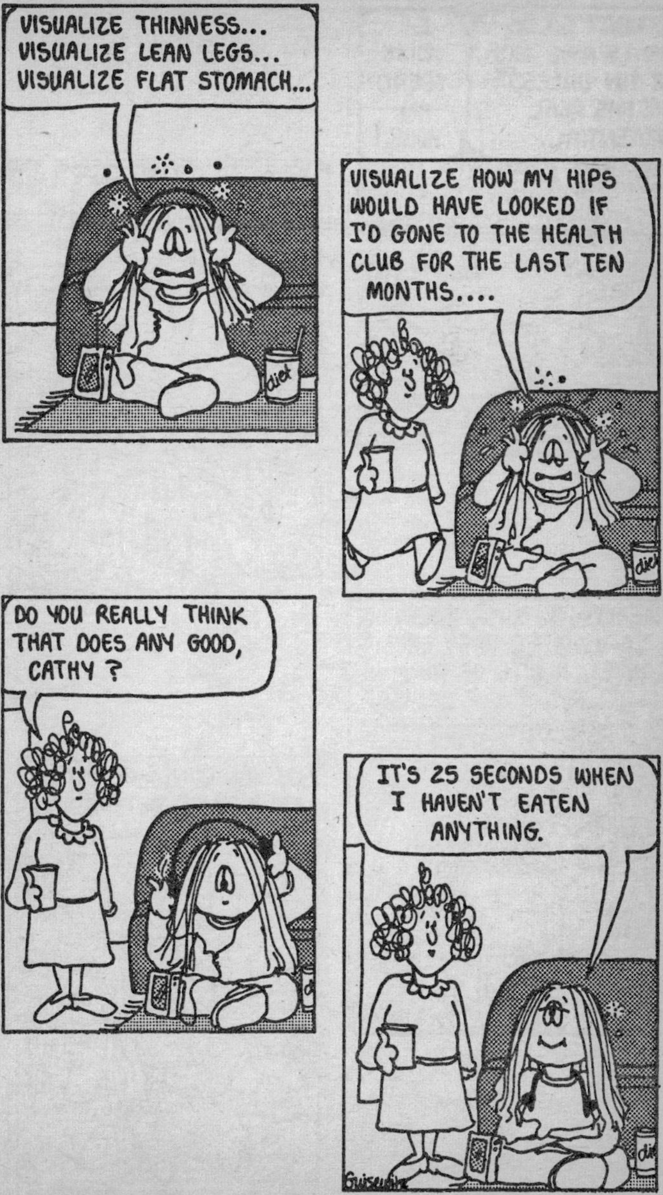
VISUALIZE THINNESS... VISUALIZE LEAN LEGS... VISUALIZE FLAT STOMACH...
VISUALIZE HOW MY HIPS WOULD HAVE LOOKED IF I'D GONE TO THE HEALTH CLUB FOR THE LAST TEN MONTHS....
DO YOU REALLY THINK THAT DOES ANY GOOD, CATHY?
IT'S 25 SECONDS WHEN I HAVEN'T EATEN ANYTHING.
diet
Guisewite

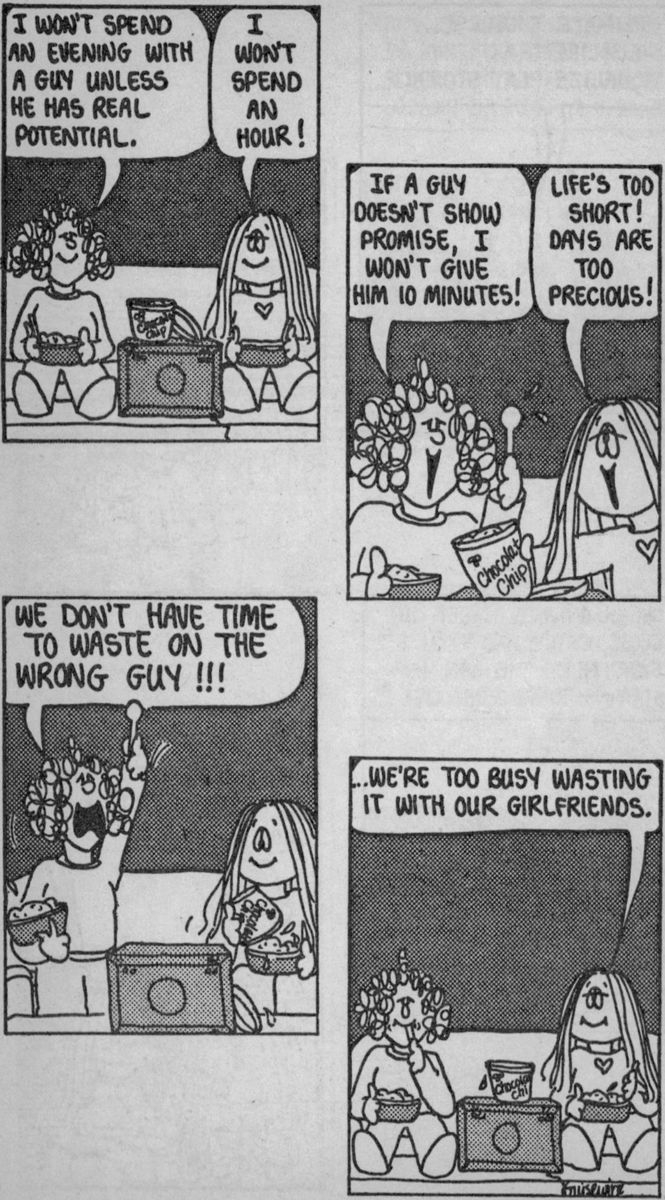
I WON'T SPEND AN EVENING WITH A GUY UNLESS HE HAS REAL POTENTIAL.
I WON'T SPEND AN HOUR!
IF A GUY DOESN'T SHOW PROMISE, I WON'T GIVE HIM 10 MINUTES!
LIFE'S TOO SHORT! DAYS ARE TOO PRECIOUS!
WE DON'T HAVE TIME TO WASTE ON THE WRONG GUY !!!
...WE'RE TOO BUSY WASTING IT WITH OUR GIRLFRIENDS.

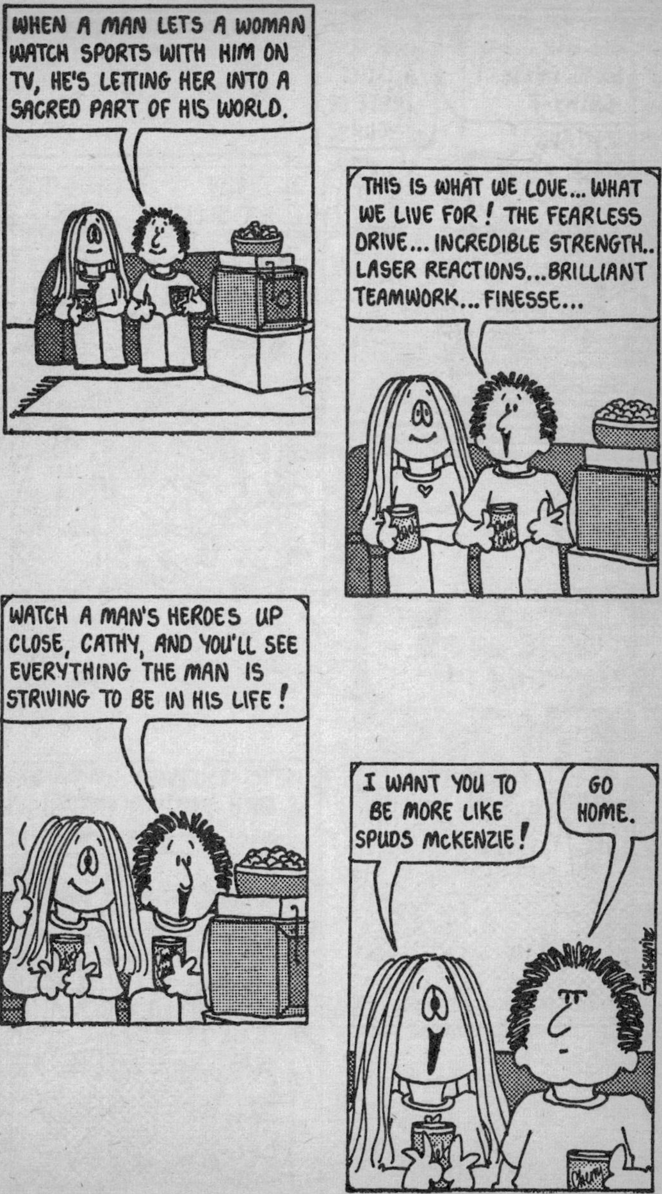
WHEN A MAN LETS A WOMAN WATCH SPORTS WITH HIM ON TV, HE'S LETTING HER INTO A SACRED PART OF HIS WORLD.
THIS IS WHAT WE LOVE... WHAT WE LIVE FOR! THE FEARLESS DRIVE... INCREDIBLE STRENGTH.. LASER REACTIONS...BRILLIANT TEAMWORK... FINESSE...
WATCH A MAN'S HEROES UP CLOSE, CATHY, AND YOU'LL SEE EVERYTHING THE MAN IS STRIVING TO BE IN HIS LIFE!
I WANT YOU TO BE MORE LIKE SPUDS McKENZIE!
GO HOME.

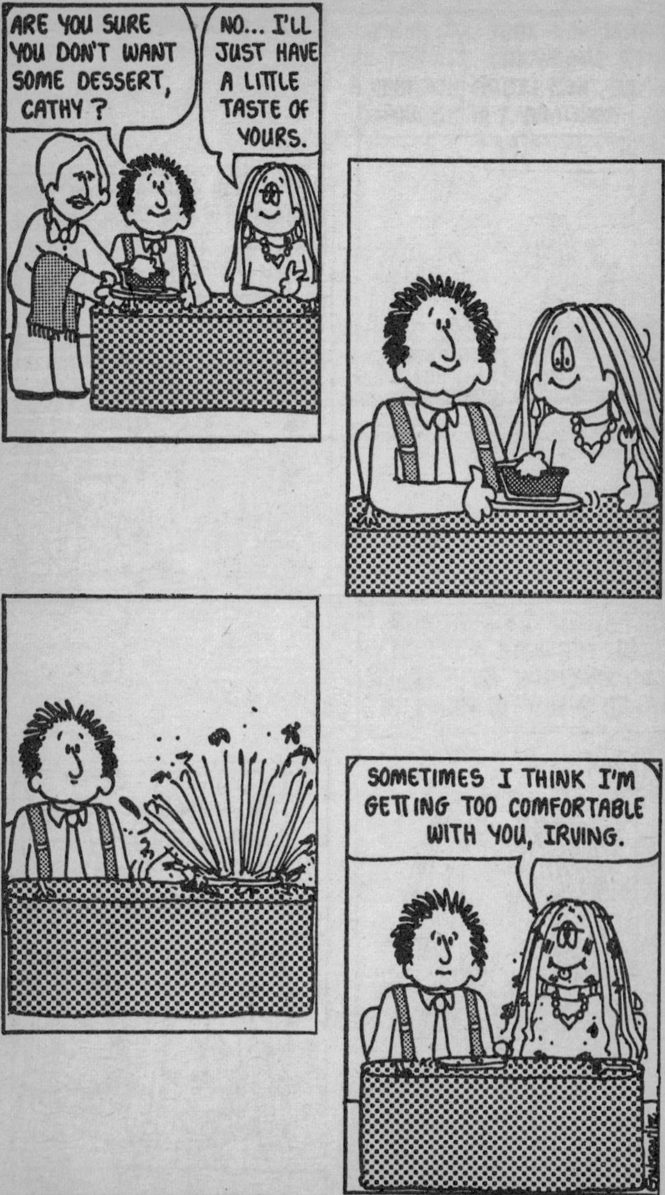
ARE YOU SURE YOU DON'T WANT SOME DESSERT, CATHY ?
NO... I'LL JUST HAVE A LITTLE TASTE OF YOURS.
SOMETIMES I THINK I'M GETTING TOO COMFORTABLE WITH YOU, IRVING.

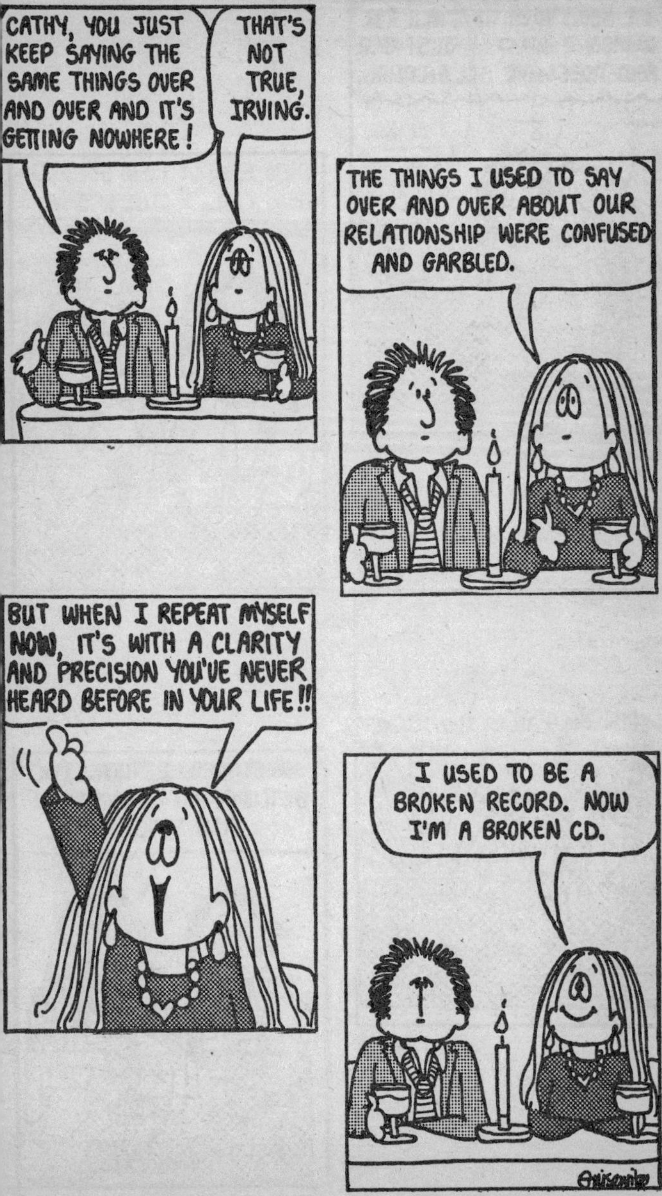
CATHY, YOU JUST KEEP SAYING THE SAME THINGS OVER AND OVER AND IT'S GETTING NOWHERE!
THAT'S NOT TRUE, IRVING.
THE THINGS I USED TO SAY OVER AND OVER ABOUT OUR RELATIONSHIP WERE CONFUSED AND GARBLED.
BUT WHEN I REPEAT MYSELF NOW, IT'S WITH A CLARITY AND PRECISION YOU'VE NEVER HEARD BEFORE IN YOUR LIFE!!
I USED TO BE A BROKEN RECORD. NOW I'M A BROKEN CD.

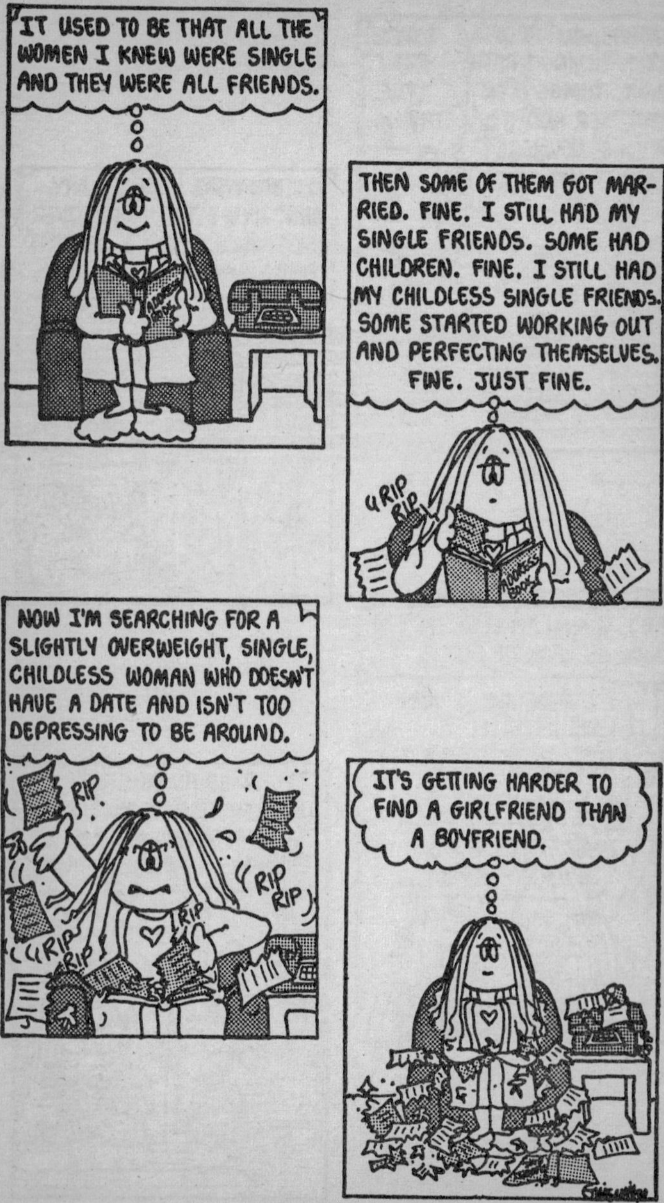
IT USED TO BE THAT ALL THE WOMEN I KNEW WERE SINGLE AND THEY WERE ALL FRIENDS.
THEN SOME OF THEM GOT MARRIED. FINE. I STILL HAD MY SINGLE FRIENDS. SOME HAD CHILDREN. FINE. I STILL HAD MY CHILDLESS SINGLE FRIENDS. SOME STARTED WORKING OUT AND PERFECTING THEMSELVES. FINE. JUST FINE.
RIP RIP
NOW I'M SEARCHING FOR A SLIGHTLY OVERWEIGHT, SINGLE, CHILDLESS WOMAN WHO DOESN'T HAVE A DATE AND ISN'T TOO DEPRESSING TO BE AROUND.
RIP
RIP RIP
RIP
RIP RIP
IT'S GETTING HARDER TO FIND A GIRLFRIEND THAN A BOYFRIEND.

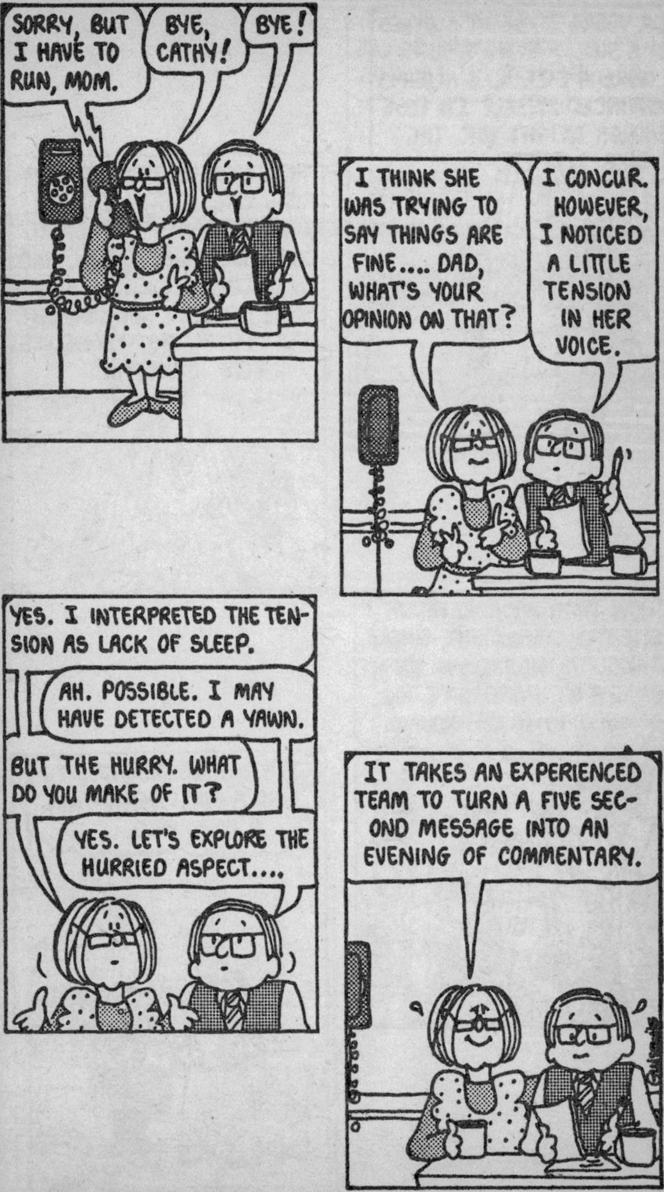
SORRY, BUT I HAVE TO RUN, MOM.
BYE, CATHY!
BYE!
I THINK SHE WAS TRYING TO SAY THINGS ARE FINE.... DAD, WHAT'S YOUR OPINION ON THAT?
I CONCUR. HOWEVER, I NOTICED A LITTLE TENSION IN HER VOICE.
YES. I INTERPRETED THE TEN-SION AS LACK OF SLEEP.
AH. POSSIBLE. I MAY HAVE DETECTED A YAWN.
BUT THE HURRY. WHAT DO YOU MAKE OF IT?
YES. LET'S EXPLORE THE HURRIED ASPECT....
IT TAKES AN EXPERIENCED TEAM TO TURN A FIVE SEC-OND MESSAGE INTO AN EVENING OF COMMENTARY.

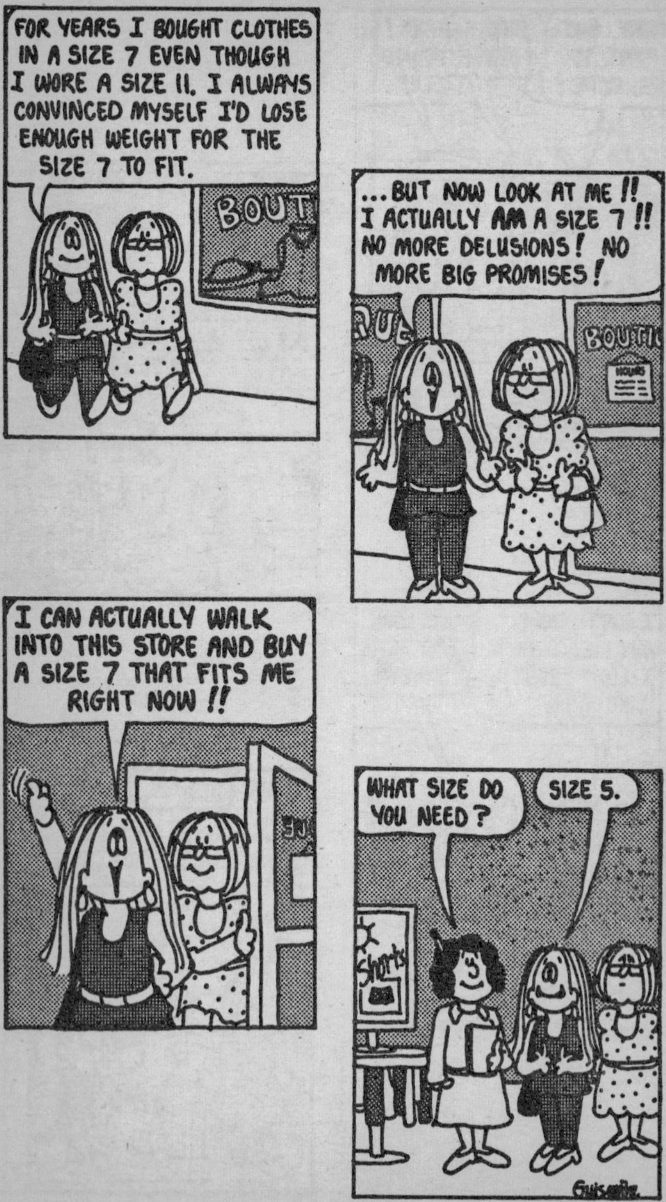
FOR YEARS I BOUGHT CLOTHES IN A SIZE 7 EVEN THOUGH I WORE A SIZE 11. I ALWAYS CONVINCED MYSELF I'D LOSE ENOUGH WEIGHT FOR THE SIZE 7 TO FIT.
...BUT NOW LOOK AT ME !! I ACTUALLY AM A SIZE 7 !! NO MORE DELUSIONS! NO MORE BIG PROMISES!
I CAN ACTUALLY WALK INTO THIS STORE AND BUY A SIZE 7 THAT FITS ME RIGHT NOW !!
WHAT SIZE DO YOU NEED?
SIZE 5.
Shorts

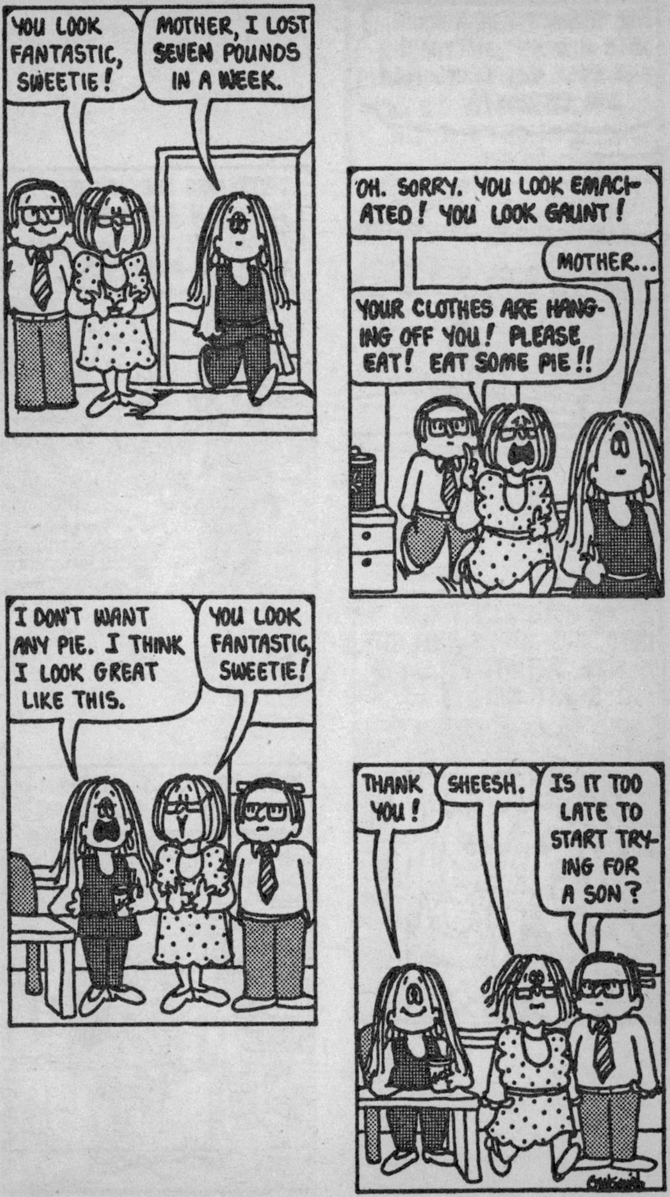
YOU LOOK FANTASTIC, SWEETIE!
MOTHER, I LOST SEVEN POUNDS IN A WEEK.
OH. SORRY. YOU LOOK EMACIATED! YOU LOOK GAUNT!
MOTHER...
YOUR CLOTHES ARE HANGING OFF YOU! PLEASE EAT! EAT SOME PIE!!
I DON'T WANT ANY PIE. I THINK I LOOK GREAT LIKE THIS.
YOU LOOK FANTASTIC, SWEETIE!
THANK YOU!
SHEESH.
IS IT TOO LATE TO START TRYING FOR A SON?

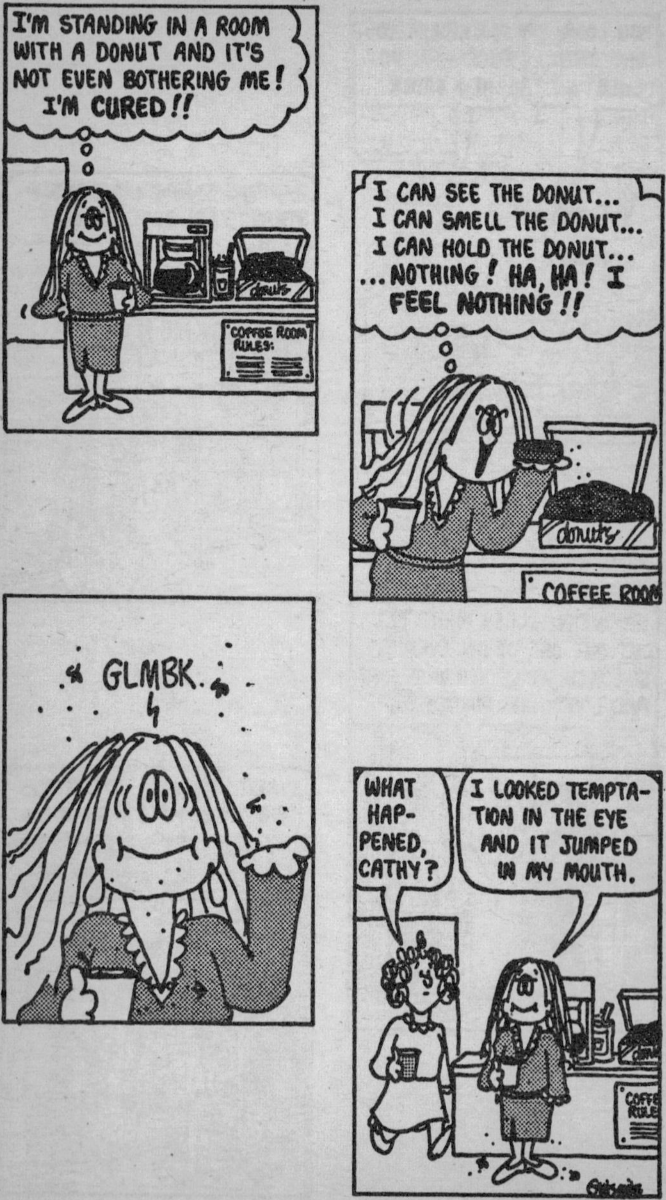
I'M STANDING IN A ROOM WITH A DONUT AND IT'S NOT EVEN BOTHERING ME! I'M CURED!!
COFFEE ROOM RULES:
I CAN SEE THE DONUT... I CAN SMELL THE DONUT... I CAN HOLD THE DONUT... ...NOTHING! HA, HA! I FEEL NOTHING!!
donuts
COFFEE ROOM
GLMBK.
WHAT HAP-PENED, CATHY?
I LOOKED TEMPTA-TION IN THE EYE AND IT JUMPED IN MY MOUTH.

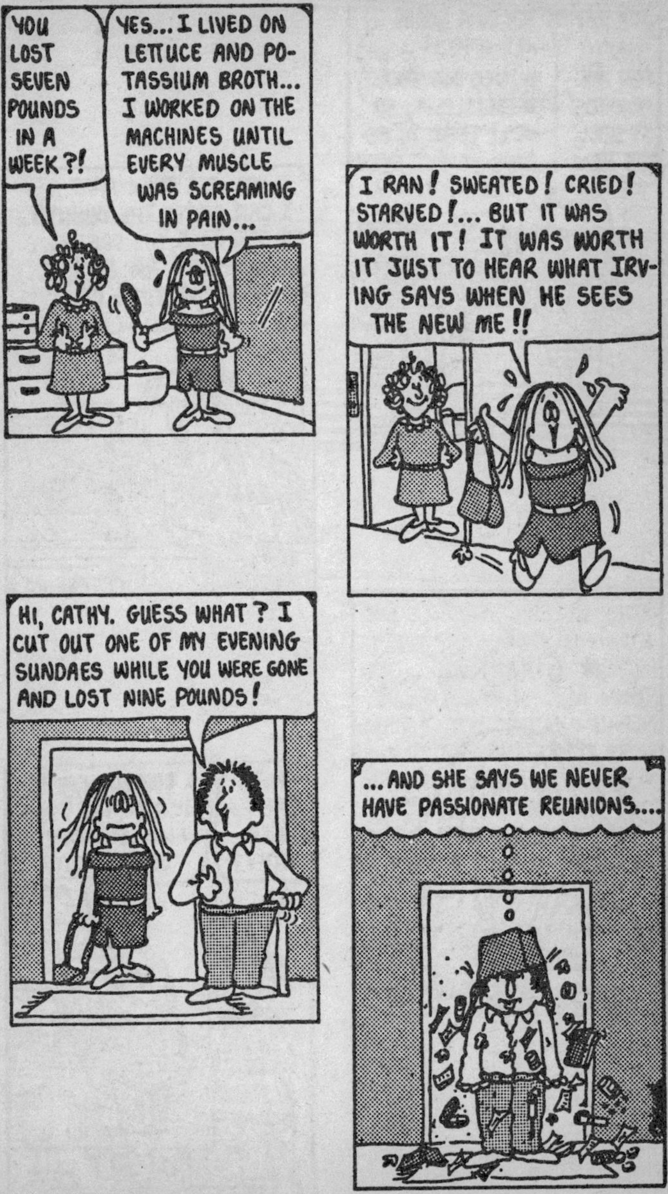

YOU LOST SEVEN POUNDS IN A WEEK ?!
YES... I LIVED ON LETTUCE AND POTASSIUM BROTH... I WORKED ON THE MACHINES UNTIL EVERY MUSCLE WAS SCREAMING IN PAIN...
I RAN! SWEATED! CRIED! STARVED!... BUT IT WAS WORTH IT! IT WAS WORTH IT JUST TO HEAR WHAT IRVING SAYS WHEN HE SEES THE NEW ME!!
HI, CATHY. GUESS WHAT? I CUT OUT ONE OF MY EVENING SUNDAES WHILE YOU WERE GONE AND LOST NINE POUNDS!
...AND SHE SAYS WE NEVER HAVE PASSIONATE REUNIONS....

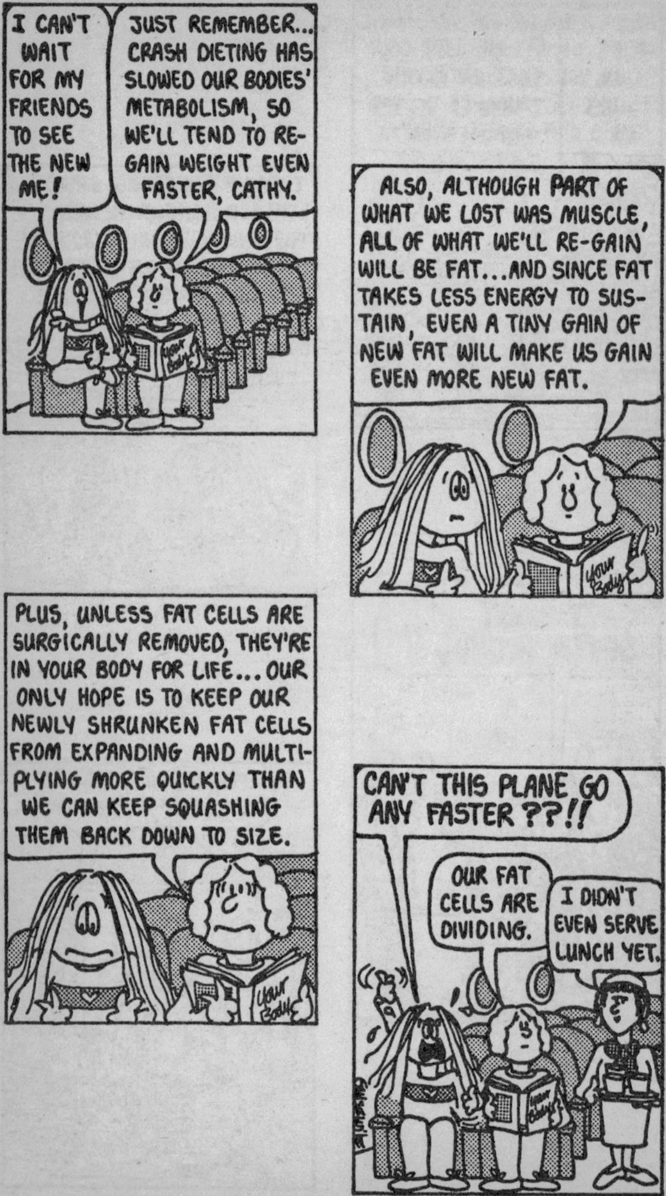
I CAN'T WAIT FOR MY FRIENDS TO SEE THE NEW ME!
JUST REMEMBER... CRASH DIETING HAS SLOWED OUR BODIES' METABOLISM, SO WE'LL TEND TO RE-GAIN WEIGHT EVEN FASTER, CATHY.
YOUR BODY
ALSO, ALTHOUGH PART OF WHAT WE LOST WAS MUSCLE, ALL OF WHAT WE'LL RE-GAIN WILL BE FAT... AND SINCE FAT TAKES LESS ENERGY TO SUS-TAIN, EVEN A TINY GAIN OF NEW FAT WILL MAKE US GAIN EVEN MORE NEW FAT.
YOUR BODY
PLUS, UNLESS FAT CELLS ARE SURGICALLY REMOVED, THEY'RE IN YOUR BODY FOR LIFE... OUR ONLY HOPE IS TO KEEP OUR NEWLY SHRUNKEN FAT CELLS FROM EXPANDING AND MULTI-PLYING MORE QUICKLY THAN WE CAN KEEP SQUASHING THEM BACK DOWN TO SIZE.
YOUR BODY
CAN'T THIS PLANE GO ANY FASTER??!!
OUR FAT CELLS ARE DIVIDING.
I DIDN'T EVEN SERVE LUNCH YET.
YOUR BODY

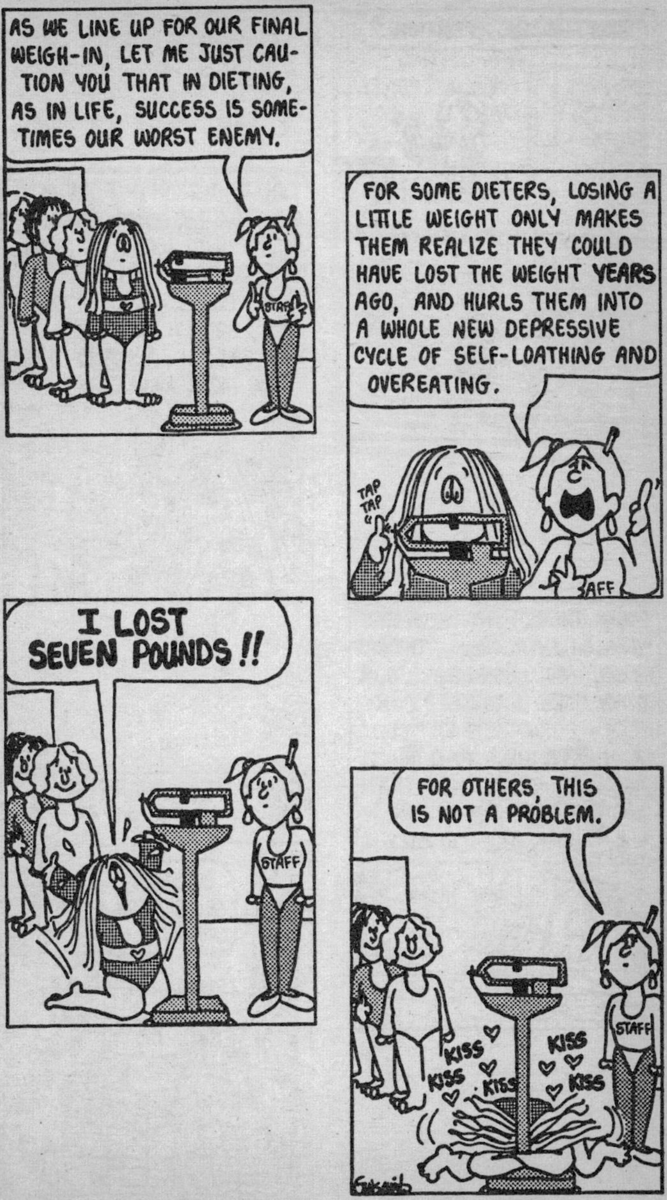
AS WE LINE UP FOR OUR FINAL WEIGH-IN, LET ME JUST CAUTION YOU THAT IN DIETING, AS IN LIFE, SUCCESS IS SOMETIMES OUR WORST ENEMY.
STAFF
FOR SOME DIETERS, LOSING A LITTLE WEIGHT ONLY MAKES THEM REALIZE THEY COULD HAVE LOST THE WEIGHT YEARS AGO, AND HURLS THEM INTO A WHOLE NEW DEPRESSIVE CYCLE OF SELF-LOATHING AND OVEREATING.
TAP TAP
I LOST SEVEN POUNDS!!
STAFF
FOR OTHERS, THIS IS NOT A PROBLEM.
KISS
KISS
KISS
KISS
KISS
STAFF

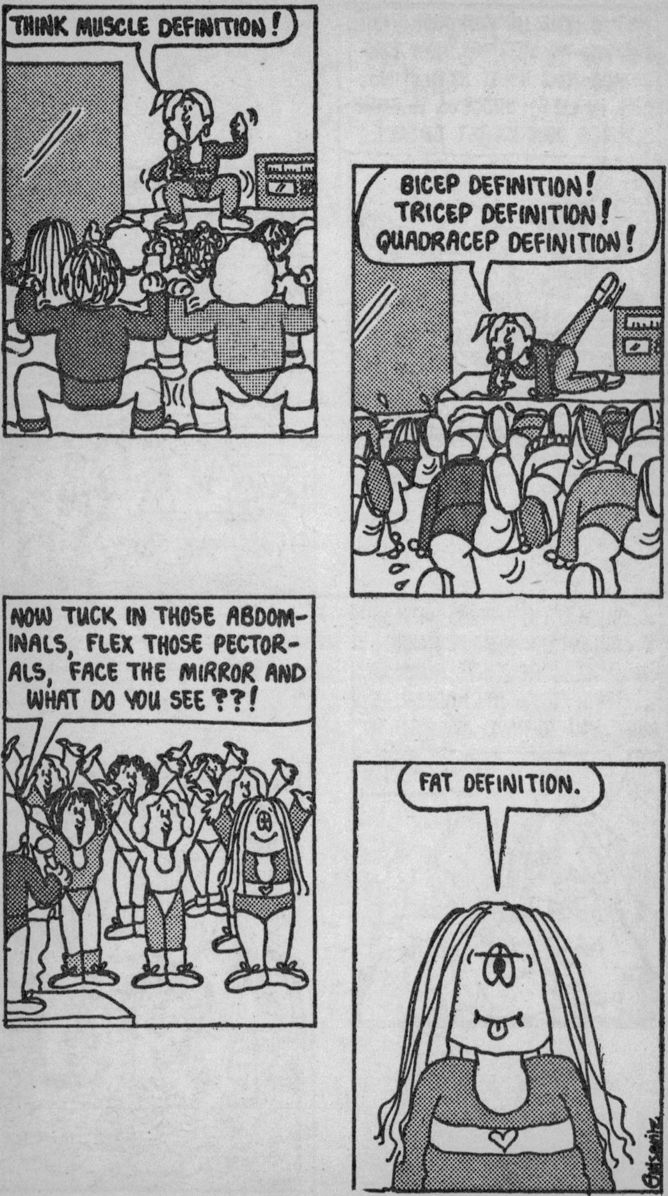
THINK MUSCLE DEFINITION!
BICEP DEFINITION! TRICEP DEFINITION! QUADRACEP DEFINITION!
NOW TUCK IN THOSE ABDOMINALS, FLEX THOSE PECTORALS, FACE THE MIRROR AND WHAT DO YOU SEE??!
FAT DEFINITION.

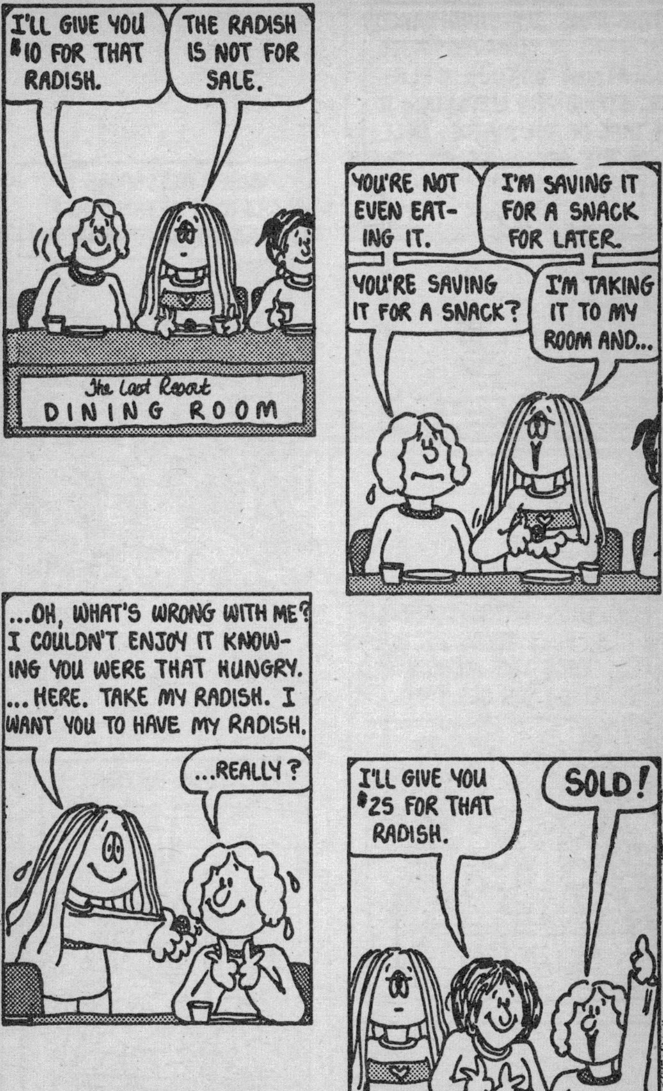
I'LL GIVE YOU $10 FOR THAT RADISH.
THE RADISH IS NOT FOR SALE.
The Last Resort
DINING ROOM
YOU'RE NOT EVEN EAT-ING IT.
I'M SAVING IT FOR A SNACK FOR LATER.
YOU'RE SAVING IT FOR A SNACK?
I'M TAKING IT TO MY ROOM AND...
...OH, WHAT'S WRONG WITH ME? I COULDN'T ENJOY IT KNOW-ING YOU WERE THAT HUNGRY. ...HERE. TAKE MY RADISH. I WANT YOU TO HAVE MY RADISH.
...REALLY?
I'LL GIVE YOU $25 FOR THAT RADISH.
SOLD!

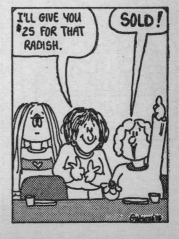

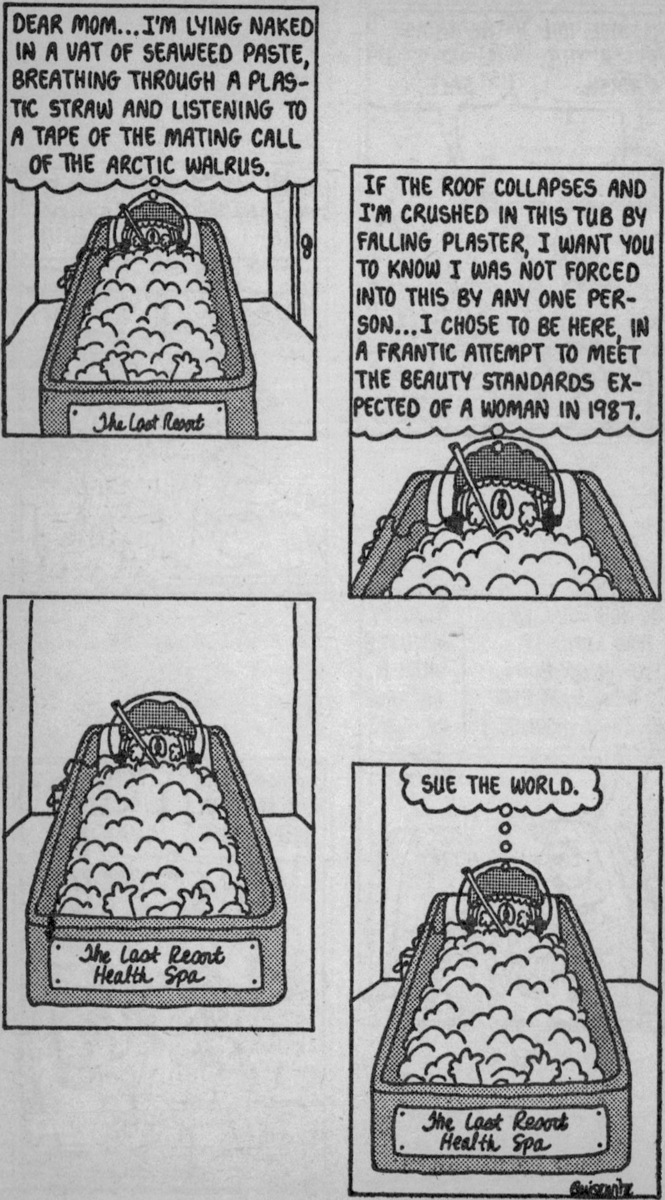
DEAR MOM...I'M LYING NAKED IN A VAT OF SEAWEED PASTE, BREATHING THROUGH A PLASTIC STRAW AND LISTENING TO A TAPE OF THE MATING CALL OF THE ARCTIC WALRUS.
The Last Resort
IF THE ROOF COLLAPSES AND I'M CRUSHED IN THIS TUB BY FALLING PLASTER, I WANT YOU TO KNOW I WAS NOT FORCED INTO THIS BY ANY ONE PERSON...I CHOSE TO BE HERE, IN A FRANTIC ATTEMPT TO MEET THE BEAUTY STANDARDS EXPECTED OF A WOMAN IN 1987.
The Last Resort Health Spa
SUE THE WORLD.
The Last Resort Health Spa
Guisewite

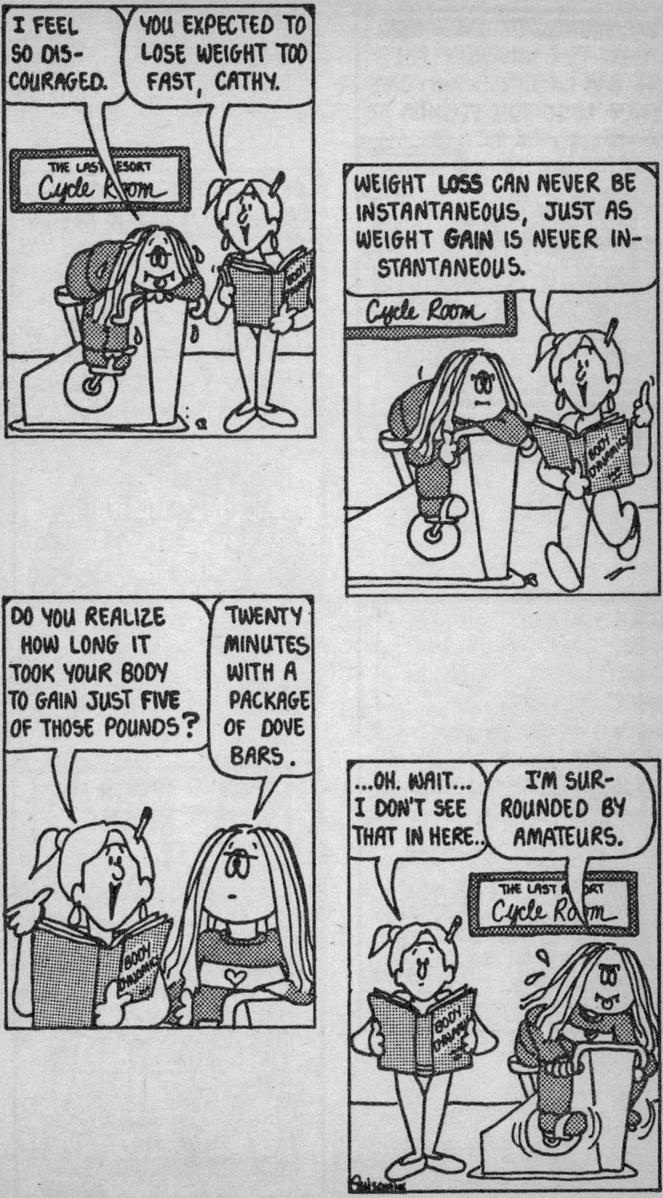
I FEEL SO DIS-COURAGED.
YOU EXPECTED TO LOSE WEIGHT TOO FAST, CATHY.
WEIGHT LOSS CAN NEVER BE INSTANTANEOUS, JUST AS WEIGHT GAIN IS NEVER IN-STANTANEOUS.
Cycle Room
DO YOU REALIZE HOW LONG IT TOOK YOUR BODY TO GAIN JUST FIVE OF THOSE POUNDS?
TWENTY MINUTES WITH A PACKAGE OF DOVE BARS.
...OH. WAIT... I DON'T SEE THAT IN HERE..
I'M SUR-ROUNDED BY AMATEURS.

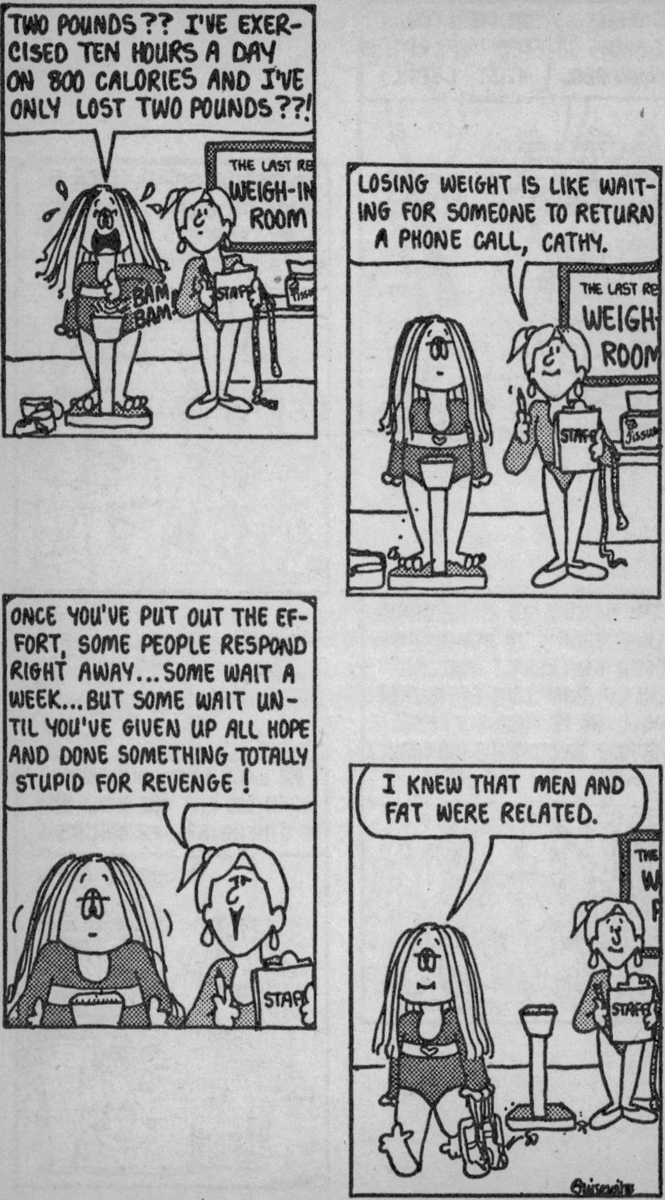
TWO POUNDS?? I'VE EXERCISED TEN HOURS A DAY ON 800 CALORIES AND I'VE ONLY LOST TWO POUNDS??!
BAM BAM
LOSING WEIGHT IS LIKE WAITING FOR SOMEONE TO RETURN A PHONE CALL, CATHY.
ONCE YOU'VE PUT OUT THE EFFORT, SOME PEOPLE RESPOND RIGHT AWAY... SOME WAIT A WEEK... BUT SOME WAIT UNTIL YOU'VE GIVEN UP ALL HOPE AND DONE SOMETHING TOTALLY STUPID FOR REVENGE!
I KNEW THAT MEN AND FAT WERE RELATED.

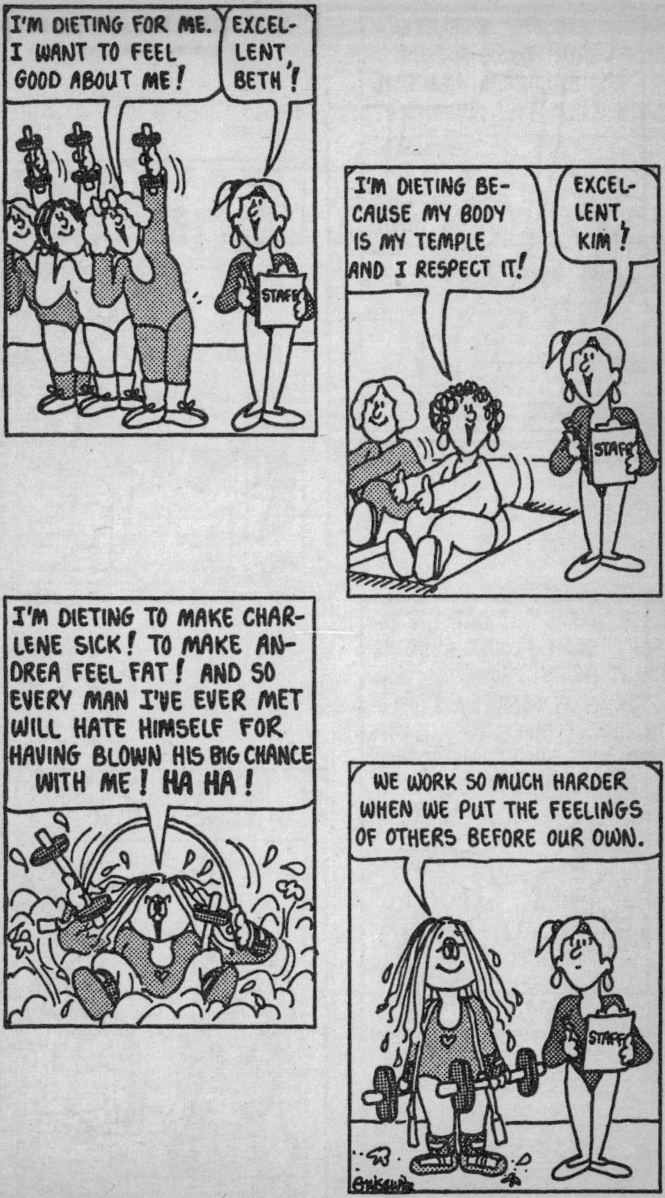
I'M DIETING FOR ME. I WANT TO FEEL GOOD ABOUT ME!
EXCEL-LENT, BETH!
STAFF
I'M DIETING BE-CAUSE MY BODY IS MY TEMPLE AND I RESPECT IT!
EXCEL-LENT, KIM!
STAFF
I'M DIETING TO MAKE CHAR-LENE SICK! TO MAKE AN-DREA FEEL FAT! AND SO EVERY MAN I'VE EVER MET WILL HATE HIMSELF FOR HAVING BLOWN HIS BIG CHANCE WITH ME! HA HA!
WE WORK SO MUCH HARDER WHEN WE PUT THE FEELINGS OF OTHERS BEFORE OUR OWN.
STAFF

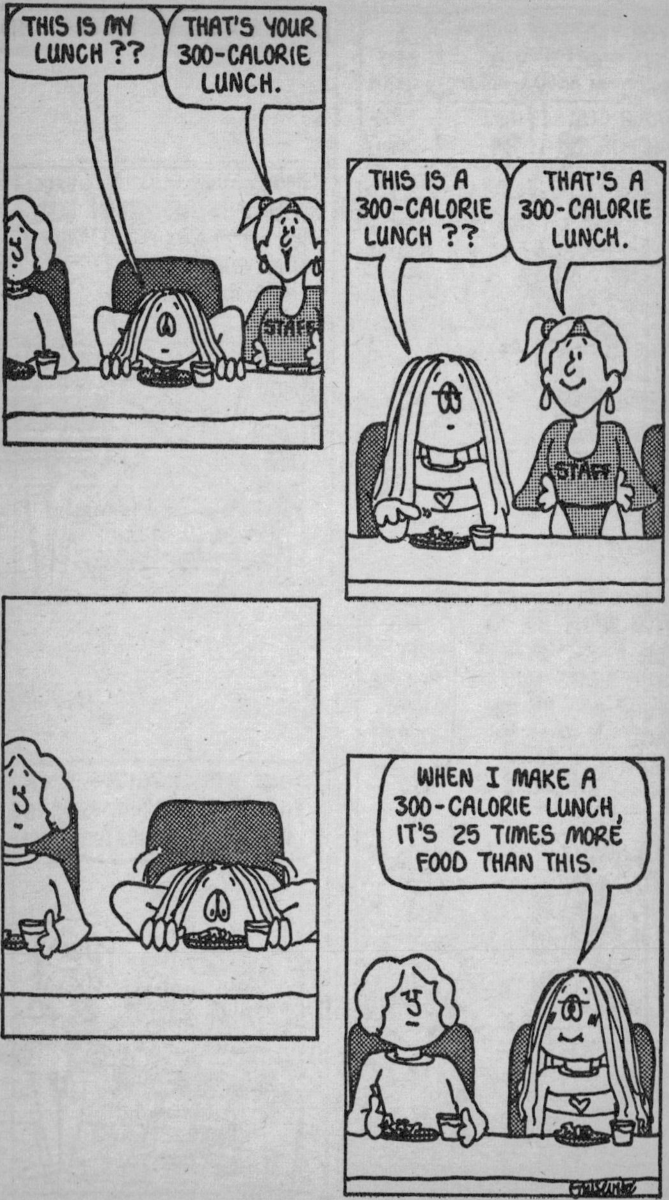
THIS IS MY LUNCH??
THAT'S YOUR 300-CALORIE LUNCH.
THIS IS A 300-CALORIE LUNCH??
THAT'S A 300-CALORIE LUNCH.
WHEN I MAKE A 300-CALORIE LUNCH, IT'S 25 TIMES MORE FOOD THAN THIS.

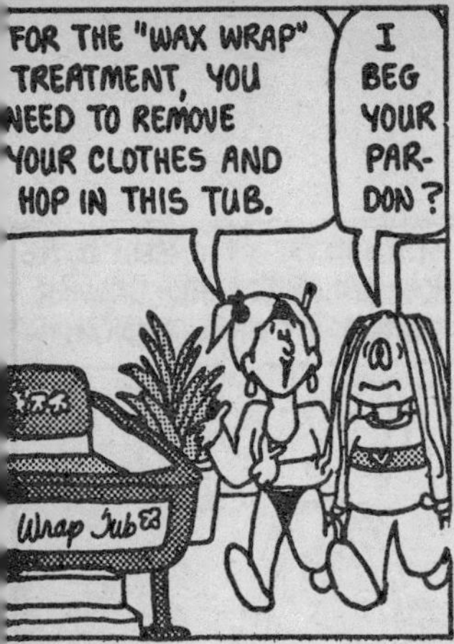
FOR THE "WAX WRAP" TREATMENT, YOU NEED TO REMOVE YOUR CLOTHES AND HOP IN THIS TUB.
I BEG YOUR PAR-DON?
Wrap Tub

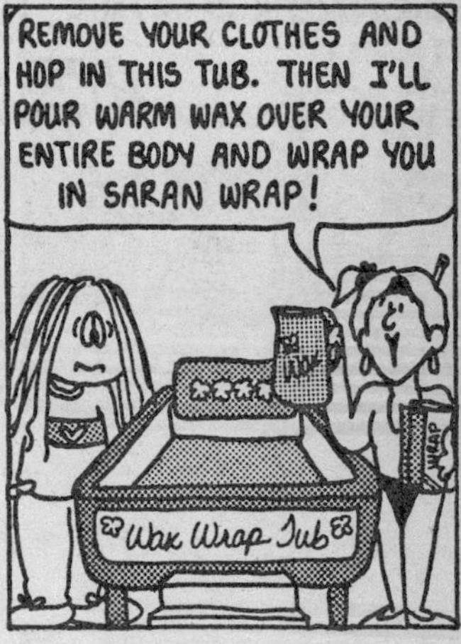
REMOVE YOUR CLOTHES AND HOP IN THIS TUB. THEN I'LL POUR WARM WAX OVER YOUR ENTIRE BODY AND WRAP YOU IN SARAN WRAP!
WRAP
Wax Wrap Tub

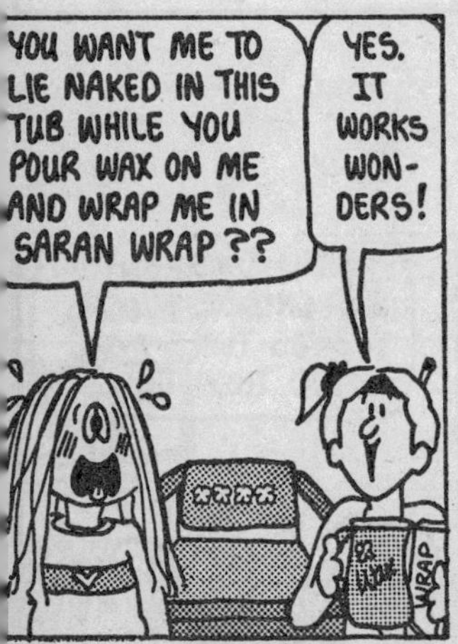
YOU WANT ME TO LIE NAKED IN THIS TUB WHILE YOU POUR WAX ON ME AND WRAP ME IN SARAN WRAP??
YES. IT WORKS WON-DERS!
WRAP

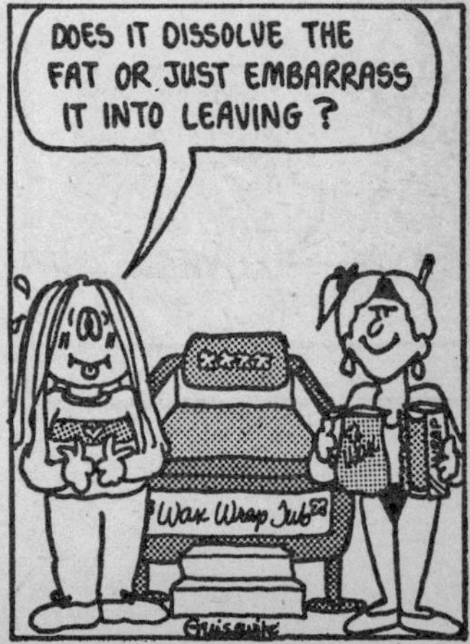
DOES IT DISSOLVE THE FAT OR JUST EMBARRASS IT INTO LEAVING?
WRAP
Wax Wrap Tub

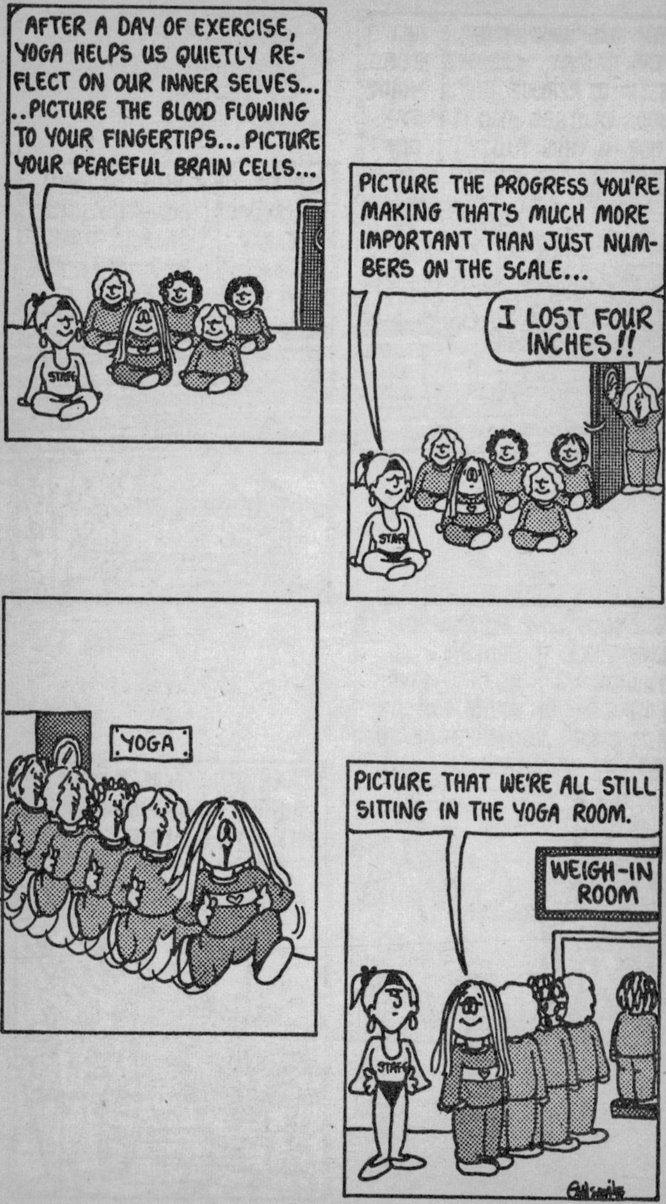
AFTER A DAY OF EXERCISE, YOGA HELPS US QUIETLY REFLECT ON OUR INNER SELVES... ..PICTURE THE BLOOD FLOWING TO YOUR FINGERTIPS... PICTURE YOUR PEACEFUL BRAIN CELLS...
PICTURE THE PROGRESS YOU'RE MAKING THAT'S MUCH MORE IMPORTANT THAN JUST NUMBERS ON THE SCALE...
I LOST FOUR INCHES!!
YOGA
PICTURE THAT WE'RE ALL STILL SITTING IN THE YOGA ROOM.
WEIGH-IN ROOM

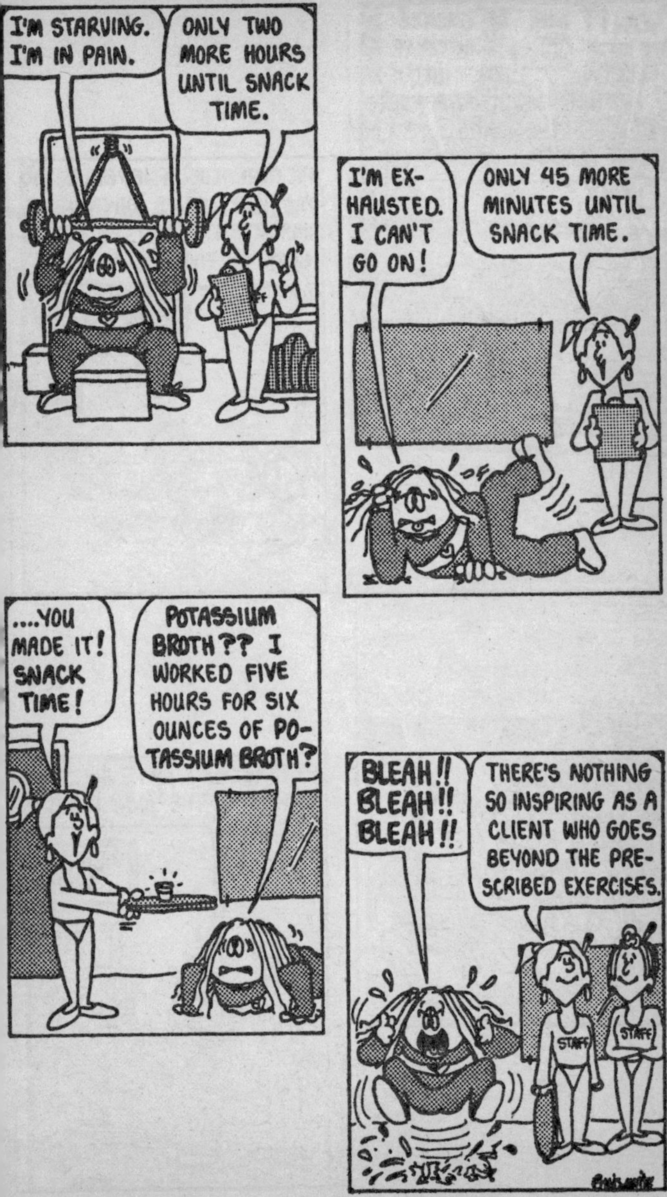
I'M STARVING. I'M IN PAIN.
ONLY TWO MORE HOURS UNTIL SNACK TIME.
I'M EX-HAUSTED. I CAN'T GO ON!
ONLY 45 MORE MINUTES UNTIL SNACK TIME.
....YOU MADE IT! SNACK TIME!
POTASSIUM BROTH?? I WORKED FIVE HOURS FOR SIX OUNCES OF PO-TASSIUM BROTH?
BLEAH!! BLEAH!! BLEAH!!
THERE'S NOTHING SO INSPIRING AS A CLIENT WHO GOES BEYOND THE PRE-SCRIBED EXERCISES.
STAFF
STAFF

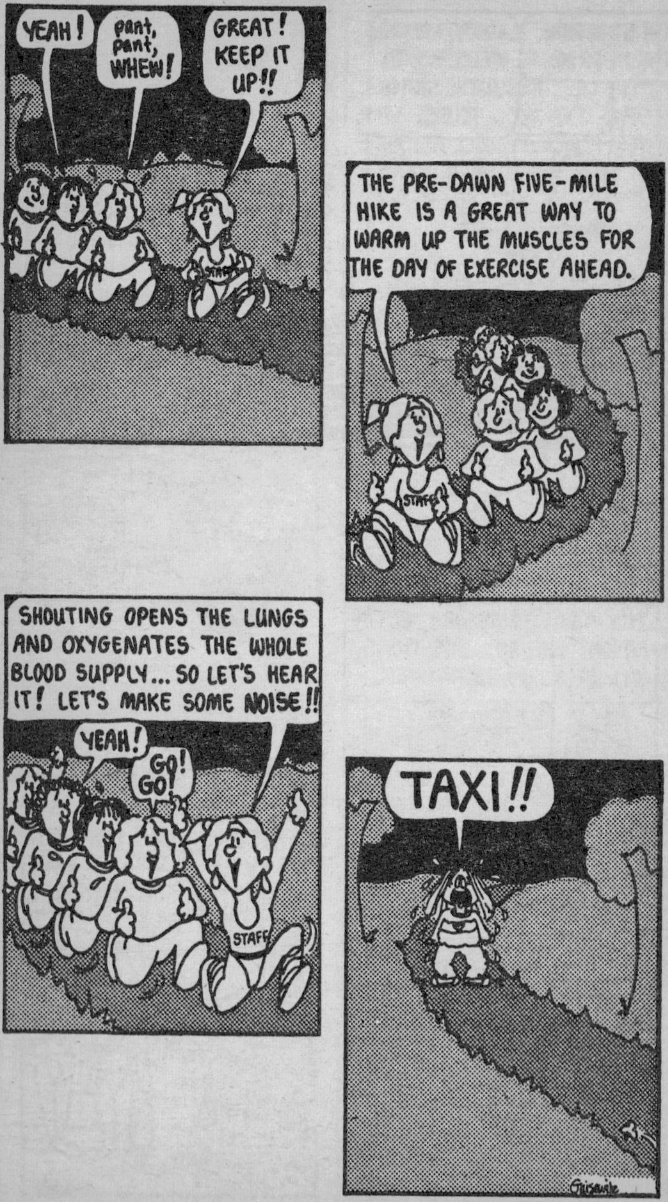
YEAH!
pant, pant, WHEW!
GREAT! KEEP IT UP!!
STAFF
THE PRE-DAWN FIVE-MILE HIKE IS A GREAT WAY TO WARM UP THE MUSCLES FOR THE DAY OF EXERCISE AHEAD.
STAFF
SHOUTING OPENS THE LUNGS AND OXYGENATES THE WHOLE BLOOD SUPPLY... SO LET'S HEAR IT! LET'S MAKE SOME NOISE!!
YEAH!
GO! GO!
STAFF
TAXI!!
Guisewite

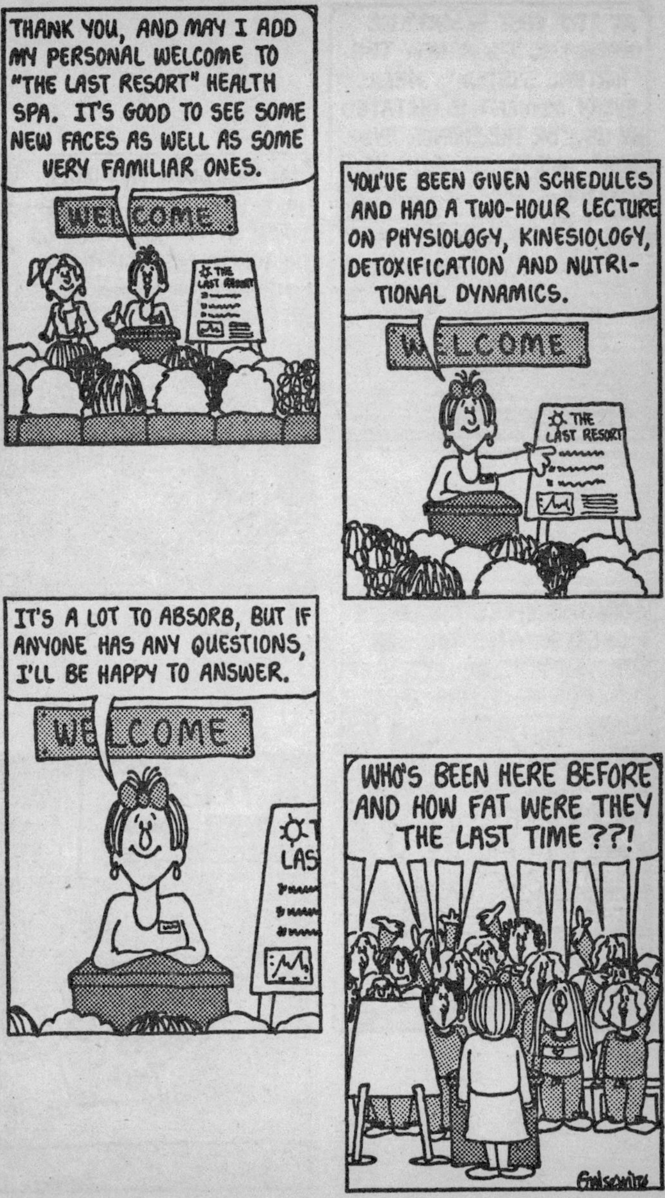
THANK YOU, AND MAY I ADD MY PERSONAL WELCOME TO "THE LAST RESORT" HEALTH SPA. IT'S GOOD TO SEE SOME NEW FACES AS WELL AS SOME VERY FAMILIAR ONES.
WELCOME
THE LAST RESORT
YOU'VE BEEN GIVEN SCHEDULES AND HAD A TWO-HOUR LECTURE ON PHYSIOLOGY, KINESIOLOGY, DETOXIFICATION AND NUTRITIONAL DYNAMICS.
WELCOME
THE LAST RESORT
IT'S A LOT TO ABSORB, BUT IF ANYONE HAS ANY QUESTIONS, I'LL BE HAPPY TO ANSWER.
WELCOME
WHO'S BEEN HERE BEFORE AND HOW FAT WERE THEY THE LAST TIME??!
Guisewite

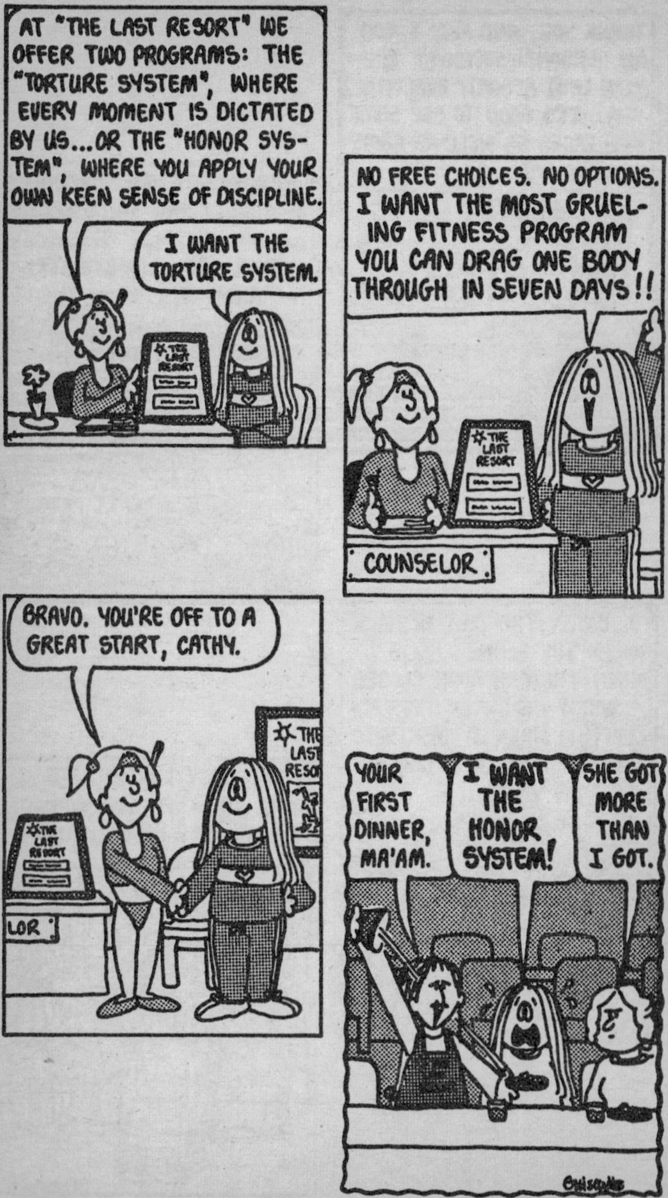
AT "THE LAST RESORT" WE OFFER TWO PROGRAMS: THE "TORTURE SYSTEM", WHERE EVERY MOMENT IS DICTATED BY US...OR THE "HONOR SYSTEM", WHERE YOU APPLY YOUR OWN KEEN SENSE OF DISCIPLINE.
I WANT THE TORTURE SYSTEM.
NO FREE CHOICES. NO OPTIONS. I WANT THE MOST GRUELING FITNESS PROGRAM YOU CAN DRAG ONE BODY THROUGH IN SEVEN DAYS!!
THE LAST RESORT
COUNSELOR
BRAVO. YOU'RE OFF TO A GREAT START, CATHY.
YOUR FIRST DINNER, MA'AM.
I WANT THE HONOR SYSTEM!
SHE GOT MORE THAN I GOT.

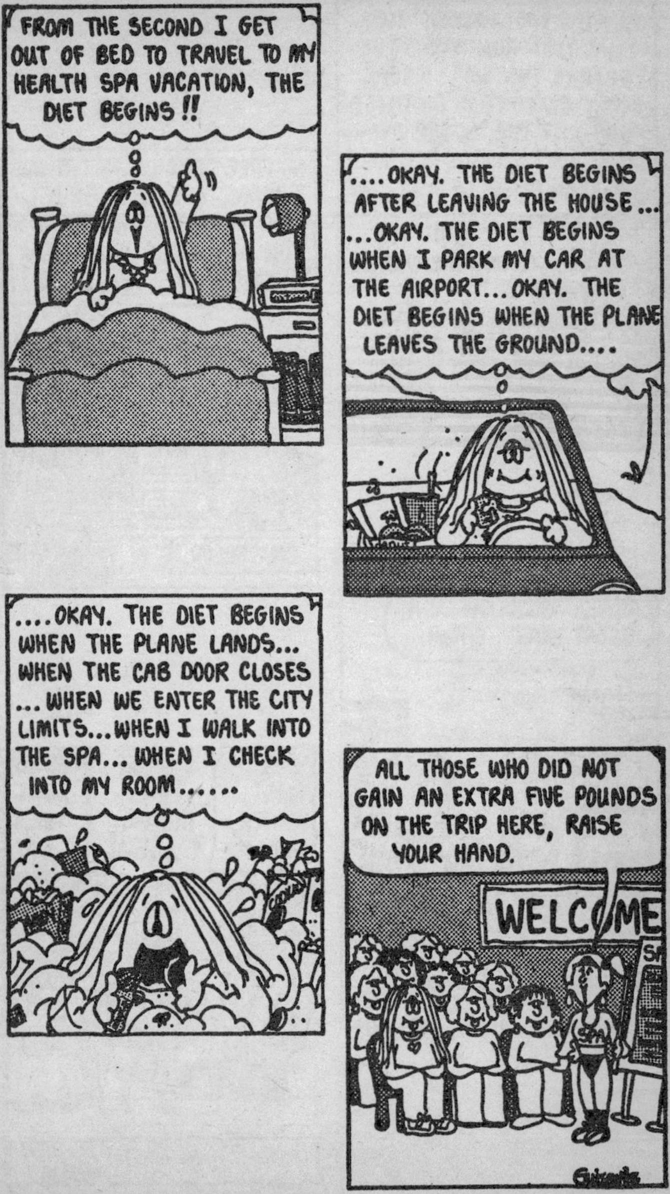

FROM THE SECOND I GET OUT OF BED TO TRAVEL TO MY HEALTH SPA VACATION, THE DIET BEGINS!!
....OKAY. THE DIET BEGINS AFTER LEAVING THE HOUSE... ...OKAY. THE DIET BEGINS WHEN I PARK MY CAR AT THE AIRPORT....OKAY. THE DIET BEGINS WHEN THE PLANE LEAVES THE GROUND....
....OKAY. THE DIET BEGINS WHEN THE PLANE LANDS... WHEN THE CAB DOOR CLOSES ...WHEN WE ENTER THE CITY LIMITS...WHEN I WALK INTO THE SPA... WHEN I CHECK INTO MY ROOM......
ALL THOSE WHO DID NOT GAIN AN EXTRA FIVE POUNDS ON THE TRIP HERE, RAISE YOUR HAND.
WELCOME

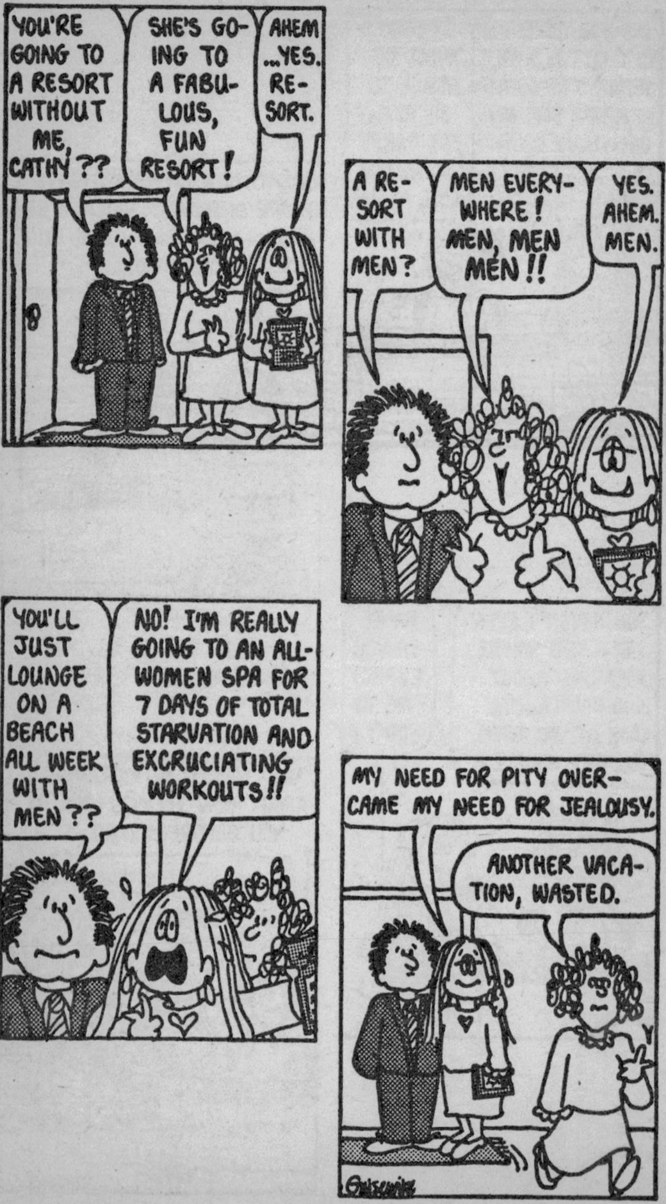
YOU'RE GOING TO A RESORT WITHOUT ME, CATHY??
SHE'S GOING TO A FABULOUS, FUN RESORT!
AHEM ...YES. RESORT.
A RESORT WITH MEN?
MEN EVERYWHERE! MEN, MEN MEN!!
YES. AHEM. MEN.
YOU'LL JUST LOUNGE ON A BEACH ALL WEEK WITH MEN??
NO! I'M REALLY GOING TO AN ALL-WOMEN SPA FOR 7 DAYS OF TOTAL STARVATION AND EXCRUCIATING WORKOUTS!!
MY NEED FOR PITY OVERCAME MY NEED FOR JEALOUSY.
ANOTHER VACATION, WASTED.
Guisewite

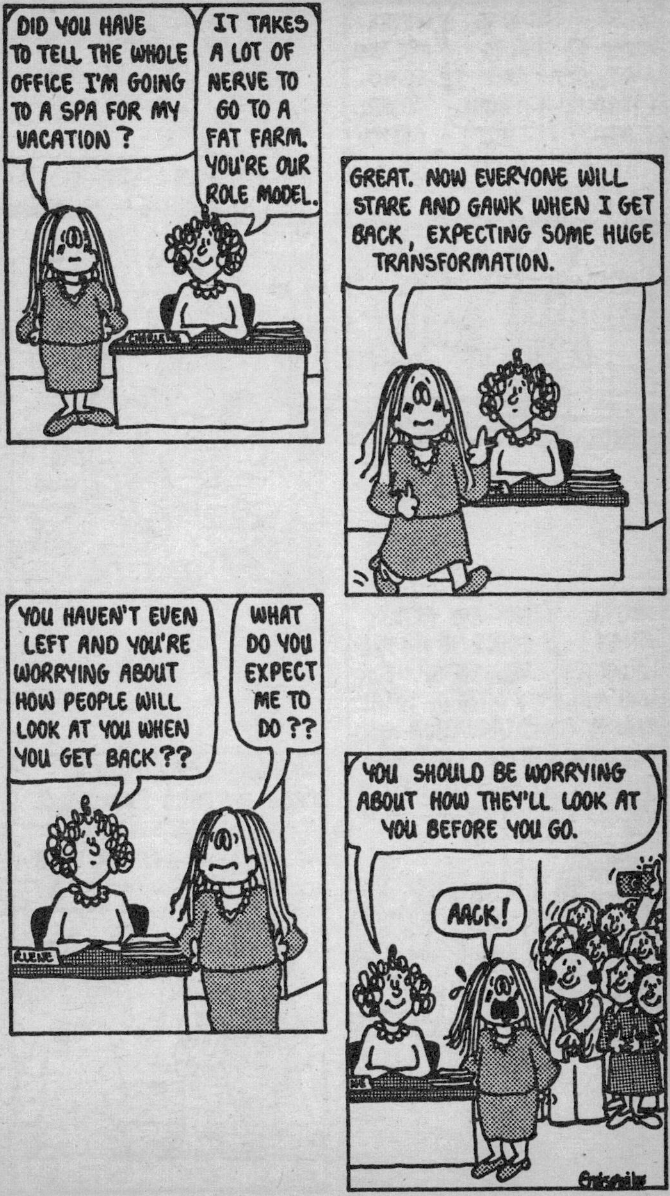
DID YOU HAVE TO TELL THE WHOLE OFFICE I'M GOING TO A SPA FOR MY VACATION?
IT TAKES A LOT OF NERVE TO GO TO A FAT FARM. YOU'RE OUR ROLE MODEL.
GREAT. NOW EVERYONE WILL STARE AND GAWK WHEN I GET BACK, EXPECTING SOME HUGE TRANSFORMATION.
YOU HAVEN'T EVEN LEFT AND YOU'RE WORRYING ABOUT HOW PEOPLE WILL LOOK AT YOU WHEN YOU GET BACK??
WHAT DO YOU EXPECT ME TO DO??
YOU SHOULD BE WORRYING ABOUT HOW THEY'LL LOOK AT YOU BEFORE YOU GO.
AACK!

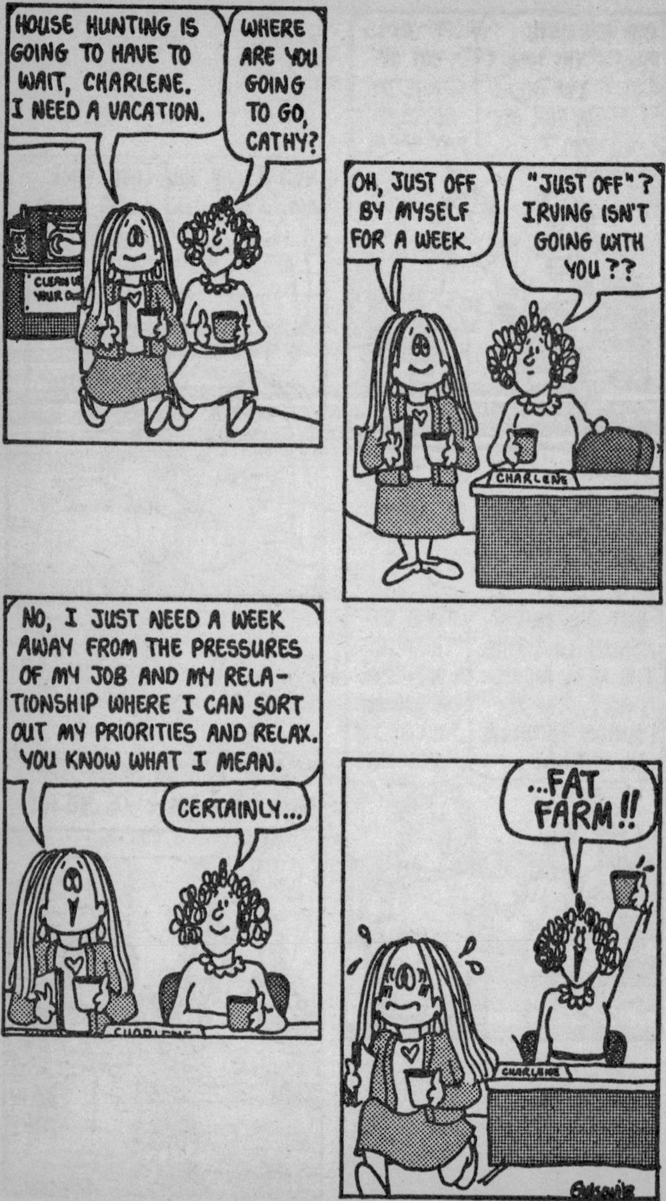
HOUSE HUNTING IS GOING TO HAVE TO WAIT, CHARLENE. I NEED A VACATION.
WHERE ARE YOU GOING TO GO, CATHY?
OH, JUST OFF BY MYSELF FOR A WEEK.
"JUST OFF"? IRVING ISN'T GOING WITH YOU??
CHARLENE
NO, I JUST NEED A WEEK AWAY FROM THE PRESSURES OF MY JOB AND MY RELATIONSHIP WHERE I CAN SORT OUT MY PRIORITIES AND RELAX. YOU KNOW WHAT I MEAN.
CERTAINLY...
...FAT FARM!!
CHARLENE
Guisewite

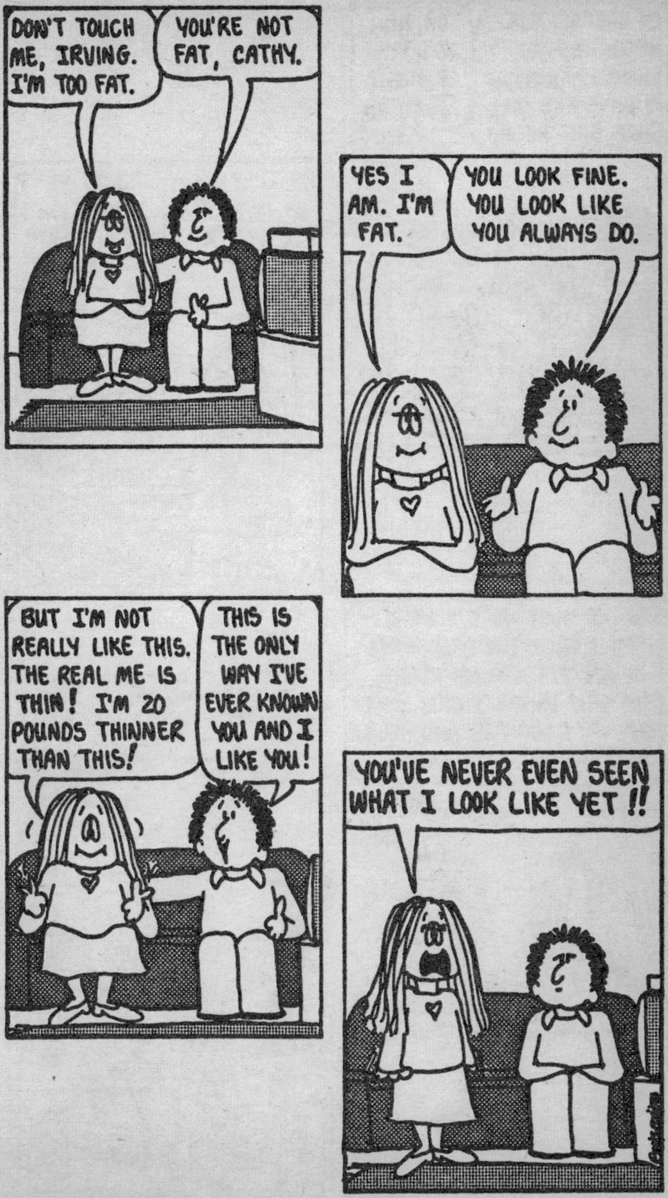
DON'T TOUCH ME, IRVING. I'M TOO FAT.
YOU'RE NOT FAT, CATHY.
YES I AM. I'M FAT.
YOU LOOK FINE. YOU LOOK LIKE YOU ALWAYS DO.
BUT I'M NOT REALLY LIKE THIS. THE REAL ME IS THIN! I'M 20 POUNDS THINNER THAN THIS!
THIS IS THE ONLY WAY I'VE EVER KNOWN YOU AND I LIKE YOU!
YOU'VE NEVER EVEN SEEN WHAT I LOOK LIKE YET !!

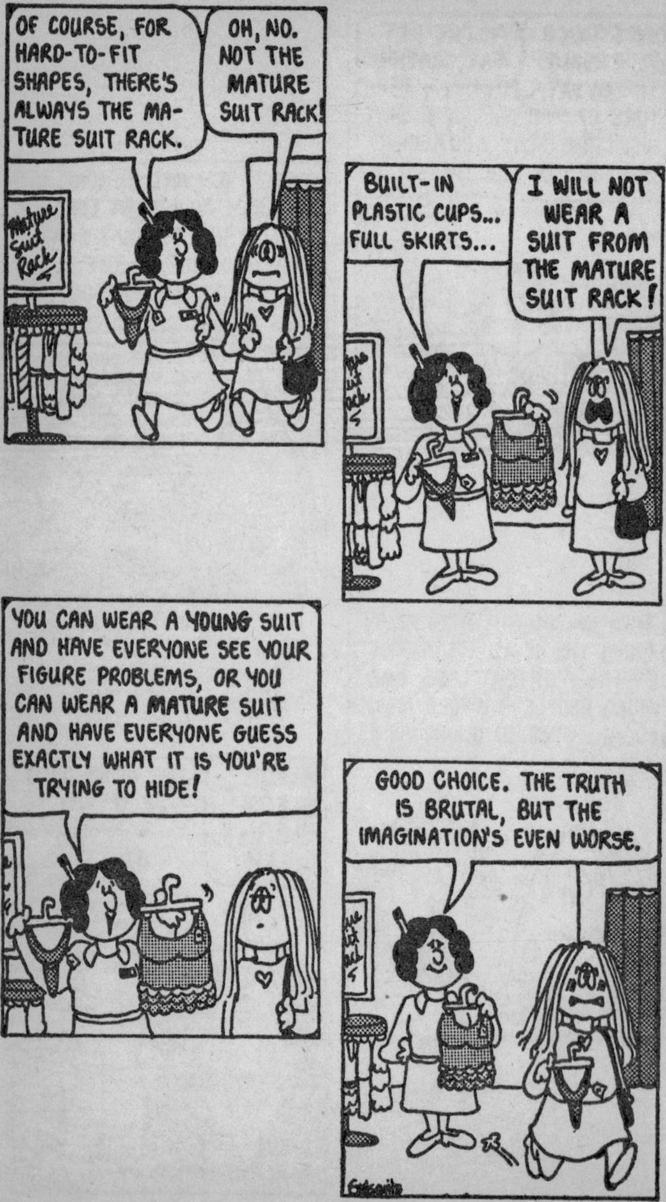
OF COURSE, FOR HARD-TO-FIT SHAPES, THERE'S ALWAYS THE MA-TURE SUIT RACK.
OH, NO. NOT THE MATURE SUIT RACK!
Mature Suit Rack
BUILT-IN PLASTIC CUPS... FULL SKIRTS...
I WILL NOT WEAR A SUIT FROM THE MATURE SUIT RACK!
YOU CAN WEAR A YOUNG SUIT AND HAVE EVERYONE SEE YOUR FIGURE PROBLEMS, OR YOU CAN WEAR A MATURE SUIT AND HAVE EVERYONE GUESS EXACTLY WHAT IT IS YOU'RE TRYING TO HIDE!
GOOD CHOICE. THE TRUTH IS BRUTAL, BUT THE IMAGINATION'S EVEN WORSE.

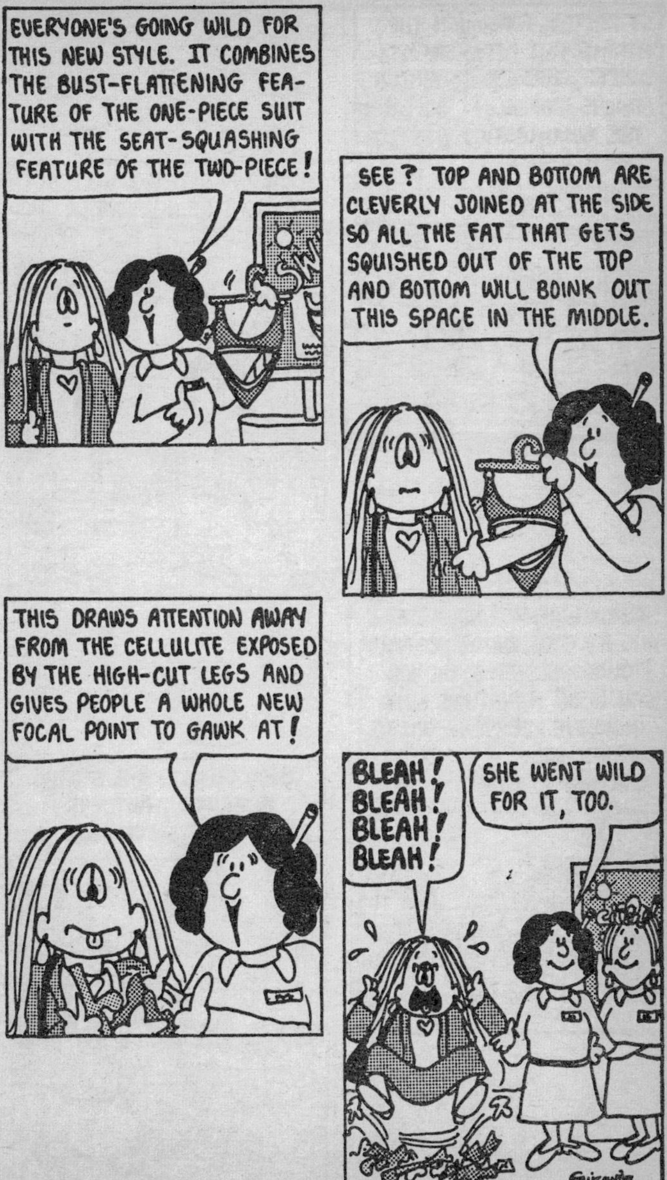
EVERYONE'S GOING WILD FOR THIS NEW STYLE. IT COMBINES THE BUST-FLATTENING FEATURE OF THE ONE-PIECE SUIT WITH THE SEAT-SQUASHING FEATURE OF THE TWO-PIECE!
SEE? TOP AND BOTTOM ARE CLEVERLY JOINED AT THE SIDE SO ALL THE FAT THAT GETS SQUISHED OUT OF THE TOP AND BOTTOM WILL BOINK OUT THIS SPACE IN THE MIDDLE.
THIS DRAWS ATTENTION AWAY FROM THE CELLULITE EXPOSED BY THE HIGH-CUT LEGS AND GIVES PEOPLE A WHOLE NEW FOCAL POINT TO GAWK AT!
BLEAH! BLEAH! BLEAH! BLEAH!
SHE WENT WILD FOR IT, TOO.

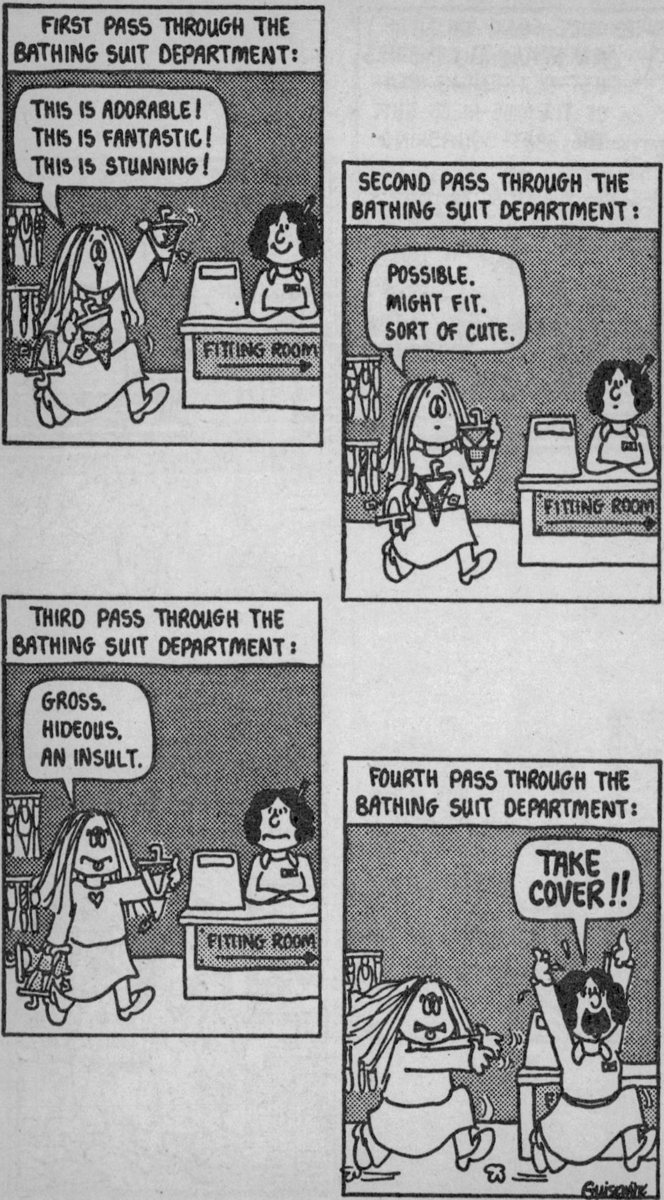
FIRST PASS THROUGH THE BATHING SUIT DEPARTMENT:
THIS IS ADORABLE! THIS IS FANTASTIC! THIS IS STUNNING!
FITTING ROOM
SECOND PASS THROUGH THE BATHING SUIT DEPARTMENT:
POSSIBLE. MIGHT FIT. SORT OF CUTE.
FITTING ROOM
THIRD PASS THROUGH THE BATHING SUIT DEPARTMENT:
GROSS. HIDEOUS. AN INSULT.
FITTING ROOM
FOURTH PASS THROUGH THE BATHING SUIT DEPARTMENT:
TAKE COVER!!

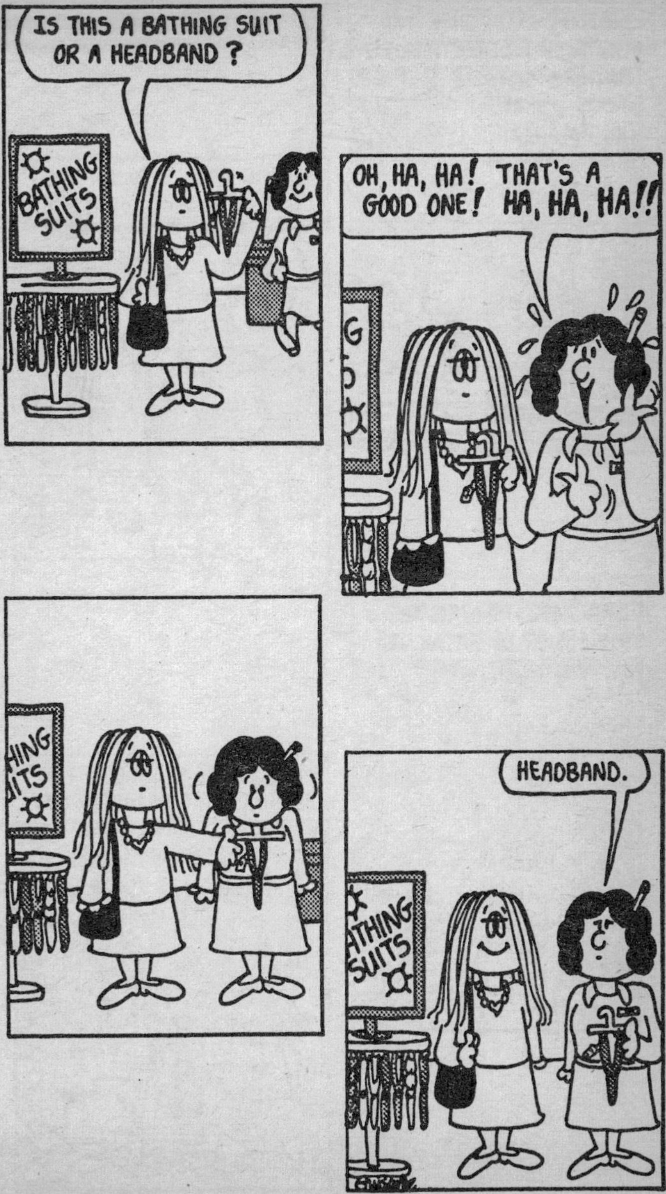
IS THIS A BATHING SUIT OR A HEADBAND?
BATHING SUITS
OH, HA, HA! THAT'S A GOOD ONE! HA, HA, HA!!
HEADBAND.

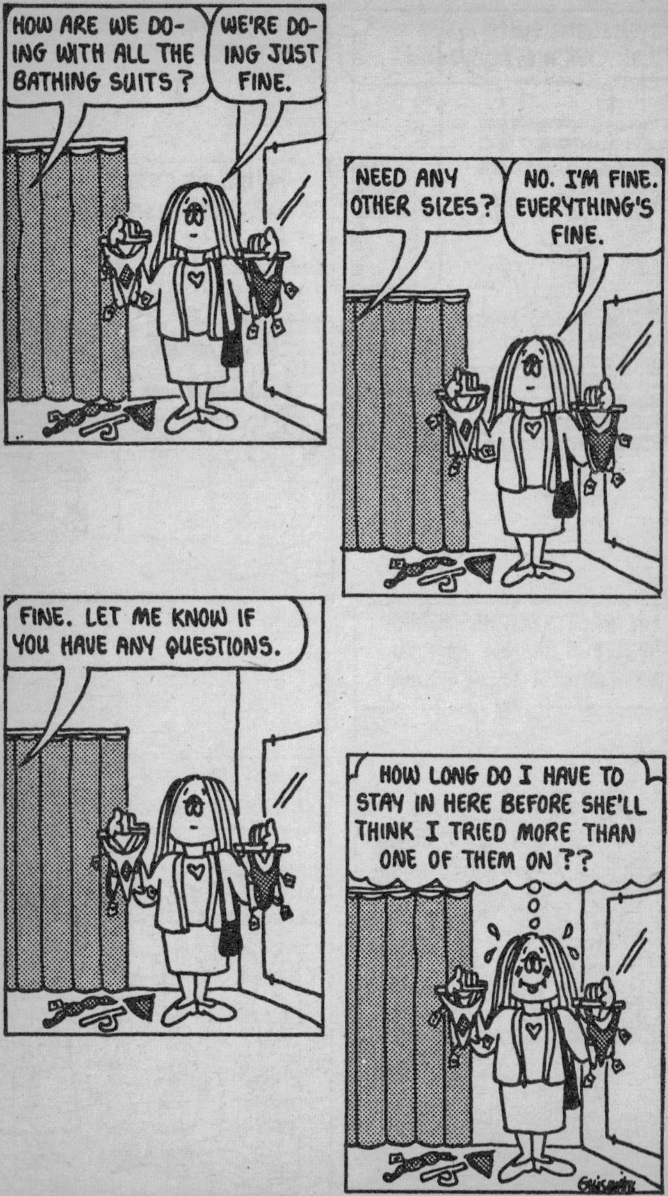
HOW ARE WE DOING WITH ALL THE BATHING SUITS?
WE'RE DOING JUST FINE.
NEED ANY OTHER SIZES?
NO. I'M FINE. EVERYTHING'S FINE.
FINE. LET ME KNOW IF YOU HAVE ANY QUESTIONS.
HOW LONG DO I HAVE TO STAY IN HERE BEFORE SHE'LL THINK I TRIED MORE THAN ONE OF THEM ON??

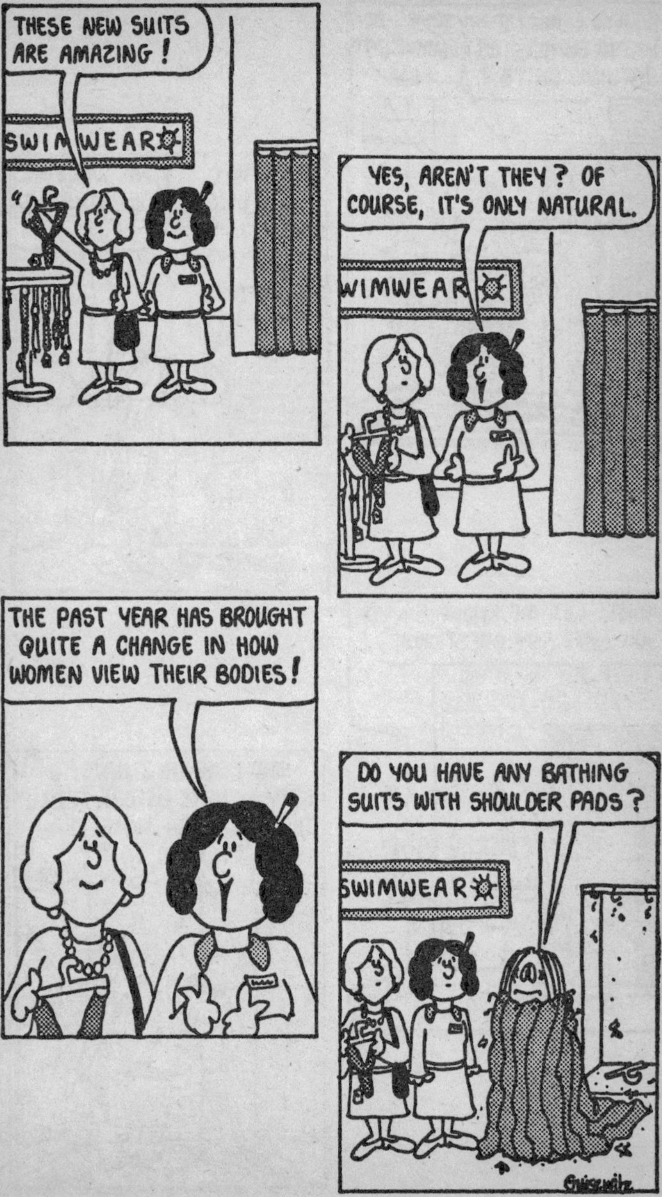
THESE NEW SUITS ARE AMAZING!
SWIMWEAR
YES, AREN'T THEY? OF COURSE, IT'S ONLY NATURAL.
WIMWEAR
THE PAST YEAR HAS BROUGHT QUITE A CHANGE IN HOW WOMEN VIEW THEIR BODIES!
DO YOU HAVE ANY BATHING SUITS WITH SHOULDER PADS?
SWIMWEAR
Guisewite

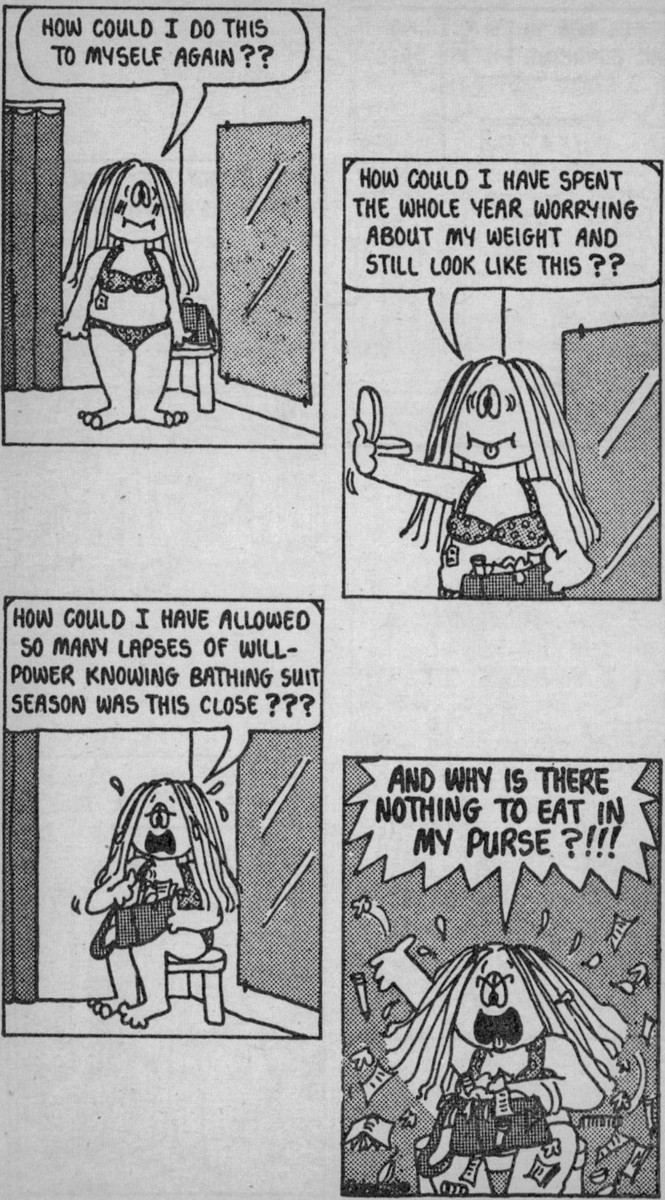
HOW COULD I DO THIS TO MYSELF AGAIN??
HOW COULD I HAVE SPENT THE WHOLE YEAR WORRYING ABOUT MY WEIGHT AND STILL LOOK LIKE THIS??
HOW COULD I HAVE ALLOWED SO MANY LAPSES OF WILL-POWER KNOWING BATHING SUIT SEASON WAS THIS CLOSE???
AND WHY IS THERE NOTHING TO EAT IN MY PURSE?!!!

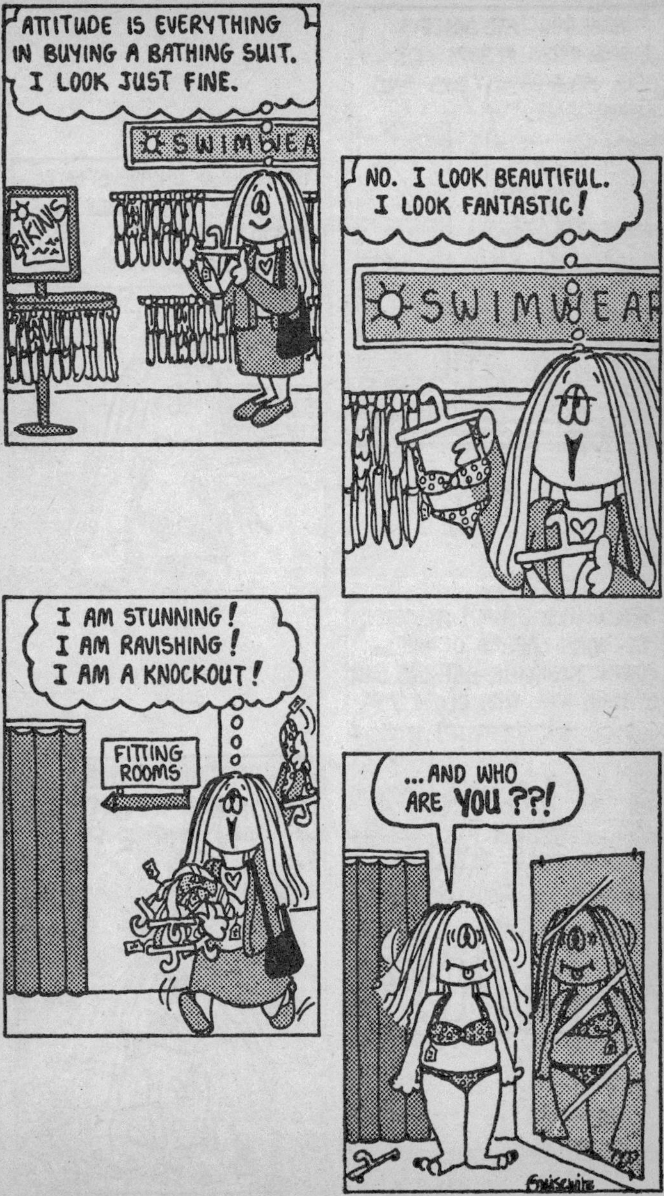

ATTITUDE IS EVERYTHING IN BUYING A BATHING SUIT. I LOOK JUST FINE.
SWIMWEA
BIKINIS
NO. I LOOK BEAUTIFUL. I LOOK FANTASTIC!
SWIMWEAR
I AM STUNNING! I AM RAVISHING! I AM A KNOCKOUT!
FITTING ROOMS
...AND WHO ARE YOU??!
Guisewite

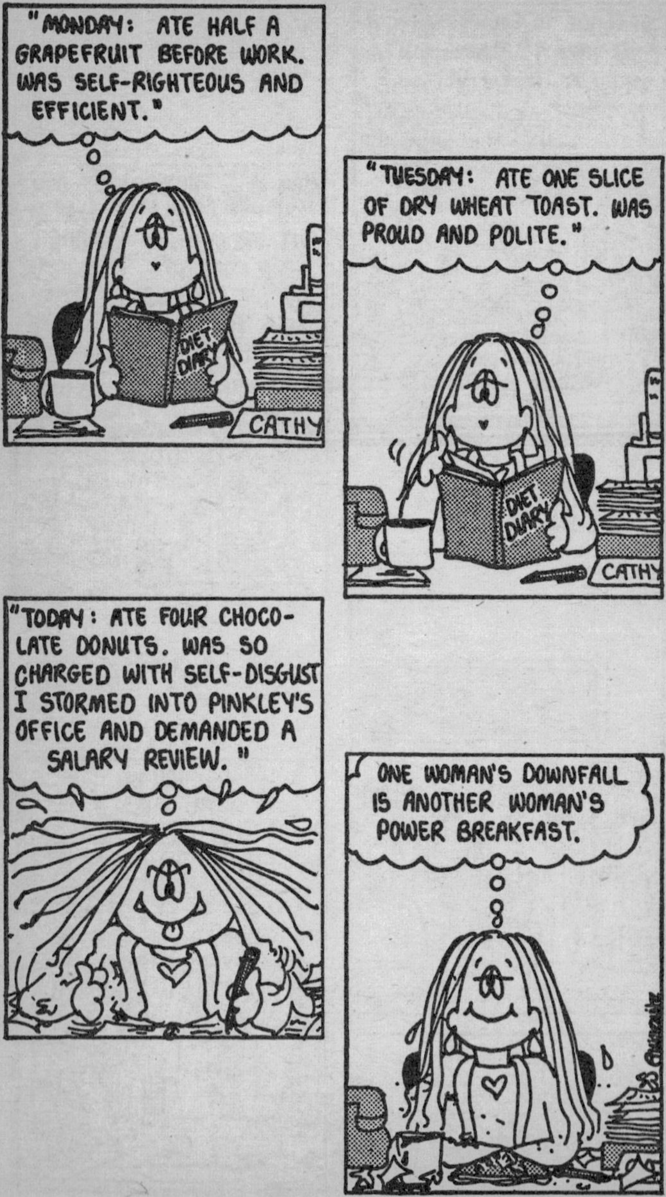
"MONDAY: ATE HALF A GRAPEFRUIT BEFORE WORK. WAS SELF-RIGHTEOUS AND EFFICIENT."
DIET DIARY
CATHY
"TUESDAY: ATE ONE SLICE OF DRY WHEAT TOAST. WAS PROUD AND POLITE."
DIET DIARY
CATHY
"TODAY: ATE FOUR CHOCO-LATE DONUTS. WAS SO CHARGED WITH SELF-DISGUST I STORMED INTO PINKLEY'S OFFICE AND DEMANDED A SALARY REVIEW."
ONE WOMAN'S DOWNFALL IS ANOTHER WOMAN'S POWER BREAKFAST.

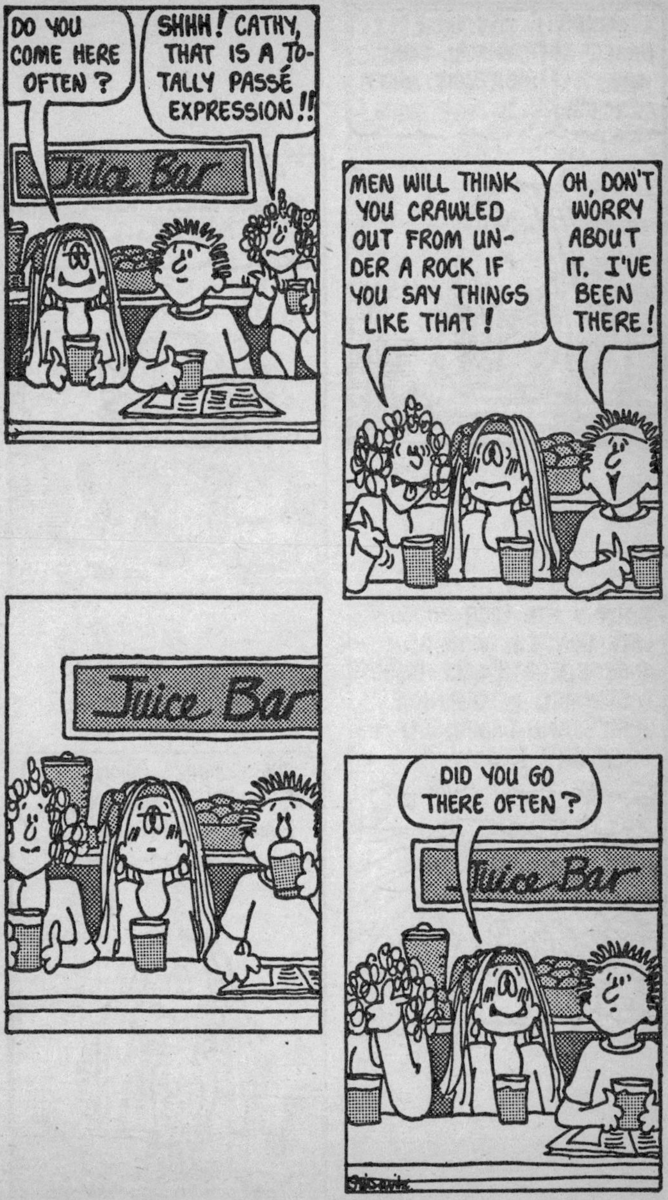
DO YOU COME HERE OFTEN ?
SHHH! CATHY, THAT IS A TOTALLY PASSÉ EXPRESSION!!
MEN WILL THINK YOU CRAWLED OUT FROM UNDER A ROCK IF YOU SAY THINGS LIKE THAT !
OH, DON'T WORRY ABOUT IT. I'VE BEEN THERE !
Juice Bar
DID YOU GO THERE OFTEN ?
Juice Bar

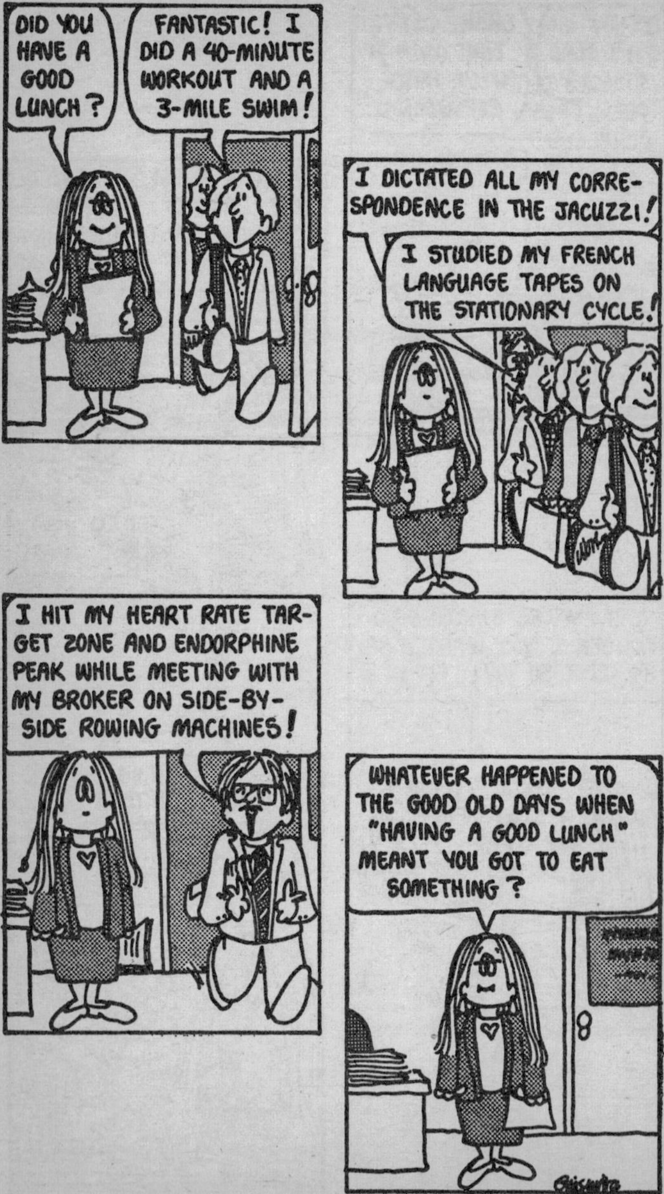
DID YOU HAVE A GOOD LUNCH?
FANTASTIC! I DID A 40-MINUTE WORKOUT AND A 3-MILE SWIM!
I DICTATED ALL MY CORRE-SPONDENCE IN THE JACUZZI!
I STUDIED MY FRENCH LANGUAGE TAPES ON THE STATIONARY CYCLE!
I HIT MY HEART RATE TAR-GET ZONE AND ENDORPHINE PEAK WHILE MEETING WITH MY BROKER ON SIDE-BY-SIDE ROWING MACHINES!
WHATEVER HAPPENED TO THE GOOD OLD DAYS WHEN "HAVING A GOOD LUNCH" MEANT YOU GOT TO EAT SOMETHING?
Guisewite

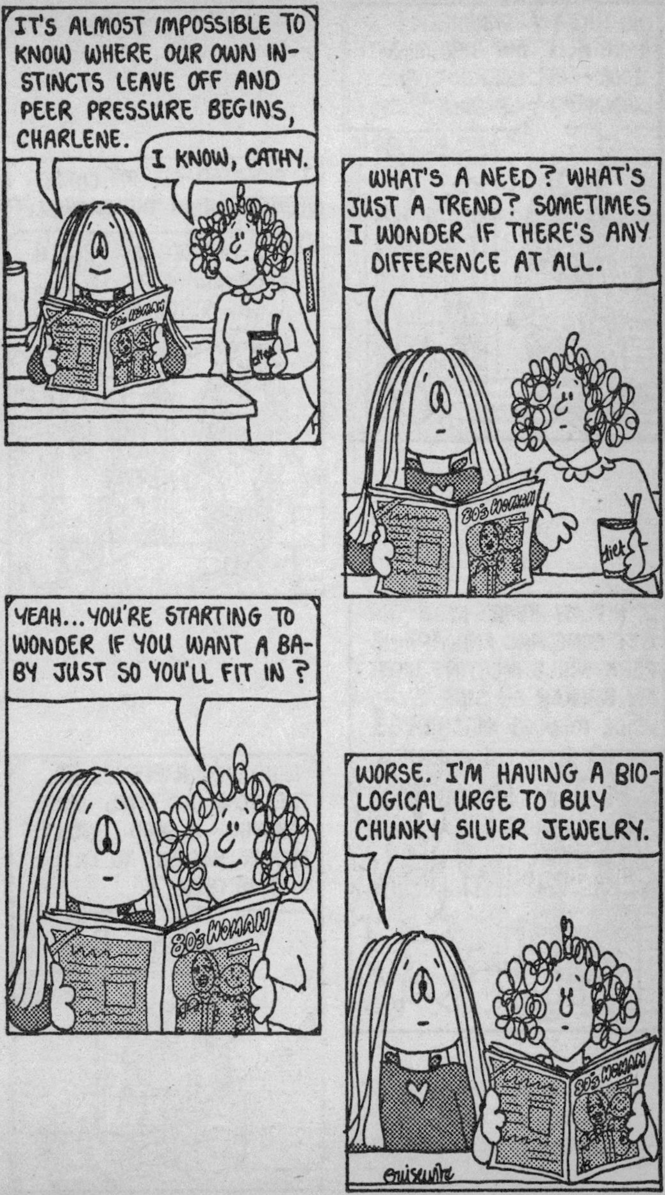
IT'S ALMOST IMPOSSIBLE TO KNOW WHERE OUR OWN INSTINCTS LEAVE OFF AND PEER PRESSURE BEGINS, CHARLENE.
I KNOW, CATHY.
WHAT'S A NEED? WHAT'S JUST A TREND? SOMETIMES I WONDER IF THERE'S ANY DIFFERENCE AT ALL.
YEAH... YOU'RE STARTING TO WONDER IF YOU WANT A BABY JUST SO YOU'LL FIT IN?
WORSE. I'M HAVING A BIOLOGICAL URGE TO BUY CHUNKY SILVER JEWELRY.
Guisewite

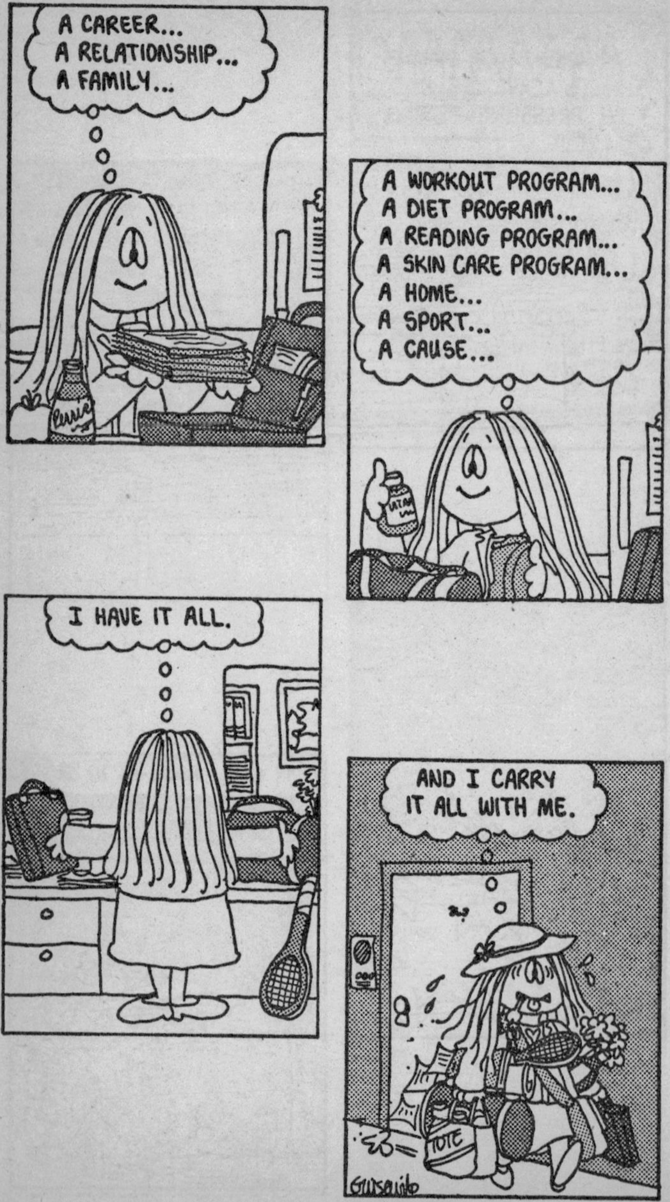
A CAREER...
A RELATIONSHIP...
A FAMILY...
A WORKOUT PROGRAM...
A DIET PROGRAM...
A READING PROGRAM...
A SKIN CARE PROGRAM...
A HOME...
A SPORT...
A CAUSE...
I HAVE IT ALL.
AND I CARRY IT ALL WITH ME.
TOTE
Guisewite

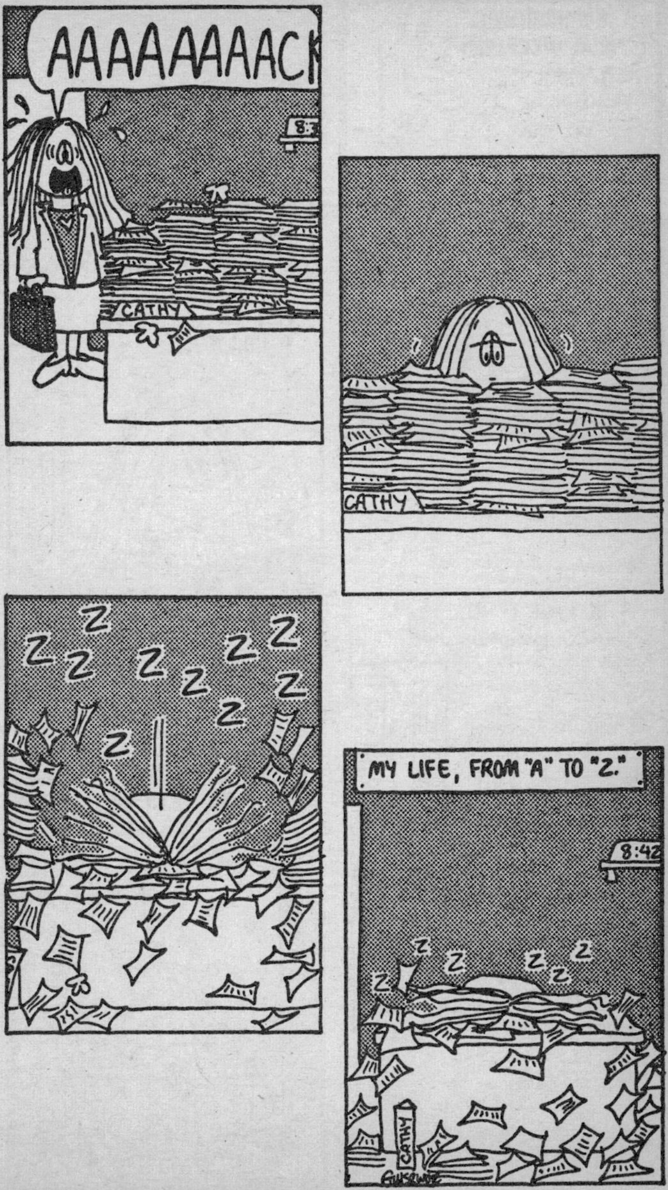
AAAAAAAACK
CATHY
CATHY
MY LIFE, FROM "A" TO "Z."
8:42

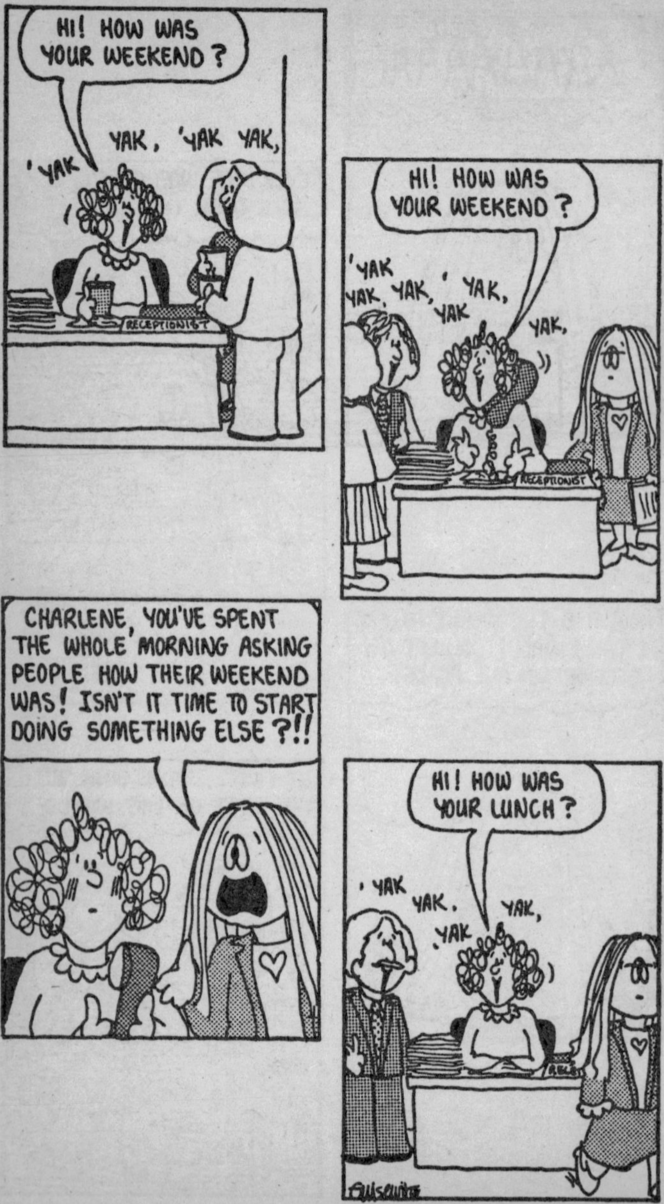
HI! HOW WAS YOUR WEEKEND?
'YAK YAK, 'YAK YAK,
RECEPTIONIST
HI! HOW WAS YOUR WEEKEND?
'YAK YAK. YAK, 'YAK, YAK YAK,
RECEPTIONIST
CHARLENE, YOU'VE SPENT THE WHOLE MORNING ASKING PEOPLE HOW THEIR WEEKEND WAS! ISN'T IT TIME TO START DOING SOMETHING ELSE?!!
HI! HOW WAS YOUR LUNCH?
YAK YAK. YAK YAK,

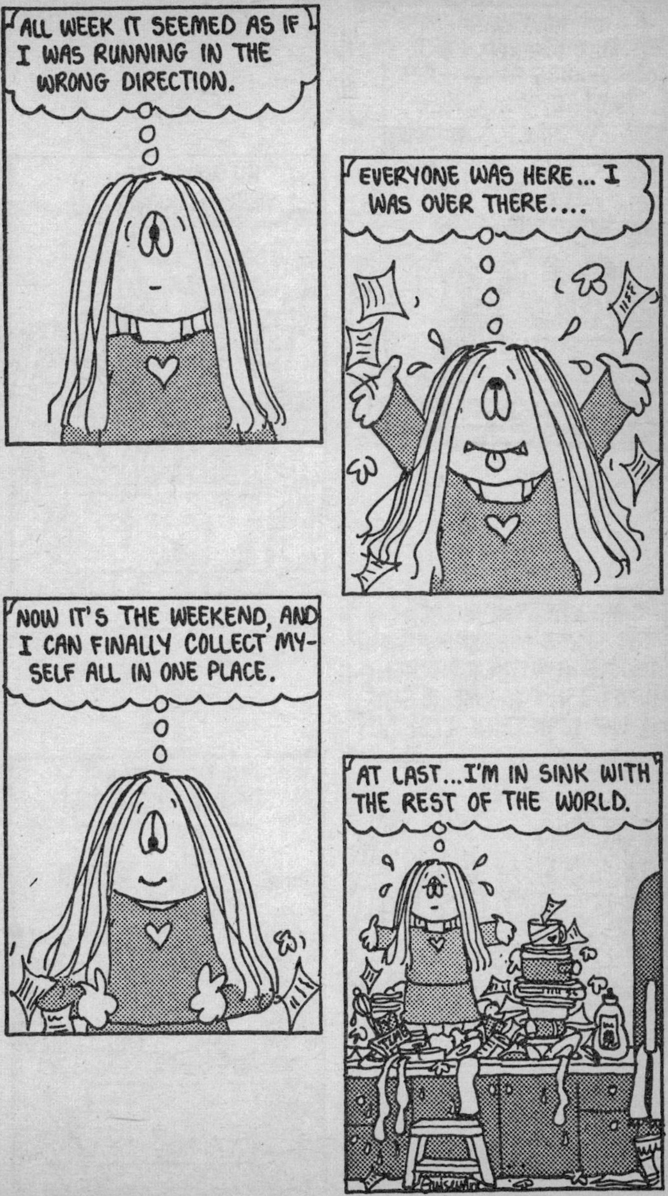
ALL WEEK IT SEEMED AS IF I WAS RUNNING IN THE WRONG DIRECTION.
EVERYONE WAS HERE... I WAS OVER THERE....
NOW IT'S THE WEEKEND, AND I CAN FINALLY COLLECT MY-SELF ALL IN ONE PLACE.
AT LAST...I'M IN SINK WITH THE REST OF THE WORLD.

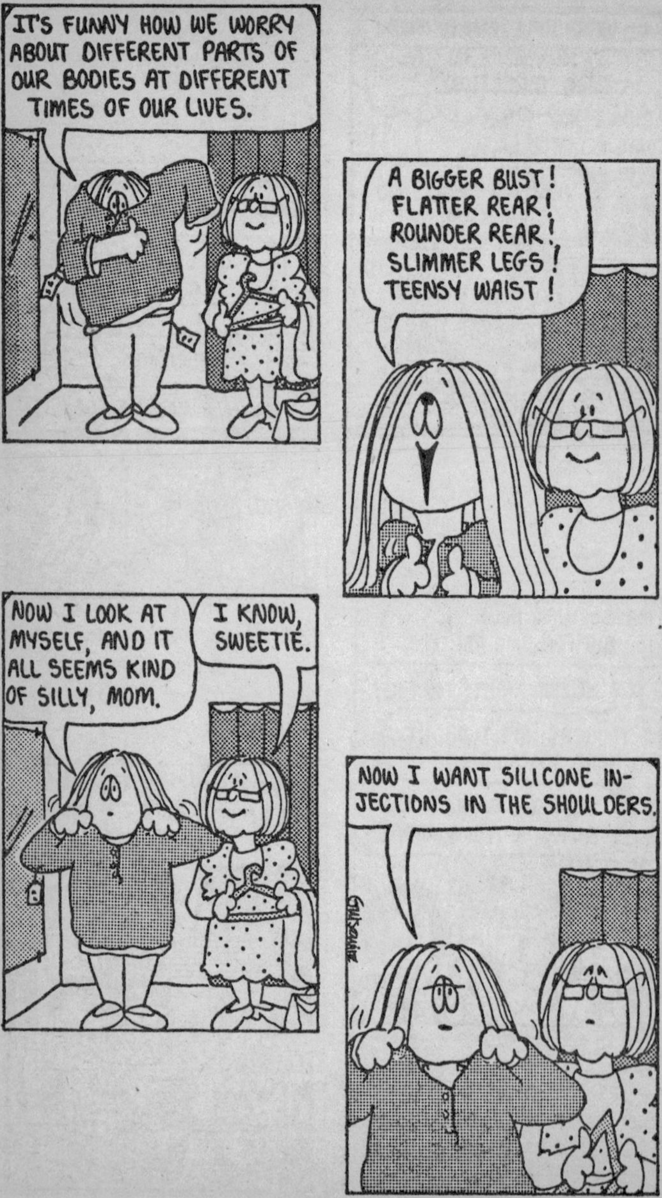
IT'S FUNNY HOW WE WORRY ABOUT DIFFERENT PARTS OF OUR BODIES AT DIFFERENT TIMES OF OUR LIVES.
A BIGGER BUST! FLATTER REAR! ROUNDER REAR! SLIMMER LEGS! TEENSY WAIST!
NOW I LOOK AT MYSELF, AND IT ALL SEEMS KIND OF SILLY, MOM.
I KNOW, SWEETIE.
NOW I WANT SILICONE INJECTIONS IN THE SHOULDERS.

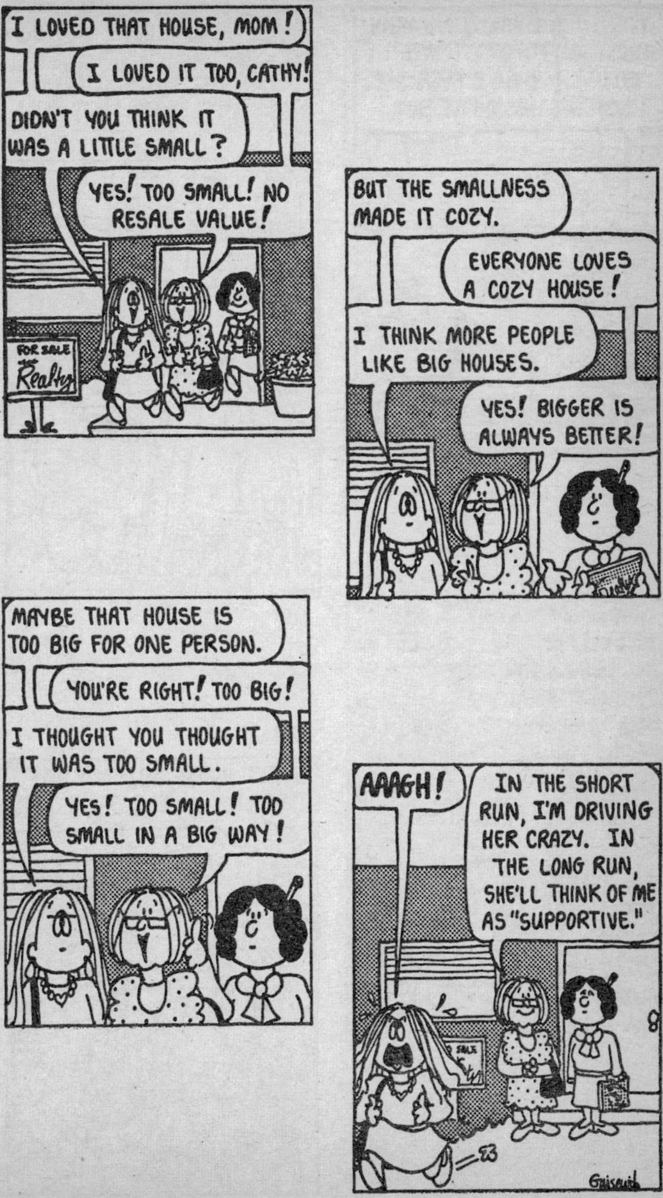
I LOVED THAT HOUSE, MOM!
I LOVED IT TOO, CATHY!
DIDN'T YOU THINK IT WAS A LITTLE SMALL?
YES! TOO SMALL! NO RESALE VALUE!
FOR SALE
Realty
BUT THE SMALLNESS MADE IT COZY.
EVERYONE LOVES A COZY HOUSE!
I THINK MORE PEOPLE LIKE BIG HOUSES.
YES! BIGGER IS ALWAYS BETTER!
MAYBE THAT HOUSE IS TOO BIG FOR ONE PERSON.
YOU'RE RIGHT! TOO BIG!
I THOUGHT YOU THOUGHT IT WAS TOO SMALL.
YES! TOO SMALL! TOO SMALL IN A BIG WAY!
AAAGH!
IN THE SHORT RUN, I'M DRIVING HER CRAZY. IN THE LONG RUN, SHE'LL THINK OF ME AS "SUPPORTIVE."

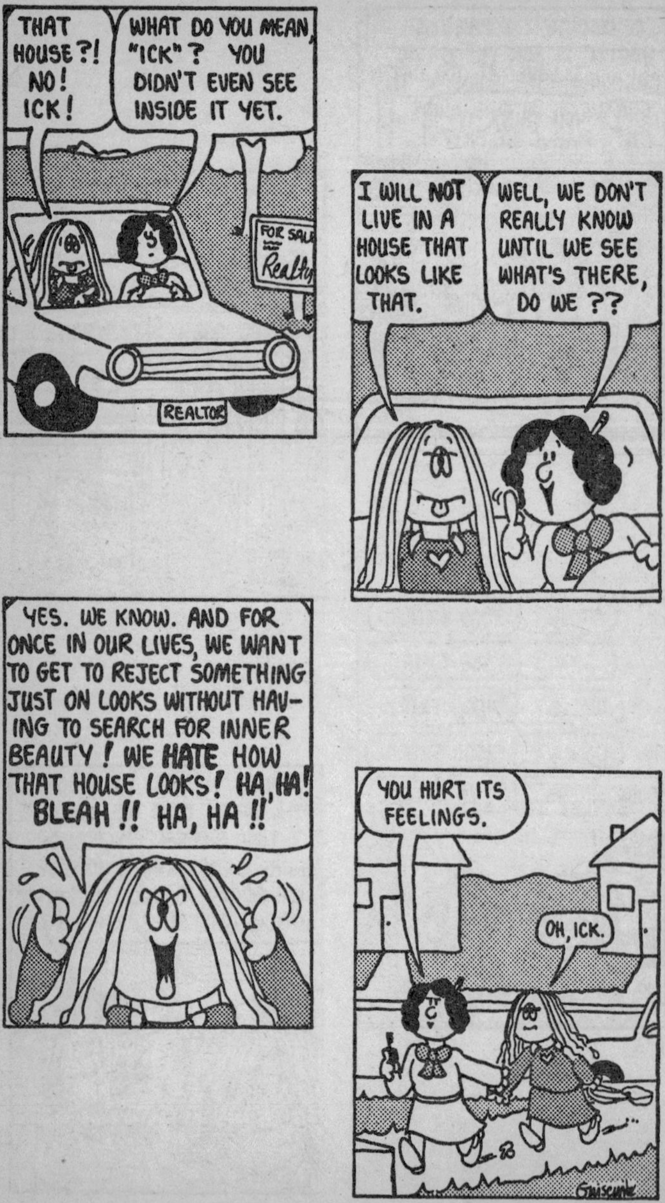
THAT HOUSE?! NO! ICK!
WHAT DO YOU MEAN, "ICK"? YOU DIDN'T EVEN SEE INSIDE IT YET.
REALTOR
I WILL NOT LIVE IN A HOUSE THAT LOOKS LIKE THAT.
WELL, WE DON'T REALLY KNOW UNTIL WE SEE WHAT'S THERE, DO WE??
YES. WE KNOW. AND FOR ONCE IN OUR LIVES, WE WANT TO GET TO REJECT SOMETHING JUST ON LOOKS WITHOUT HAV-ING TO SEARCH FOR INNER BEAUTY! WE HATE HOW THAT HOUSE LOOKS! HA, HA! BLEAH!! HA, HA!!
YOU HURT ITS FEELINGS.
OH, ICK.
Guisewite

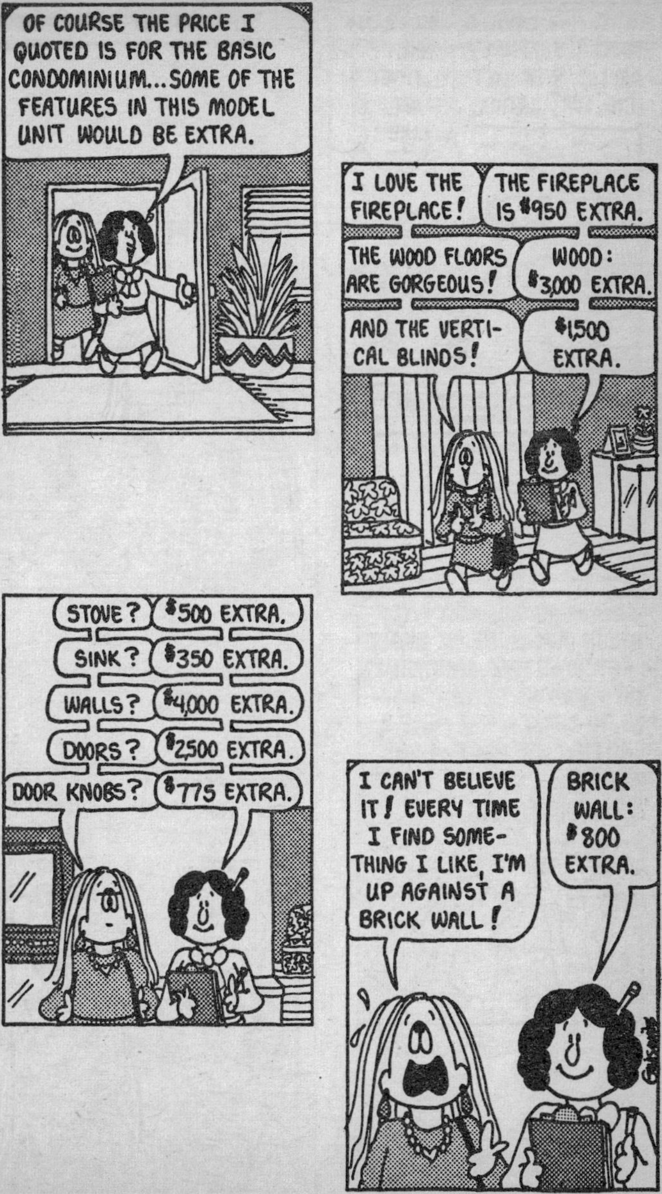
OF COURSE THE PRICE I QUOTED IS FOR THE BASIC CONDOMINIUM...SOME OF THE FEATURES IN THIS MODEL UNIT WOULD BE EXTRA.
I LOVE THE FIREPLACE!
THE FIREPLACE IS $950 EXTRA.
THE WOOD FLOORS ARE GORGEOUS!
WOOD: $3,000 EXTRA.
AND THE VERTICAL BLINDS!
$1,500 EXTRA.
STOVE?
$500 EXTRA.
SINK?
$350 EXTRA.
WALLS?
$4,000 EXTRA.
DOORS?
$2,500 EXTRA.
DOOR KNOBS?
$775 EXTRA.
I CAN'T BELIEVE IT! EVERY TIME I FIND SOMETHING I LIKE, I'M UP AGAINST A BRICK WALL!
BRICK WALL: $800 EXTRA.

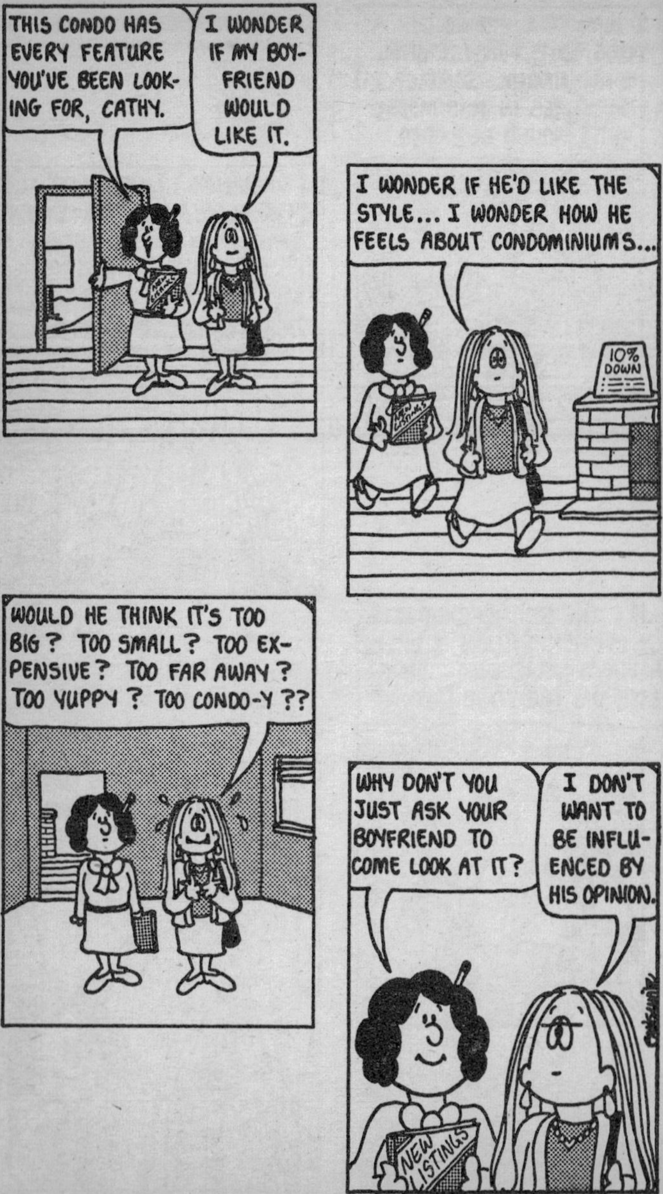
THIS CONDO HAS EVERY FEATURE YOU'VE BEEN LOOKING FOR, CATHY.
I WONDER IF MY BOYFRIEND WOULD LIKE IT.
I WONDER IF HE'D LIKE THE STYLE... I WONDER HOW HE FEELS ABOUT CONDOMINIUMS...
10% DOWN
WOULD HE THINK IT'S TOO BIG? TOO SMALL? TOO EXPENSIVE? TOO FAR AWAY? TOO YUPPY? TOO CONDO-Y??
WHY DON'T YOU JUST ASK YOUR BOYFRIEND TO COME LOOK AT IT?
I DON'T WANT TO BE INFLUENCED BY HIS OPINION.
NEW LISTINGS

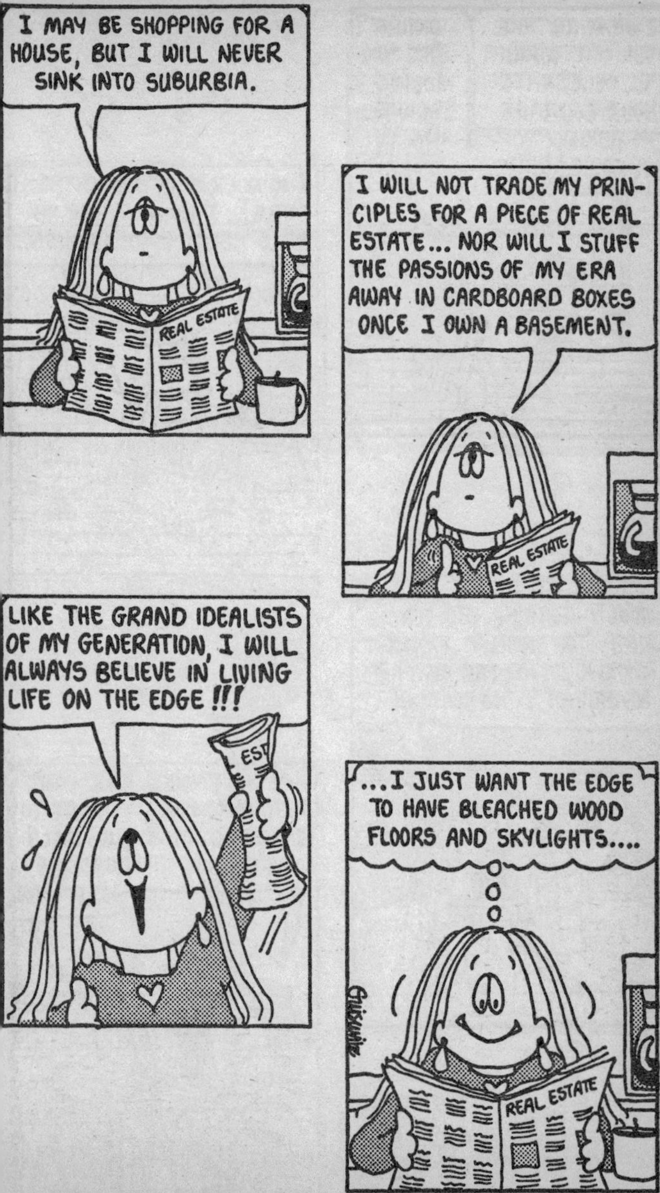
I MAY BE SHOPPING FOR A HOUSE, BUT I WILL NEVER SINK INTO SUBURBIA.
REAL ESTATE
I WILL NOT TRADE MY PRINCIPLES FOR A PIECE OF REAL ESTATE... NOR WILL I STUFF THE PASSIONS OF MY ERA AWAY IN CARDBOARD BOXES ONCE I OWN A BASEMENT.
REAL ESTATE
LIKE THE GRAND IDEALISTS OF MY GENERATION, I WILL ALWAYS BELIEVE IN LIVING LIFE ON THE EDGE!!!
...I JUST WANT THE EDGE TO HAVE BLEACHED WOOD FLOORS AND SKYLIGHTS....
REAL ESTATE

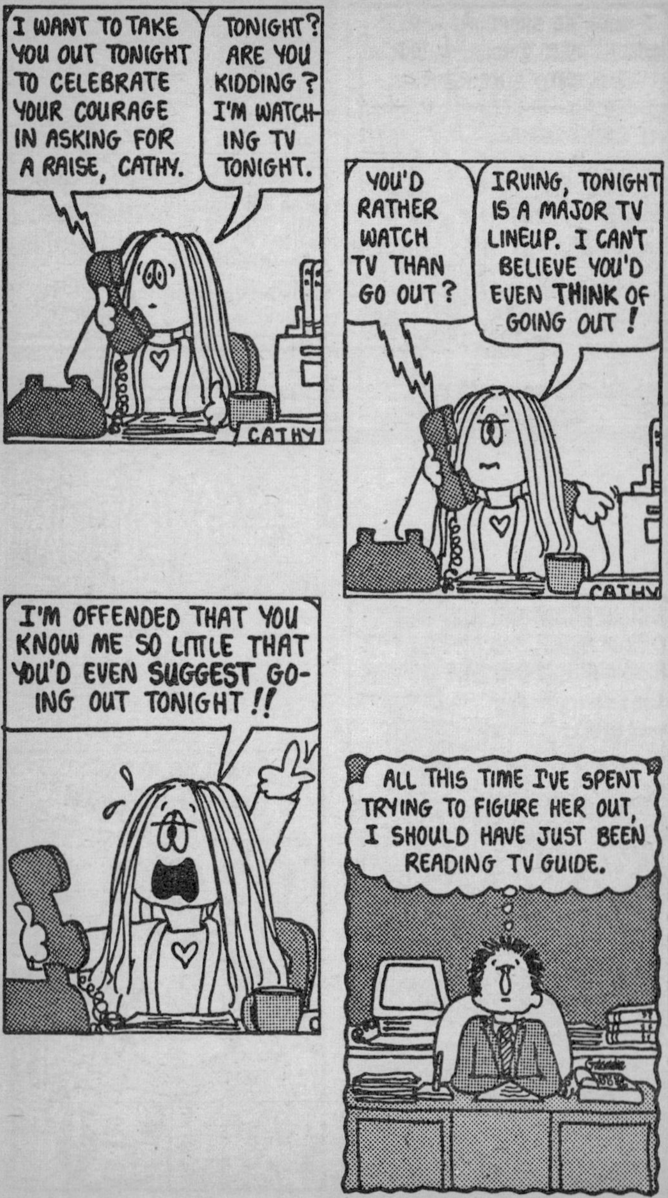
I WANT TO TAKE YOU OUT TONIGHT TO CELEBRATE YOUR COURAGE IN ASKING FOR A RAISE, CATHY.
TONIGHT? ARE YOU KIDDING? I'M WATCHING TV TONIGHT.
CATHY
YOU'D RATHER WATCH TV THAN GO OUT?
IRVING, TONIGHT IS A MAJOR TV LINEUP. I CAN'T BELIEVE YOU'D EVEN THINK OF GOING OUT!
CATHY
I'M OFFENDED THAT YOU KNOW ME SO LITTLE THAT YOU'D EVEN SUGGEST GOING OUT TONIGHT!!
ALL THIS TIME I'VE SPENT TRYING TO FIGURE HER OUT, I SHOULD HAVE JUST BEEN READING TV GUIDE.

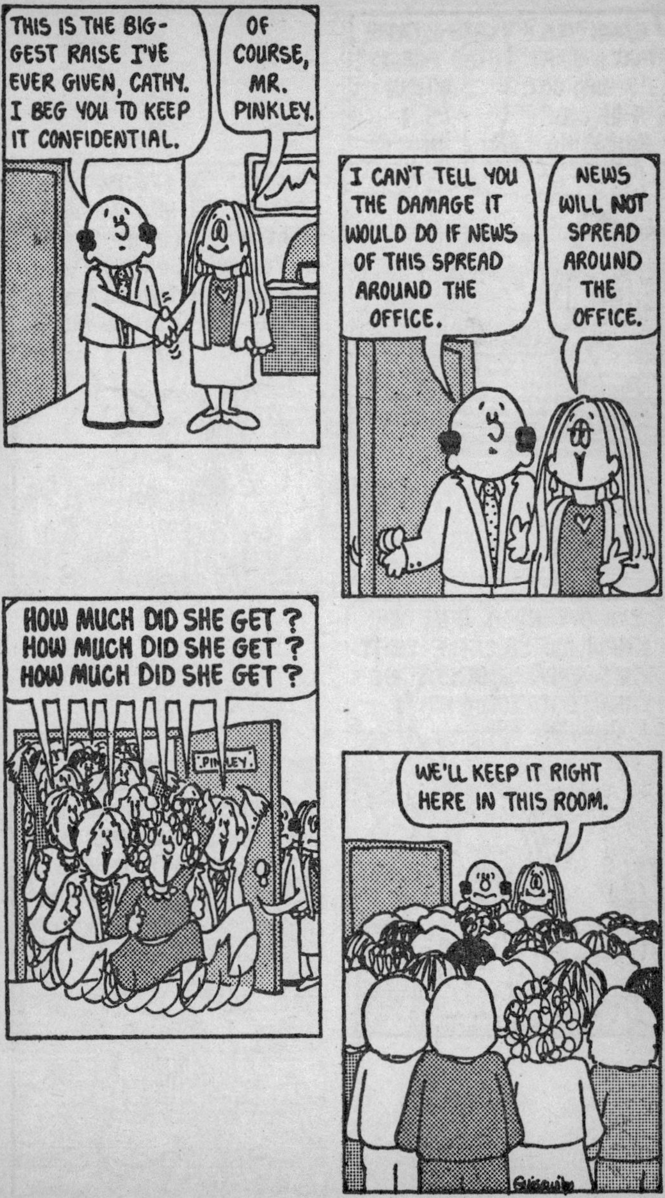
THIS IS THE BIGGEST RAISE I'VE EVER GIVEN, CATHY. I BEG YOU TO KEEP IT CONFIDENTIAL.
OF COURSE, MR. PINKLEY.
I CAN'T TELL YOU THE DAMAGE IT WOULD DO IF NEWS OF THIS SPREAD AROUND THE OFFICE.
NEWS WILL NOT SPREAD AROUND THE OFFICE.
HOW MUCH DID SHE GET ? HOW MUCH DID SHE GET ? HOW MUCH DID SHE GET ?
WE'LL KEEP IT RIGHT HERE IN THIS ROOM.

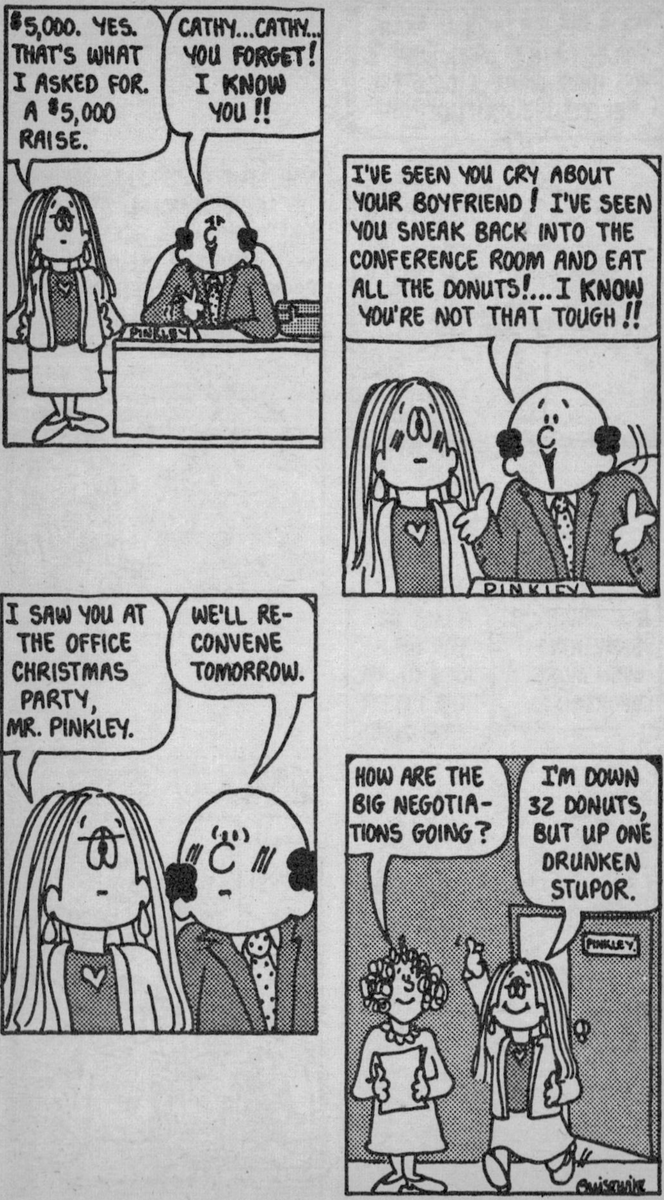

$5,000. YES. THAT'S WHAT I ASKED FOR. A $5,000 RAISE.
CATHY...CATHY... YOU FORGET! I KNOW YOU!!
I'VE SEEN YOU CRY ABOUT YOUR BOYFRIEND! I'VE SEEN YOU SNEAK BACK INTO THE CONFERENCE ROOM AND EAT ALL THE DONUTS!...I KNOW YOU'RE NOT THAT TOUGH!!
I SAW YOU AT THE OFFICE CHRISTMAS PARTY, MR. PINKLEY.
WE'LL RE-CONVENE TOMORROW.
HOW ARE THE BIG NEGOTIATIONS GOING?
I'M DOWN 32 DONUTS, BUT UP ONE DRUNKEN STUPOR.
PINKLEY
Guisewite

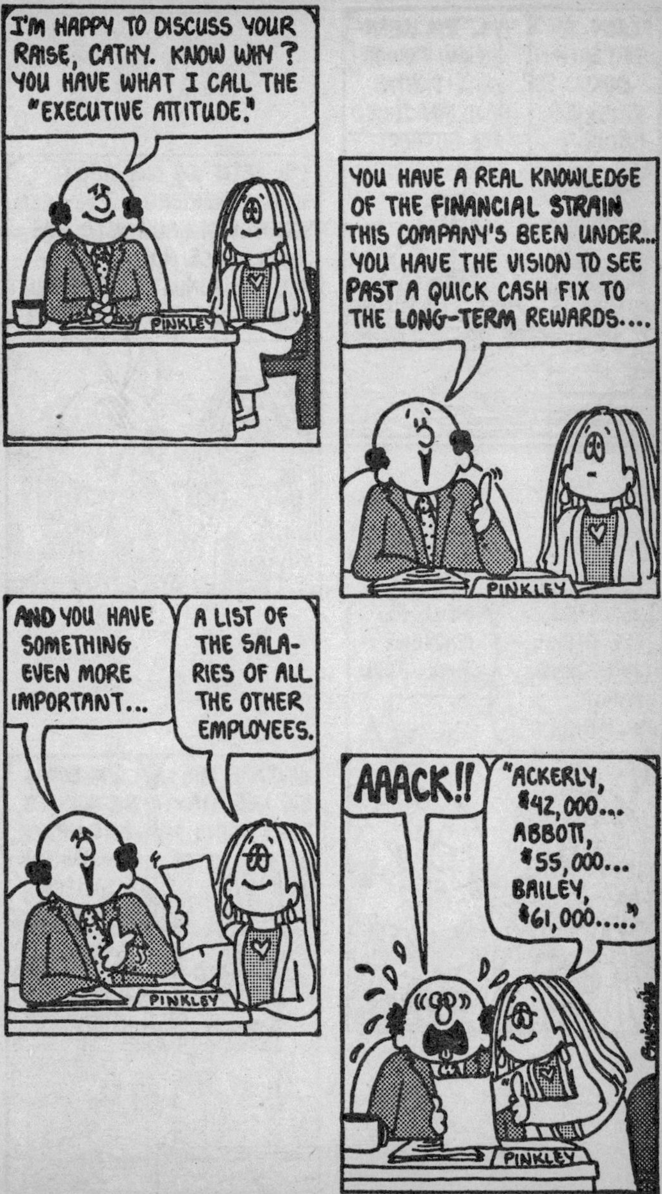
I'M HAPPY TO DISCUSS YOUR RAISE, CATHY. KNOW WHY? YOU HAVE WHAT I CALL THE "EXECUTIVE ATTITUDE."
PINKLEY
YOU HAVE A REAL KNOWLEDGE OF THE FINANCIAL STRAIN THIS COMPANY'S BEEN UNDER... YOU HAVE THE VISION TO SEE PAST A QUICK CASH FIX TO THE LONG-TERM REWARDS....
PINKLEY
AND YOU HAVE SOMETHING EVEN MORE IMPORTANT...
A LIST OF THE SALARIES OF ALL THE OTHER EMPLOYEES.
PINKLEY
AAACK!!
"ACKERLY, $42,000... ABBOTT, $55,000... BAILEY, $61,000....."
PINKLEY

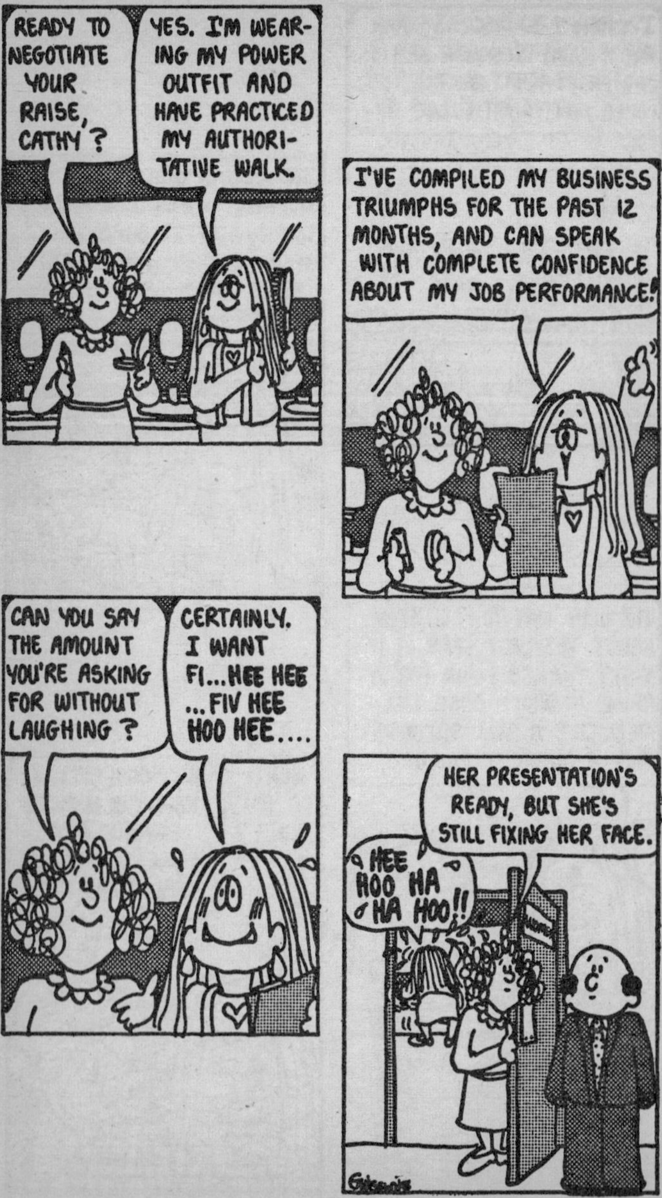
READY TO NEGOTIATE YOUR RAISE, CATHY ?
YES. I'M WEARING MY POWER OUTFIT AND HAVE PRACTICED MY AUTHORITATIVE WALK.
I'VE COMPILED MY BUSINESS TRIUMPHS FOR THE PAST 12 MONTHS, AND CAN SPEAK WITH COMPLETE CONFIDENCE ABOUT MY JOB PERFORMANCE!
CAN YOU SAY THE AMOUNT YOU'RE ASKING FOR WITHOUT LAUGHING ?
CERTAINLY. I WANT FI...HEE HEE ...FIV HEE HOO HEE....
HER PRESENTATION'S READY, BUT SHE'S STILL FIXING HER FACE.
HEE HOO HA HA HOO!!

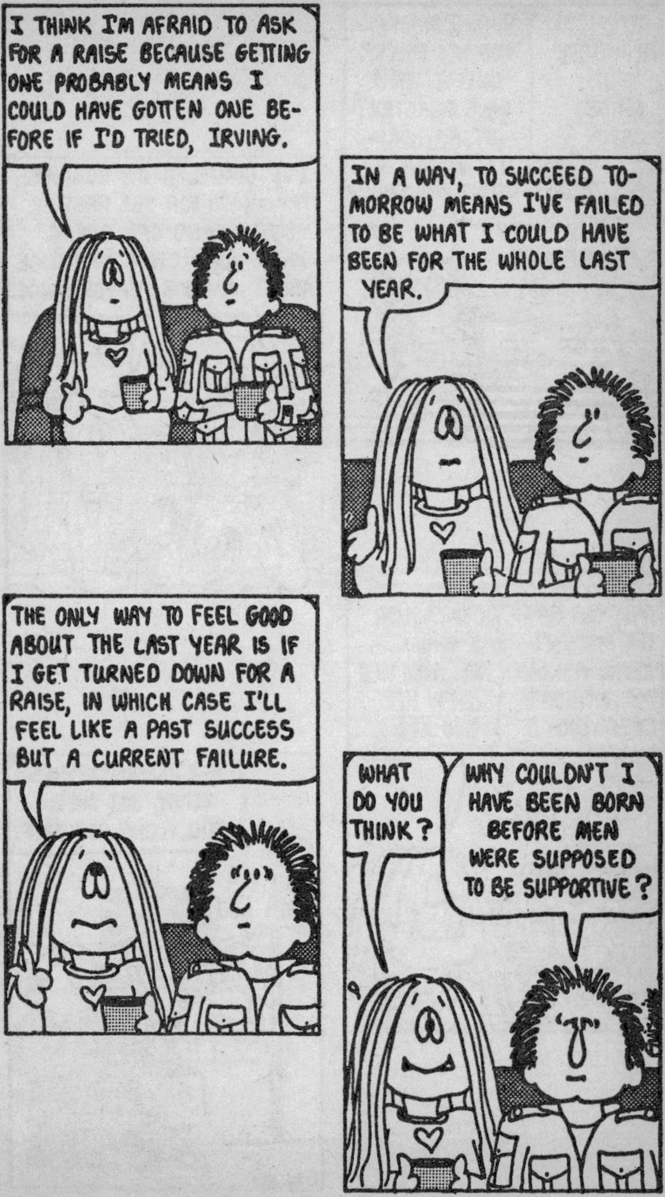

I THINK I'M AFRAID TO ASK FOR A RAISE BECAUSE GETTING ONE PROBABLY MEANS I COULD HAVE GOTTEN ONE BEFORE IF I'D TRIED, IRVING.
IN A WAY, TO SUCCEED TOMORROW MEANS I'VE FAILED TO BE WHAT I COULD HAVE BEEN FOR THE WHOLE LAST YEAR.
THE ONLY WAY TO FEEL GOOD ABOUT THE LAST YEAR IS IF I GET TURNED DOWN FOR A RAISE, IN WHICH CASE I'LL FEEL LIKE A PAST SUCCESS BUT A CURRENT FAILURE.
WHAT DO YOU THINK?
WHY COULDN'T I HAVE BEEN BORN BEFORE MEN WERE SUPPOSED TO BE SUPPORTIVE?

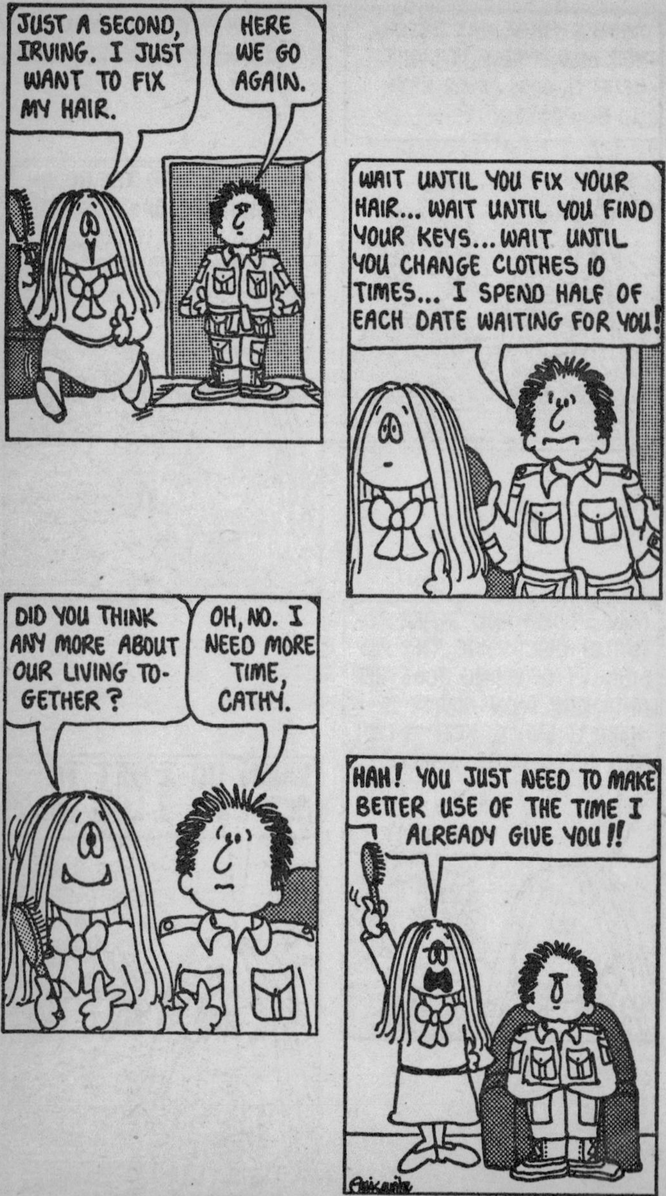
JUST A SECOND, IRVING. I JUST WANT TO FIX MY HAIR.
HERE WE GO AGAIN.
WAIT UNTIL YOU FIX YOUR HAIR... WAIT UNTIL YOU FIND YOUR KEYS... WAIT UNTIL YOU CHANGE CLOTHES 10 TIMES... I SPEND HALF OF EACH DATE WAITING FOR YOU!
DID YOU THINK ANY MORE ABOUT OUR LIVING TO-GETHER?
OH, NO. I NEED MORE TIME, CATHY.
HAH! YOU JUST NEED TO MAKE BETTER USE OF THE TIME I ALREADY GIVE YOU!!

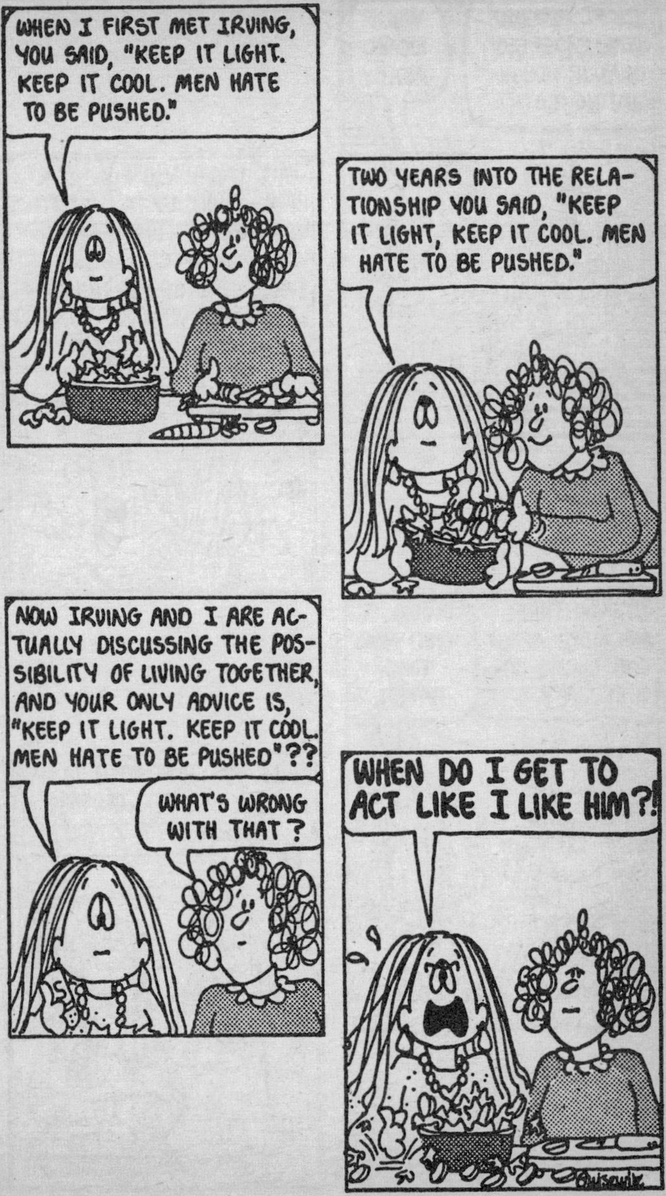
WHEN I FIRST MET IRVING, YOU SAID, "KEEP IT LIGHT. KEEP IT COOL. MEN HATE TO BE PUSHED."
TWO YEARS INTO THE RELATIONSHIP YOU SAID, "KEEP IT LIGHT, KEEP IT COOL. MEN HATE TO BE PUSHED."
NOW IRVING AND I ARE ACTUALLY DISCUSSING THE POSSIBILITY OF LIVING TOGETHER, AND YOUR ONLY ADVICE IS, "KEEP IT LIGHT. KEEP IT COOL. MEN HATE TO BE PUSHED"??
WHAT'S WRONG WITH THAT?
WHEN DO I GET TO ACT LIKE I LIKE HIM?!
Guisewite

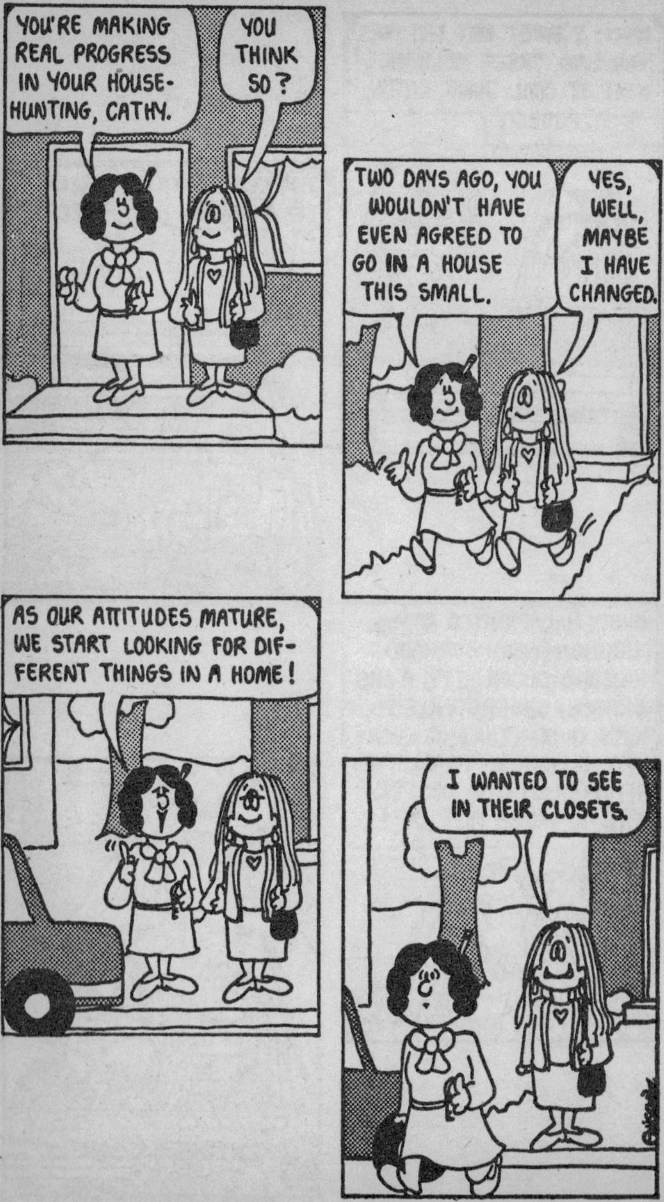
YOU'RE MAKING REAL PROGRESS IN YOUR HOUSE-HUNTING, CATHY.
YOU THINK SO?
TWO DAYS AGO, YOU WOULDN'T HAVE EVEN AGREED TO GO IN A HOUSE THIS SMALL.
YES, WELL, MAYBE I HAVE CHANGED.
AS OUR ATTITUDES MATURE, WE START LOOKING FOR DIFFERENT THINGS IN A HOME!
I WANTED TO SEE IN THEIR CLOSETS.

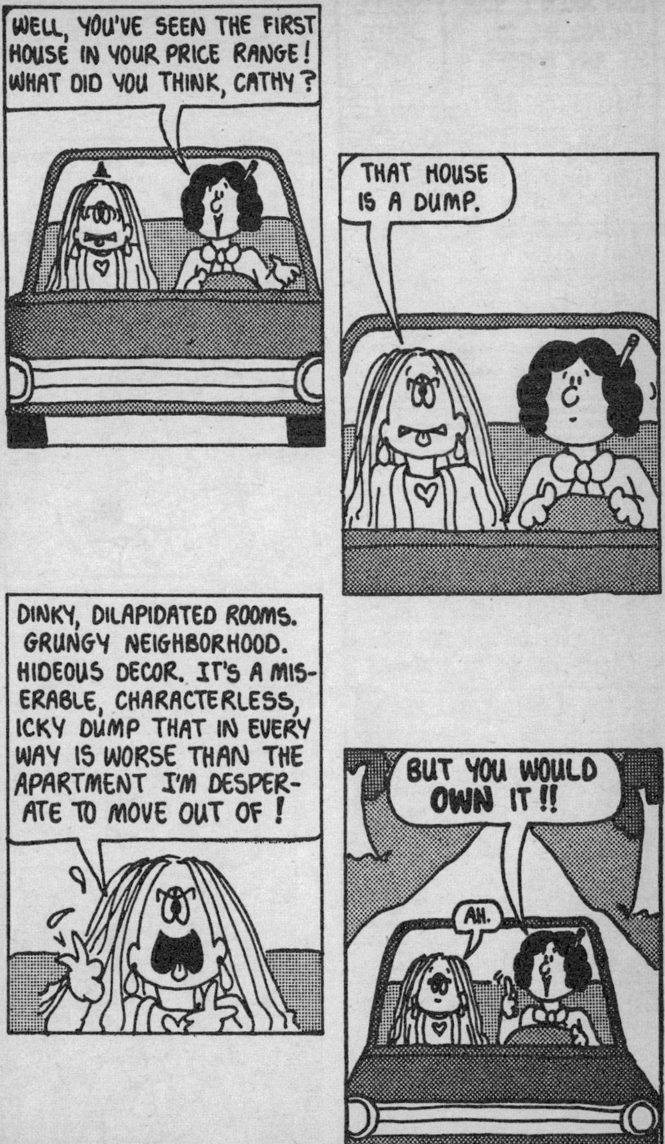
WELL, YOU'VE SEEN THE FIRST HOUSE IN YOUR PRICE RANGE! WHAT DID YOU THINK, CATHY?
THAT HOUSE IS A DUMP.
DINKY, DILAPIDATED ROOMS. GRUNGY NEIGHBORHOOD. HIDEOUS DECOR. IT'S A MISERABLE, CHARACTERLESS, ICKY DUMP THAT IN EVERY WAY IS WORSE THAN THE APARTMENT I'M DESPERATE TO MOVE OUT OF!
BUT YOU WOULD OWN IT!!
AH.

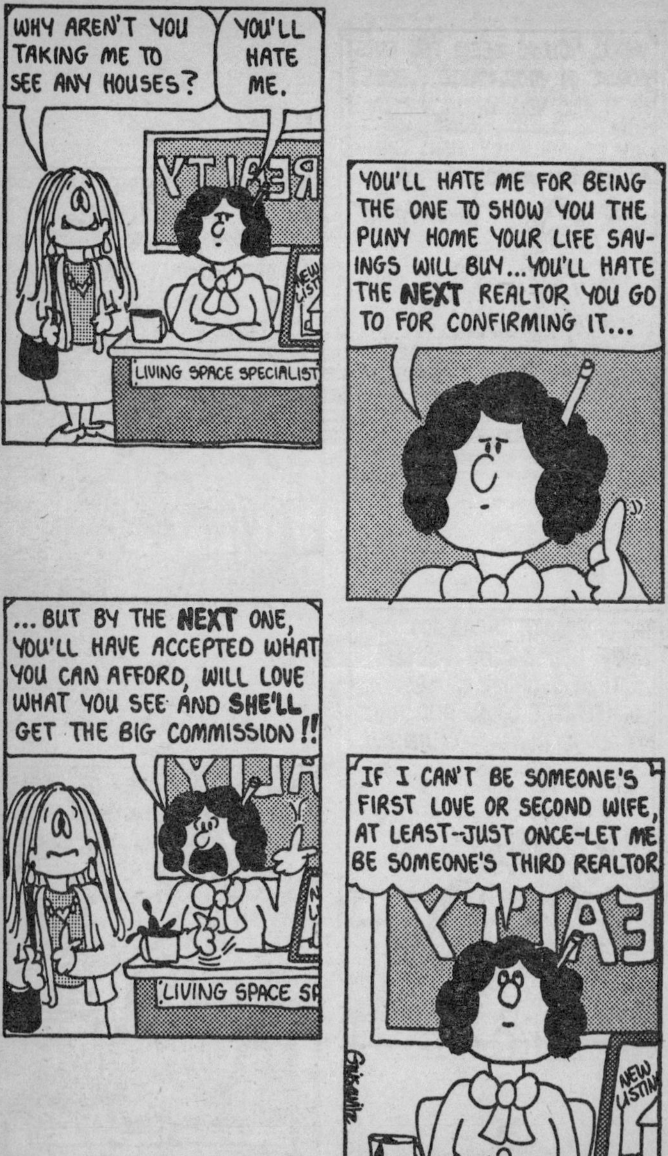
WHY AREN'T YOU TAKING ME TO SEE ANY HOUSES?
YOU'LL HATE ME.
LIVING SPACE SPECIALIST
YOU'LL HATE ME FOR BEING THE ONE TO SHOW YOU THE PUNY HOME YOUR LIFE SAVINGS WILL BUY... YOU'LL HATE THE **NEXT** REALTOR YOU GO TO FOR CONFIRMING IT...
... BUT BY THE **NEXT** ONE, YOU'LL HAVE ACCEPTED WHAT YOU CAN AFFORD, WILL LOVE WHAT YOU SEE AND **SHE'LL** GET THE BIG COMMISSION!!
LIVING SPACE SP
IF I CAN'T BE SOMEONE'S FIRST LOVE OR SECOND WIFE, AT LEAST--JUST ONCE--LET ME BE SOMEONE'S THIRD REALTOR.
NEW LISTIN
Guisewite

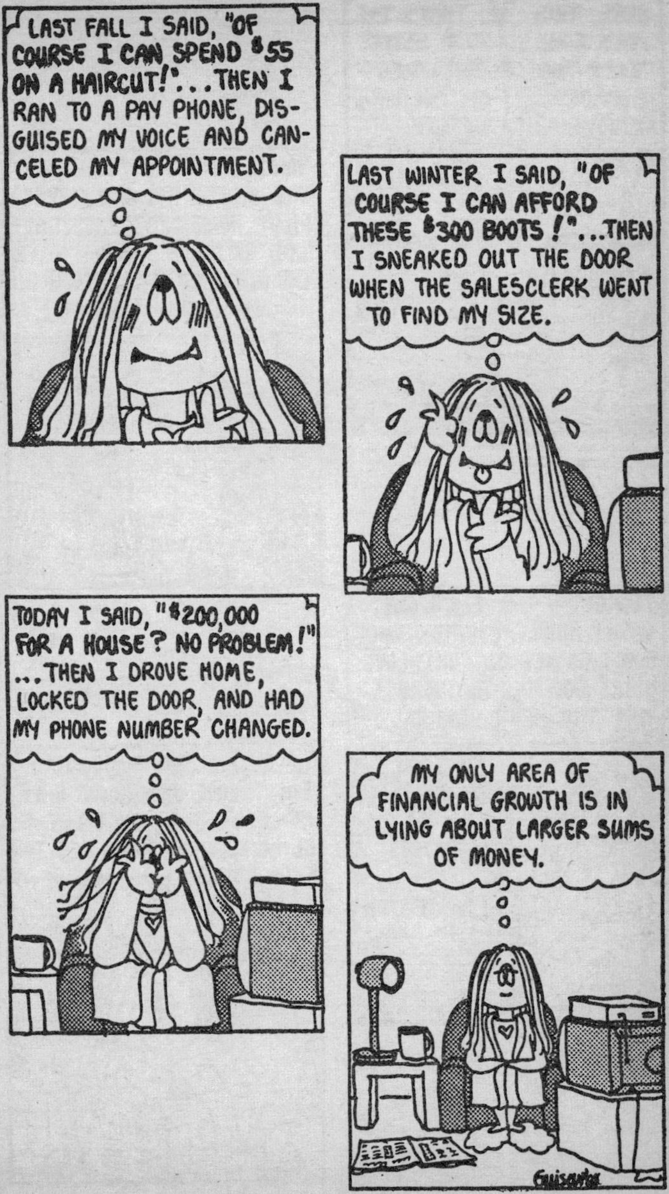
LAST FALL I SAID, "OF COURSE I CAN SPEND $55 ON A HAIRCUT!"...THEN I RAN TO A PAY PHONE, DISGUISED MY VOICE AND CANCELED MY APPOINTMENT.
LAST WINTER I SAID, "OF COURSE I CAN AFFORD THESE $300 BOOTS!"...THEN I SNEAKED OUT THE DOOR WHEN THE SALESCLERK WENT TO FIND MY SIZE.
TODAY I SAID, "$200,000 FOR A HOUSE? NO PROBLEM!" ...THEN I DROVE HOME, LOCKED THE DOOR, AND HAD MY PHONE NUMBER CHANGED.
MY ONLY AREA OF FINANCIAL GROWTH IS IN LYING ABOUT LARGER SUMS OF MONEY.

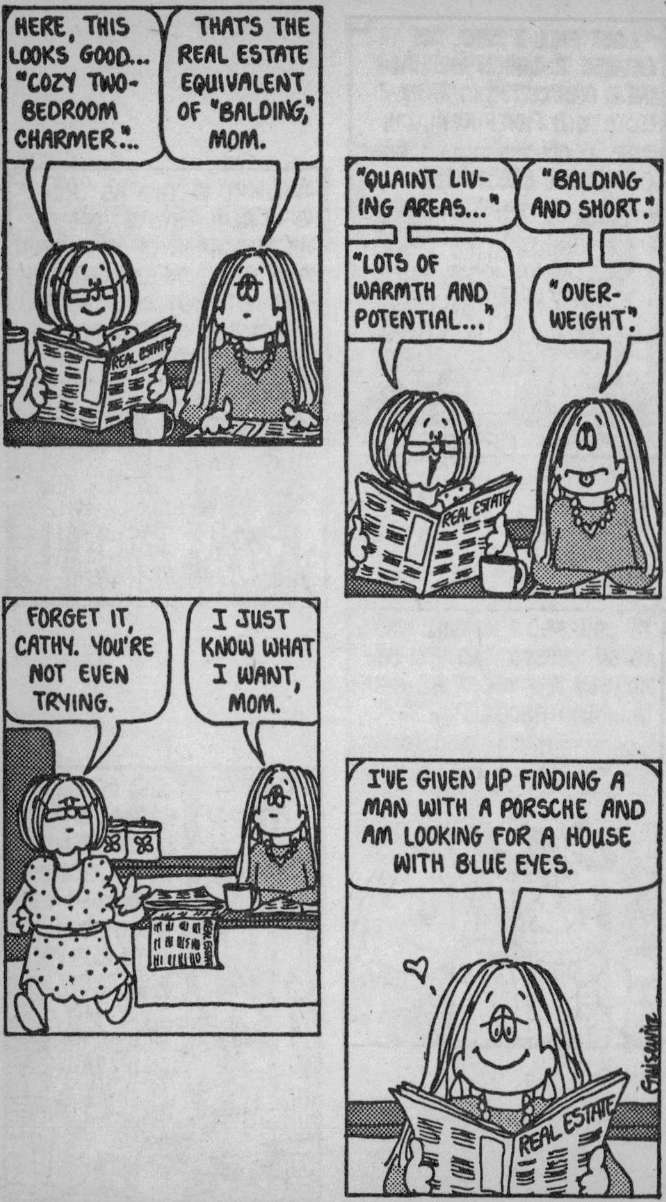
HERE, THIS LOOKS GOOD... "COZY TWO-BEDROOM CHARMER."...
THAT'S THE REAL ESTATE EQUIVALENT OF "BALDING," MOM.
REAL ESTATE
"QUAINT LIVING AREAS..."
"BALDING AND SHORT."
"LOTS OF WARMTH AND POTENTIAL..."
"OVER-WEIGHT."
REAL ESTATE
FORGET IT, CATHY. YOU'RE NOT EVEN TRYING.
I JUST KNOW WHAT I WANT, MOM.
REAL ESTATE
I'VE GIVEN UP FINDING A MAN WITH A PORSCHE AND AM LOOKING FOR A HOUSE WITH BLUE EYES.
REAL ESTATE
GUISEWITE

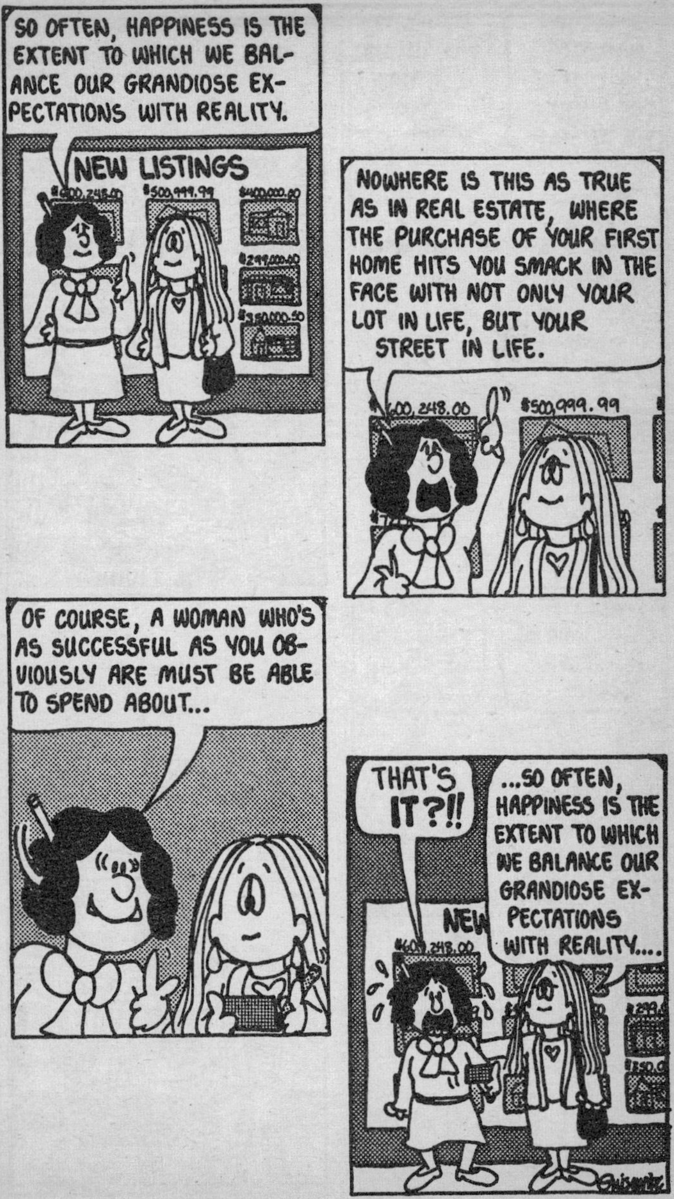
SO OFTEN, HAPPINESS IS THE EXTENT TO WHICH WE BALANCE OUR GRANDIOSE EXPECTATIONS WITH REALITY.
NEW LISTINGS
$500,999.99
NOWHERE IS THIS AS TRUE AS IN REAL ESTATE, WHERE THE PURCHASE OF YOUR FIRST HOME HITS YOU SMACK IN THE FACE WITH NOT ONLY YOUR LOT IN LIFE, BUT YOUR STREET IN LIFE.
$600,248.00
$500,999.99
OF COURSE, A WOMAN WHO'S AS SUCCESSFUL AS YOU OBVIOUSLY ARE MUST BE ABLE TO SPEND ABOUT...
THAT'S IT?!!
...SO OFTEN, HAPPINESS IS THE EXTENT TO WHICH WE BALANCE OUR GRANDIOSE EXPECTATIONS WITH REALITY....
NEW
$600,248.00

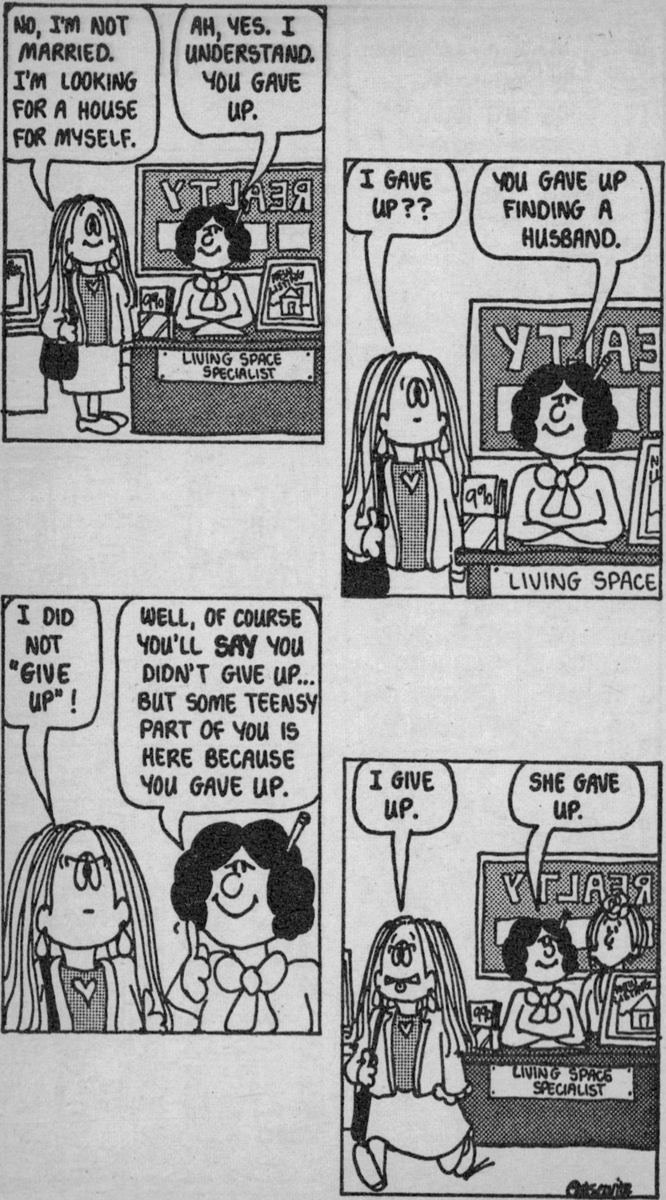

NO, I'M NOT MARRIED. I'M LOOKING FOR A HOUSE FOR MYSELF.
AH, YES. I UNDERSTAND. YOU GAVE UP.
9%
LIVING SPACE SPECIALIST
I GAVE UP??
YOU GAVE UP FINDING A HUSBAND.
9%
LIVING SPACE
I DID NOT "GIVE UP"!
WELL, OF COURSE YOU'LL SAY YOU DIDN'T GIVE UP... BUT SOME TEENSY PART OF YOU IS HERE BECAUSE YOU GAVE UP.
I GIVE UP.
SHE GAVE UP.
LIVING SPACE SPECIALIST

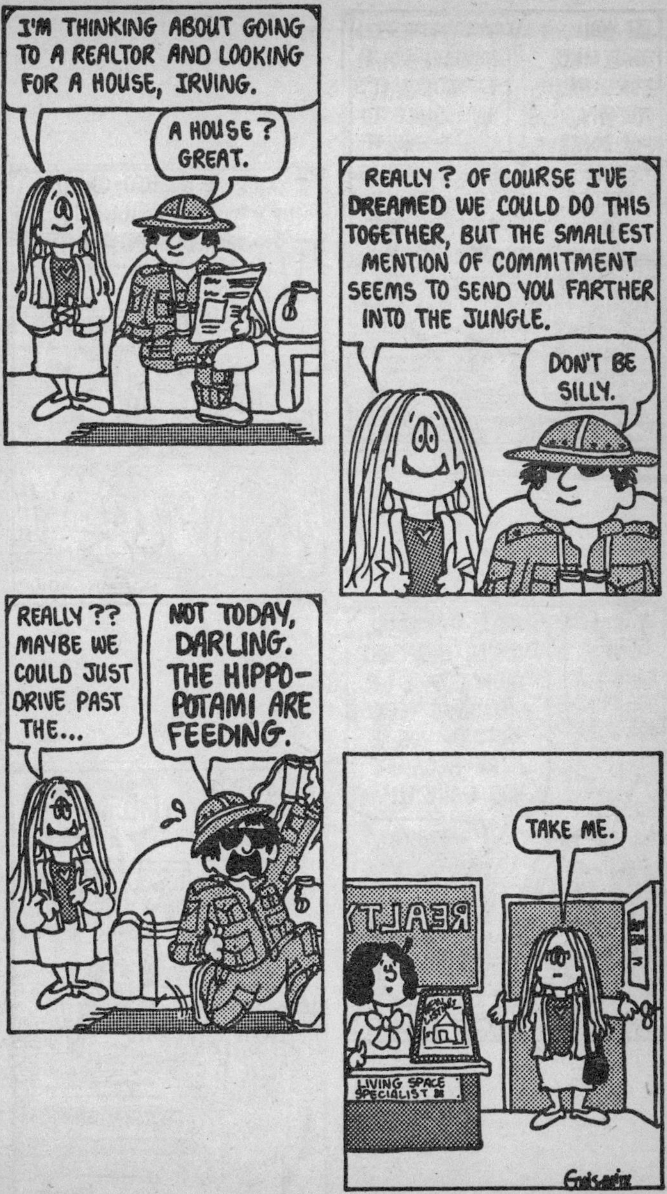
I'M THINKING ABOUT GOING TO A REALTOR AND LOOKING FOR A HOUSE, IRVING.
A HOUSE? GREAT.
REALLY? OF COURSE I'VE DREAMED WE COULD DO THIS TOGETHER, BUT THE SMALLEST MENTION OF COMMITMENT SEEMS TO SEND YOU FARTHER INTO THE JUNGLE.
DON'T BE SILLY.
REALLY?? MAYBE WE COULD JUST DRIVE PAST THE...
NOT TODAY, DARLING. THE HIPPO-POTAMI ARE FEEDING.
LIVING SPACE SPECIALIST
TAKE ME.
Guisewite

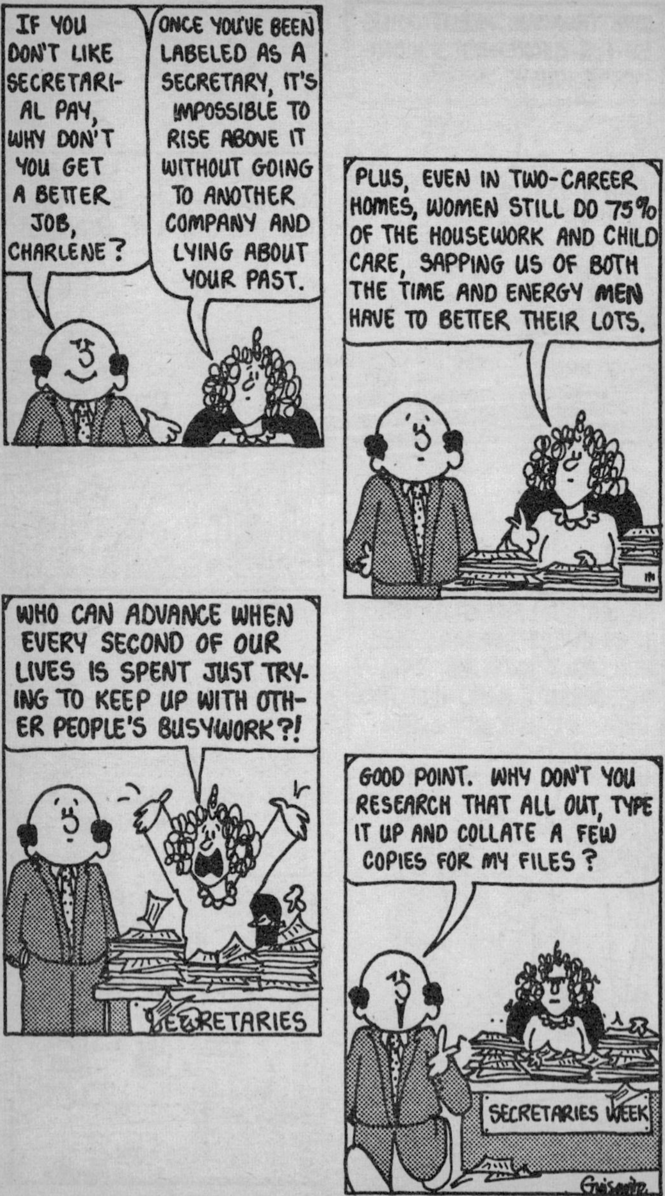
IF YOU DON'T LIKE SECRETARIAL PAY, WHY DON'T YOU GET A BETTER JOB, CHARLENE?
ONCE YOU'VE BEEN LABELED AS A SECRETARY, IT'S IMPOSSIBLE TO RISE ABOVE IT WITHOUT GOING TO ANOTHER COMPANY AND LYING ABOUT YOUR PAST.
PLUS, EVEN IN TWO-CAREER HOMES, WOMEN STILL DO 75% OF THE HOUSEWORK AND CHILD CARE, SAPPING US OF BOTH THE TIME AND ENERGY MEN HAVE TO BETTER THEIR LOTS.
WHO CAN ADVANCE WHEN EVERY SECOND OF OUR LIVES IS SPENT JUST TRYING TO KEEP UP WITH OTHER PEOPLE'S BUSYWORK?!
SECRETARIES
GOOD POINT. WHY DON'T YOU RESEARCH THAT ALL OUT, TYPE IT UP AND COLLATE A FEW COPIES FOR MY FILES?
SECRETARIES WEEK
Guisewite

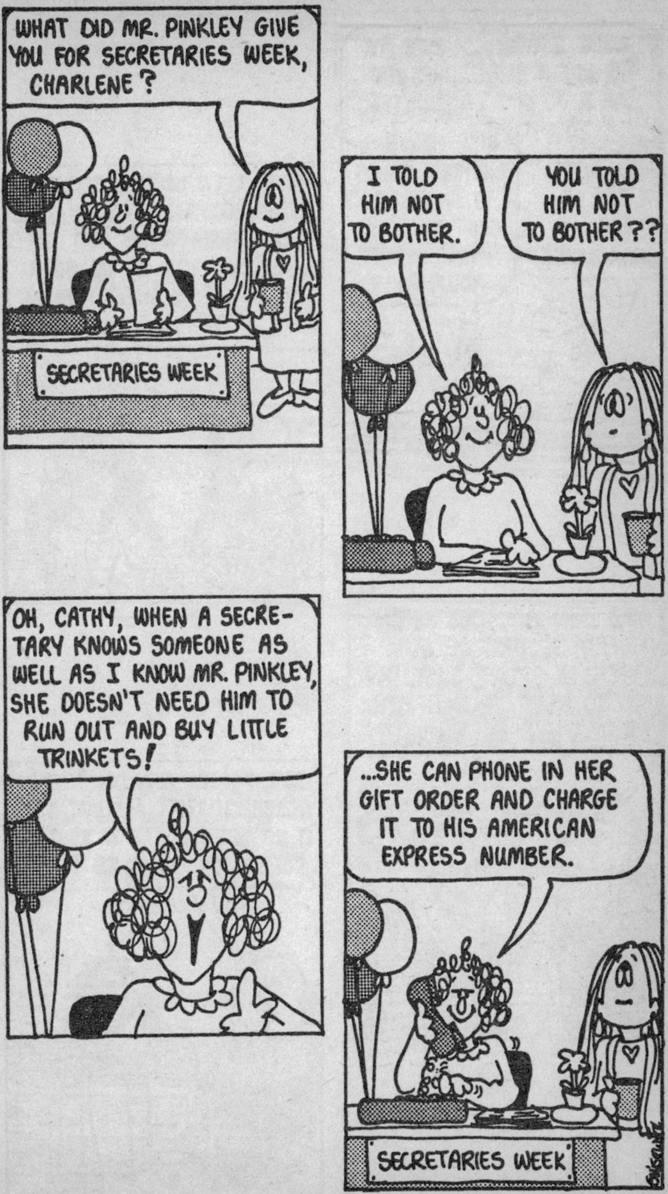
WHAT DID MR. PINKLEY GIVE YOU FOR SECRETARIES WEEK, CHARLENE?
SECRETARIES WEEK
I TOLD HIM NOT TO BOTHER.
YOU TOLD HIM NOT TO BOTHER??
OH, CATHY, WHEN A SECRETARY KNOWS SOMEONE AS WELL AS I KNOW MR. PINKLEY, SHE DOESN'T NEED HIM TO RUN OUT AND BUY LITTLE TRINKETS!
...SHE CAN PHONE IN HER GIFT ORDER AND CHARGE IT TO HIS AMERICAN EXPRESS NUMBER.
SECRETARIES WEEK

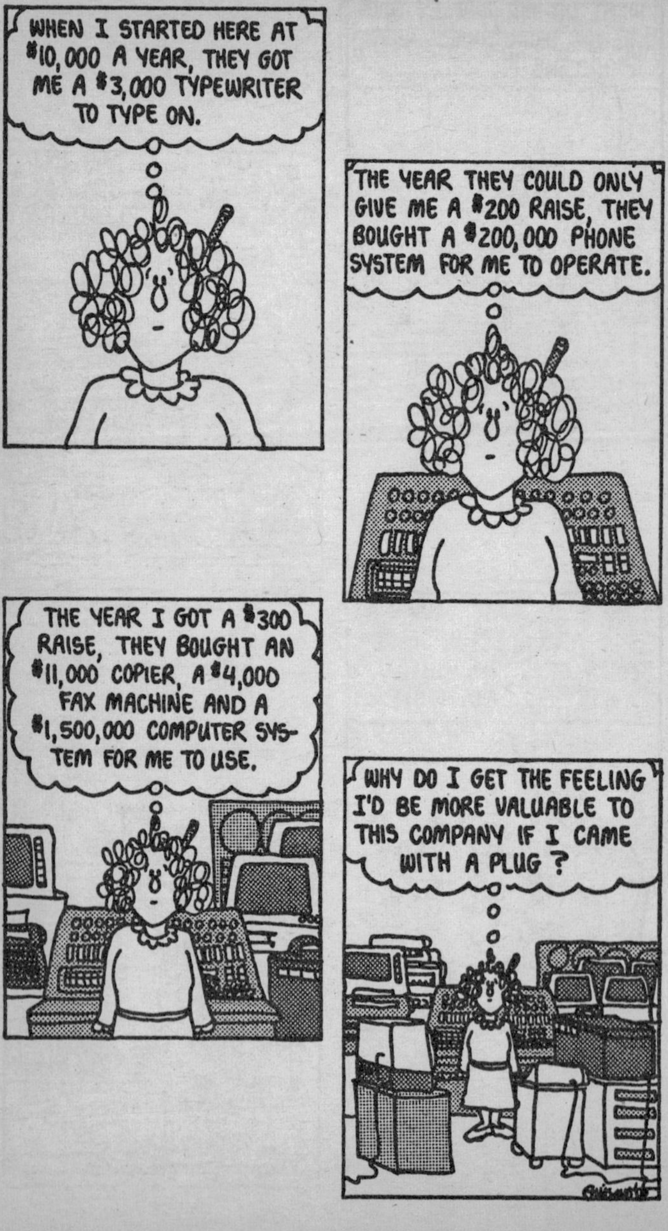
WHEN I STARTED HERE AT $10,000 A YEAR, THEY GOT ME A $3,000 TYPEWRITER TO TYPE ON.
THE YEAR THEY COULD ONLY GIVE ME A $200 RAISE, THEY BOUGHT A $200,000 PHONE SYSTEM FOR ME TO OPERATE.
THE YEAR I GOT A $300 RAISE, THEY BOUGHT AN $11,000 COPIER, A $4,000 FAX MACHINE AND A $1,500,000 COMPUTER SYS-TEM FOR ME TO USE.
WHY DO I GET THE FEELING I'D BE MORE VALUABLE TO THIS COMPANY IF I CAME WITH A PLUG?

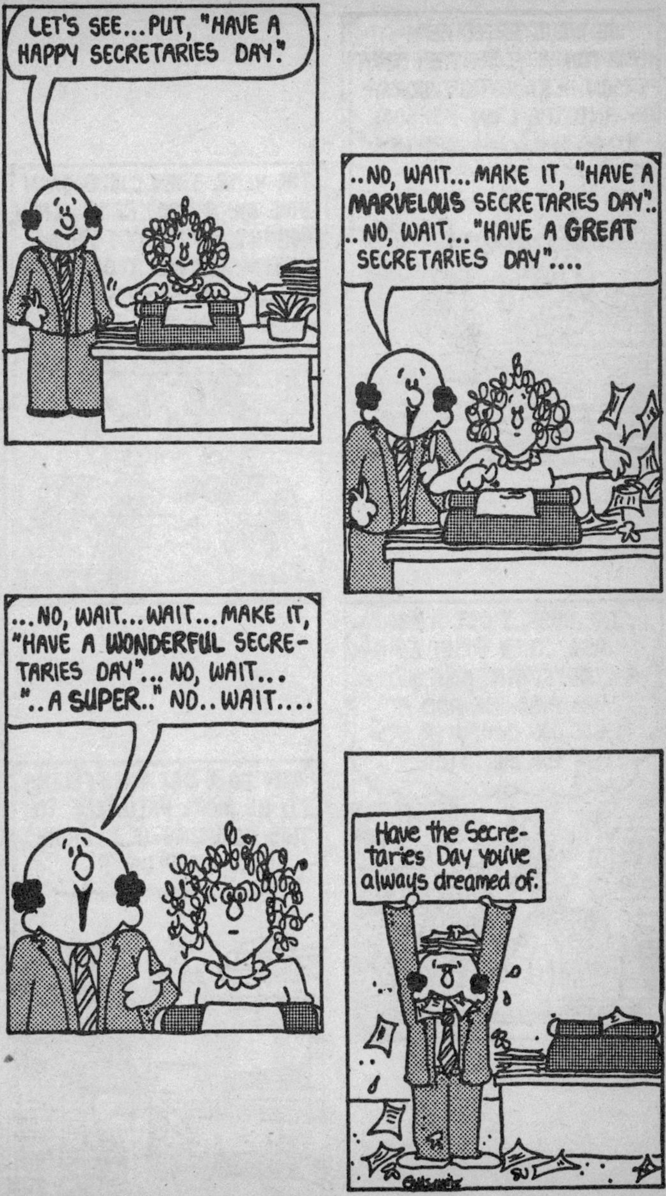
LET'S SEE...PUT, "HAVE A HAPPY SECRETARIES DAY."
..NO, WAIT...MAKE IT, "HAVE A MARVELOUS SECRETARIES DAY"...NO, WAIT..."HAVE A GREAT SECRETARIES DAY"....
...NO, WAIT...WAIT...MAKE IT, "HAVE A WONDERFUL SECRETARIES DAY"... NO, WAIT... "..A SUPER.." NO..WAIT....
Have the Secretaries Day you've always dreamed of.

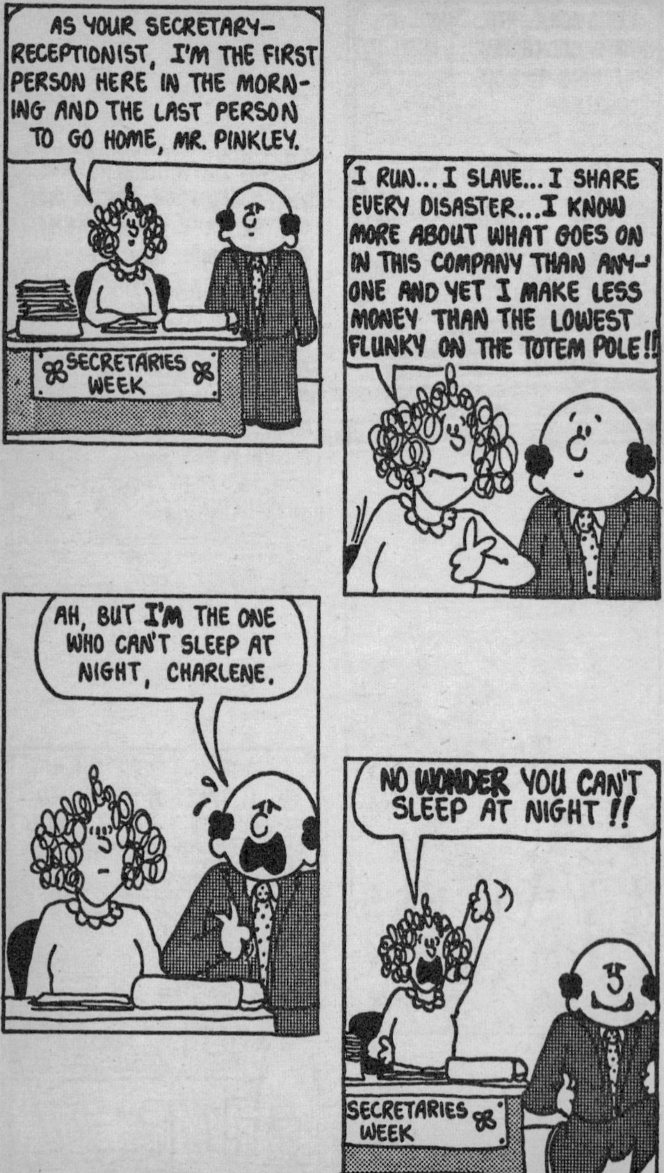
AS YOUR SECRETARY-RECEPTIONIST, I'M THE FIRST PERSON HERE IN THE MORNING AND THE LAST PERSON TO GO HOME, MR. PINKLEY.
SECRETARIES WEEK
I RUN... I SLAVE... I SHARE EVERY DISASTER... I KNOW MORE ABOUT WHAT GOES ON IN THIS COMPANY THAN ANYONE AND YET I MAKE LESS MONEY THAN THE LOWEST FLUNKY ON THE TOTEM POLE!!
AH, BUT I'M THE ONE WHO CAN'T SLEEP AT NIGHT, CHARLENE.
NO WONDER YOU CAN'T SLEEP AT NIGHT!!
SECRETARIES WEEK

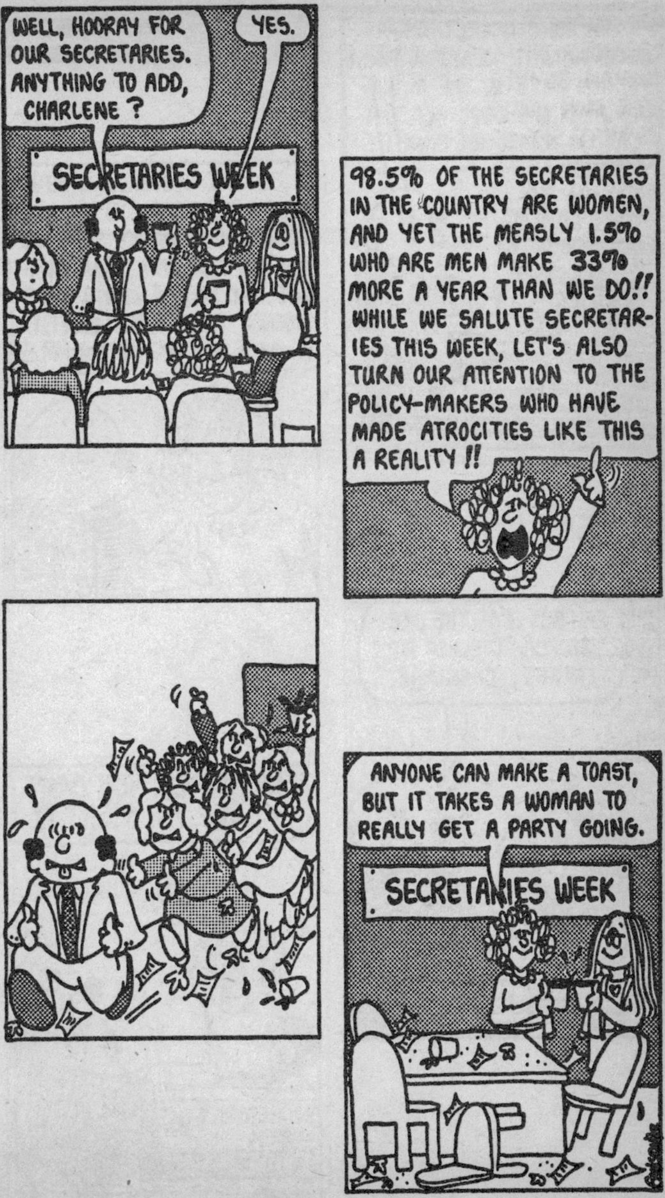
WELL, HOORAY FOR OUR SECRETARIES. ANYTHING TO ADD, CHARLENE ?
YES.
SECRETARIES WEEK
98.5% OF THE SECRETARIES IN THE COUNTRY ARE WOMEN, AND YET THE MEASLY 1.5% WHO ARE MEN MAKE 33% MORE A YEAR THAN WE DO!! WHILE WE SALUTE SECRETARIES THIS WEEK, LET'S ALSO TURN OUR ATTENTION TO THE POLICY-MAKERS WHO HAVE MADE ATROCITIES LIKE THIS A REALITY !!
ANYONE CAN MAKE A TOAST, BUT IT TAKES A WOMAN TO REALLY GET A PARTY GOING.
SECRETARIES WEEK

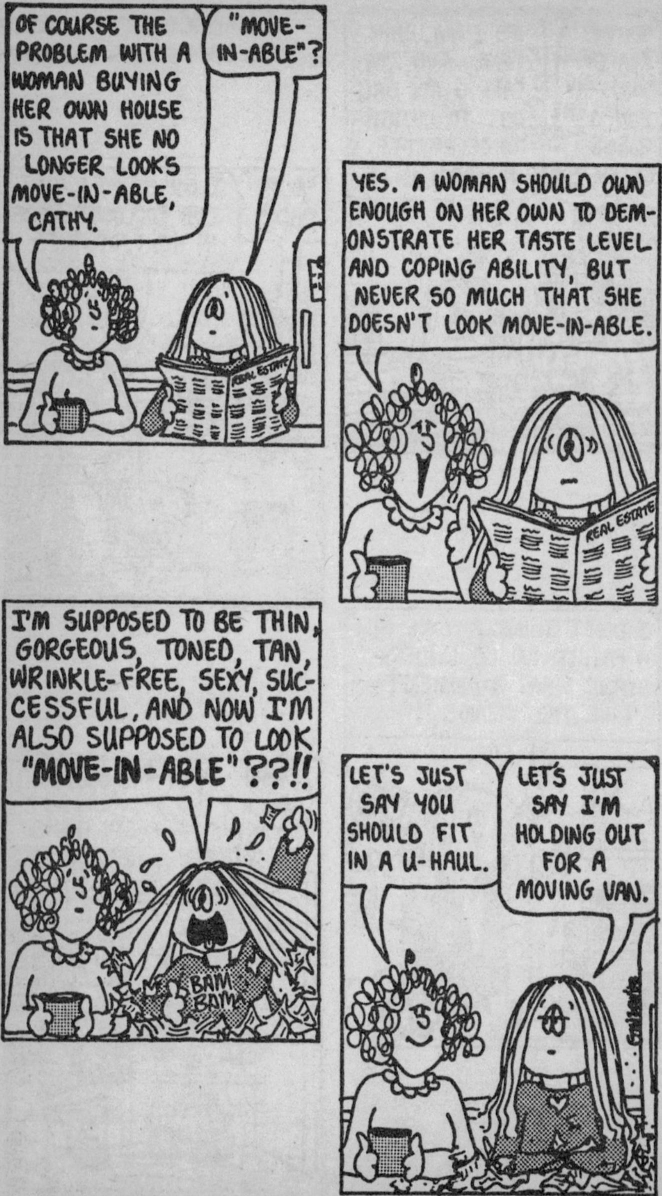
OF COURSE THE PROBLEM WITH A WOMAN BUYING HER OWN HOUSE IS THAT SHE NO LONGER LOOKS MOVE-IN-ABLE, CATHY.
"MOVE-IN-ABLE"?
REAL ESTATE
YES. A WOMAN SHOULD OWN ENOUGH ON HER OWN TO DEMONSTRATE HER TASTE LEVEL AND COPING ABILITY, BUT NEVER SO MUCH THAT SHE DOESN'T LOOK MOVE-IN-ABLE.
REAL ESTATE
I'M SUPPOSED TO BE THIN, GORGEOUS, TONED, TAN, WRINKLE-FREE, SEXY, SUCCESSFUL, AND NOW I'M ALSO SUPPOSED TO LOOK "MOVE-IN-ABLE"??!!
BAM BAM
LET'S JUST SAY YOU SHOULD FIT IN A U-HAUL.
LET'S JUST SAY I'M HOLDING OUT FOR A MOVING VAN.

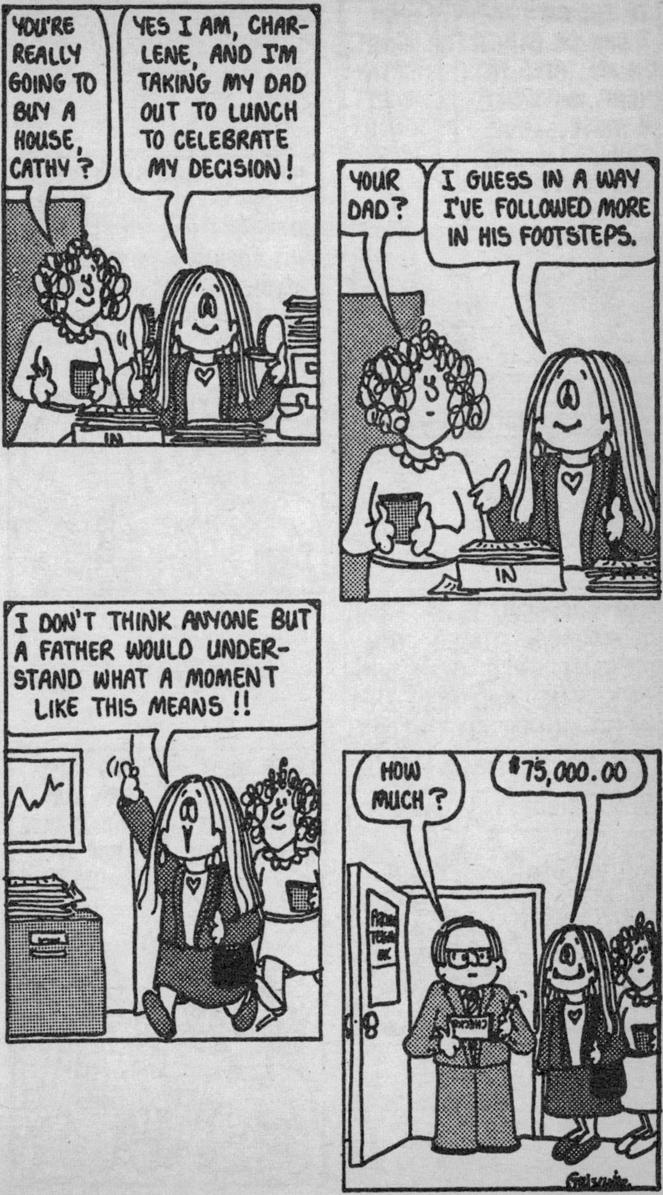
YOU'RE REALLY GOING TO BUY A HOUSE, CATHY?
YES I AM, CHARLENE, AND I'M TAKING MY DAD OUT TO LUNCH TO CELEBRATE MY DECISION!
IN
YOUR DAD?
I GUESS IN A WAY I'VE FOLLOWED MORE IN HIS FOOTSTEPS.
IN
I DON'T THINK ANYONE BUT A FATHER WOULD UNDERSTAND WHAT A MOMENT LIKE THIS MEANS!!
HOW MUCH?
$75,000.00

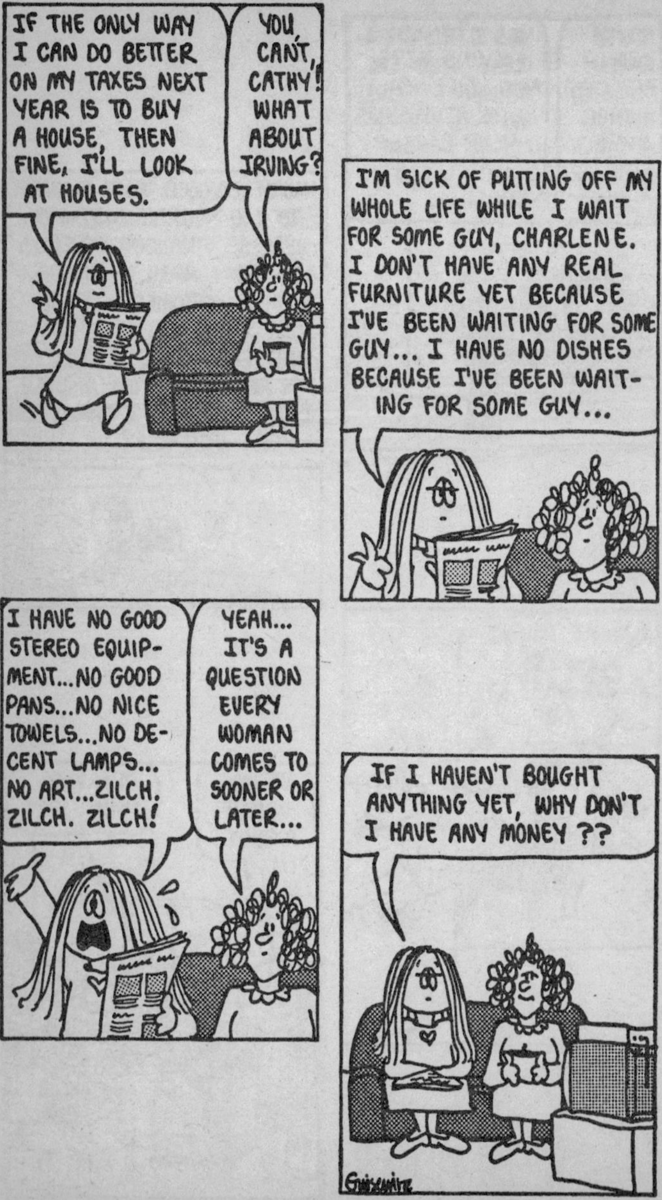
IF THE ONLY WAY I CAN DO BETTER ON MY TAXES NEXT YEAR IS TO BUY A HOUSE, THEN FINE, I'LL LOOK AT HOUSES.
YOU CAN'T, CATHY! WHAT ABOUT IRVING?
I'M SICK OF PUTTING OFF MY WHOLE LIFE WHILE I WAIT FOR SOME GUY, CHARLENE. I DON'T HAVE ANY REAL FURNITURE YET BECAUSE I'VE BEEN WAITING FOR SOME GUY... I HAVE NO DISHES BECAUSE I'VE BEEN WAITING FOR SOME GUY...
I HAVE NO GOOD STEREO EQUIPMENT...NO GOOD PANS...NO NICE TOWELS...NO DECENT LAMPS... NO ART...ZILCH. ZILCH. ZILCH!
YEAH... IT'S A QUESTION EVERY WOMAN COMES TO SOONER OR LATER...
IF I HAVEN'T BOUGHT ANYTHING YET, WHY DON'T I HAVE ANY MONEY ??

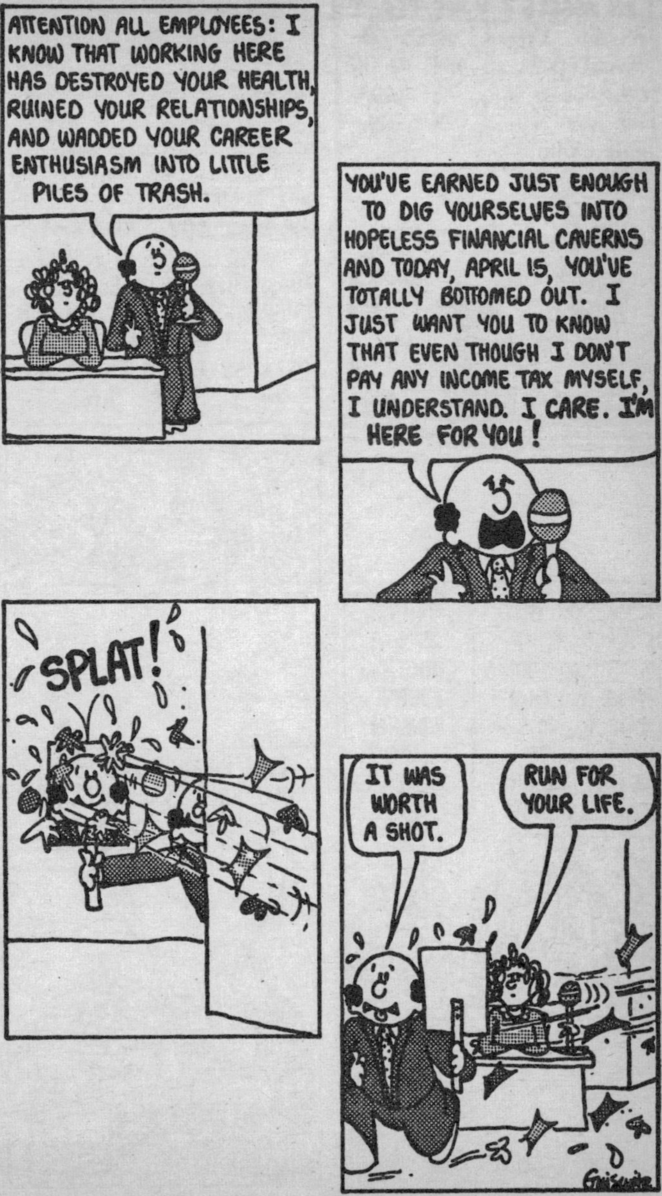
ATTENTION ALL EMPLOYEES: I KNOW THAT WORKING HERE HAS DESTROYED YOUR HEALTH, RUINED YOUR RELATIONSHIPS, AND WADDED YOUR CAREER ENTHUSIASM INTO LITTLE PILES OF TRASH.
YOU'VE EARNED JUST ENOUGH TO DIG YOURSELVES INTO HOPELESS FINANCIAL CAVERNS AND TODAY, APRIL 15, YOU'VE TOTALLY BOTTOMED OUT. I JUST WANT YOU TO KNOW THAT EVEN THOUGH I DON'T PAY ANY INCOME TAX MYSELF, I UNDERSTAND. I CARE. I'M HERE FOR YOU!
SPLAT!
IT WAS WORTH A SHOT.
RUN FOR YOUR LIFE.

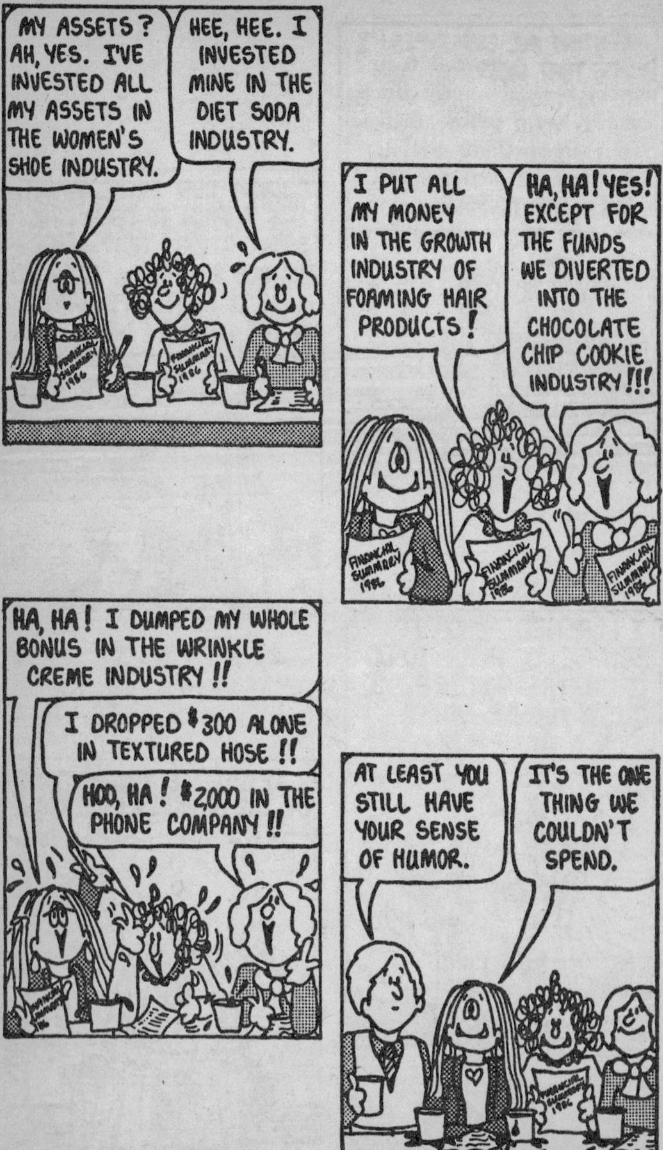
MY ASSETS? AH, YES. I'VE INVESTED ALL MY ASSETS IN THE WOMEN'S SHOE INDUSTRY.
HEE, HEE. I INVESTED MINE IN THE DIET SODA INDUSTRY.
I PUT ALL MY MONEY IN THE GROWTH INDUSTRY OF FOAMING HAIR PRODUCTS!
HA, HA! YES! EXCEPT FOR THE FUNDS WE DIVERTED INTO THE CHOCOLATE CHIP COOKIE INDUSTRY!!!
HA, HA! I DUMPED MY WHOLE BONUS IN THE WRINKLE CREME INDUSTRY!!
I DROPPED $300 ALONE IN TEXTURED HOSE!!
HOO, HA! $2,000 IN THE PHONE COMPANY!!
AT LEAST YOU STILL HAVE YOUR SENSE OF HUMOR.
IT'S THE ONE THING WE COULDN'T SPEND.
Guisewite

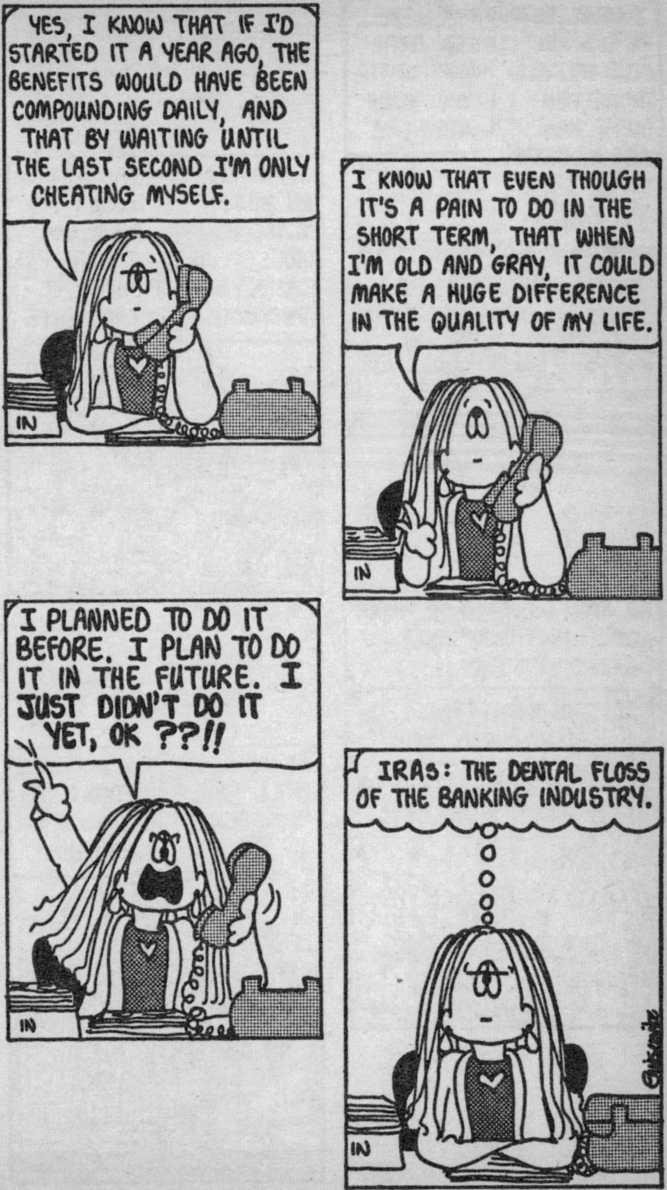
YES, I KNOW THAT IF I'D STARTED IT A YEAR AGO, THE BENEFITS WOULD HAVE BEEN COMPOUNDING DAILY, AND THAT BY WAITING UNTIL THE LAST SECOND I'M ONLY CHEATING MYSELF.
IN
I KNOW THAT EVEN THOUGH IT'S A PAIN TO DO IN THE SHORT TERM, THAT WHEN I'M OLD AND GRAY, IT COULD MAKE A HUGE DIFFERENCE IN THE QUALITY OF MY LIFE.
IN
I PLANNED TO DO IT BEFORE. I PLAN TO DO IT IN THE FUTURE. I JUST DIDN'T DO IT YET, OK ??!!
IN
IRAS: THE DENTAL FLOSS OF THE BANKING INDUSTRY.
IN

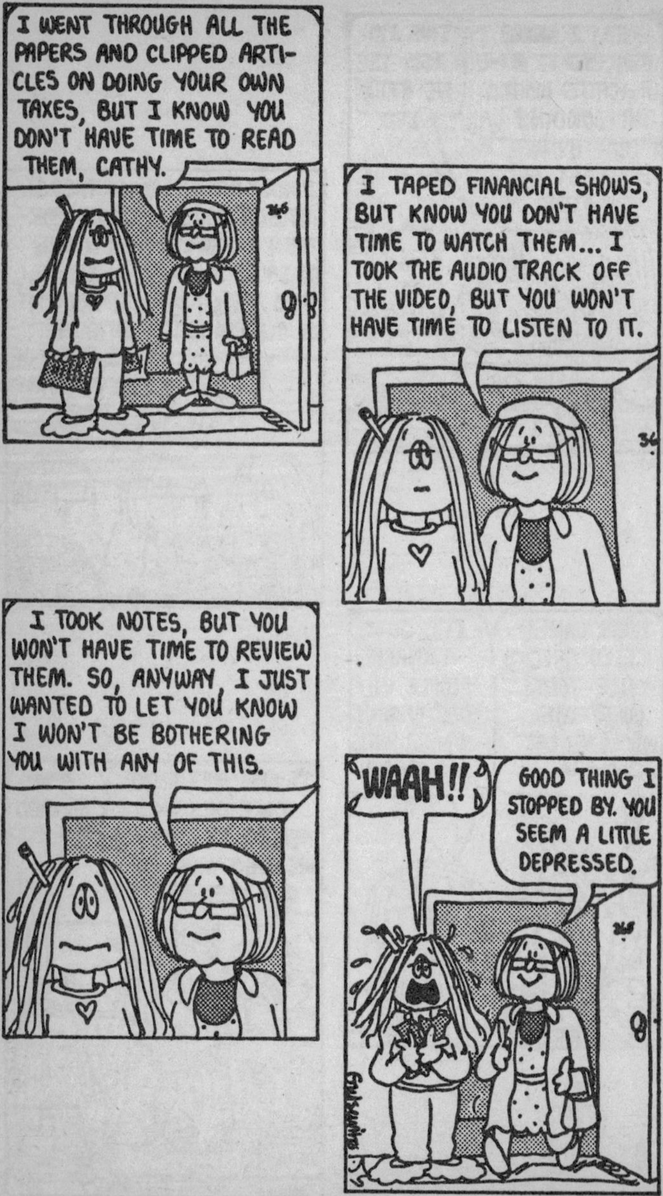
I WENT THROUGH ALL THE PAPERS AND CLIPPED ARTICLES ON DOING YOUR OWN TAXES, BUT I KNOW YOU DON'T HAVE TIME TO READ THEM, CATHY.
I TAPED FINANCIAL SHOWS, BUT KNOW YOU DON'T HAVE TIME TO WATCH THEM... I TOOK THE AUDIO TRACK OFF THE VIDEO, BUT YOU WON'T HAVE TIME TO LISTEN TO IT.
I TOOK NOTES, BUT YOU WON'T HAVE TIME TO REVIEW THEM. SO, ANYWAY, I JUST WANTED TO LET YOU KNOW I WON'T BE BOTHERING YOU WITH ANY OF THIS.
WAAH!!
GOOD THING I STOPPED BY. YOU SEEM A LITTLE DEPRESSED.

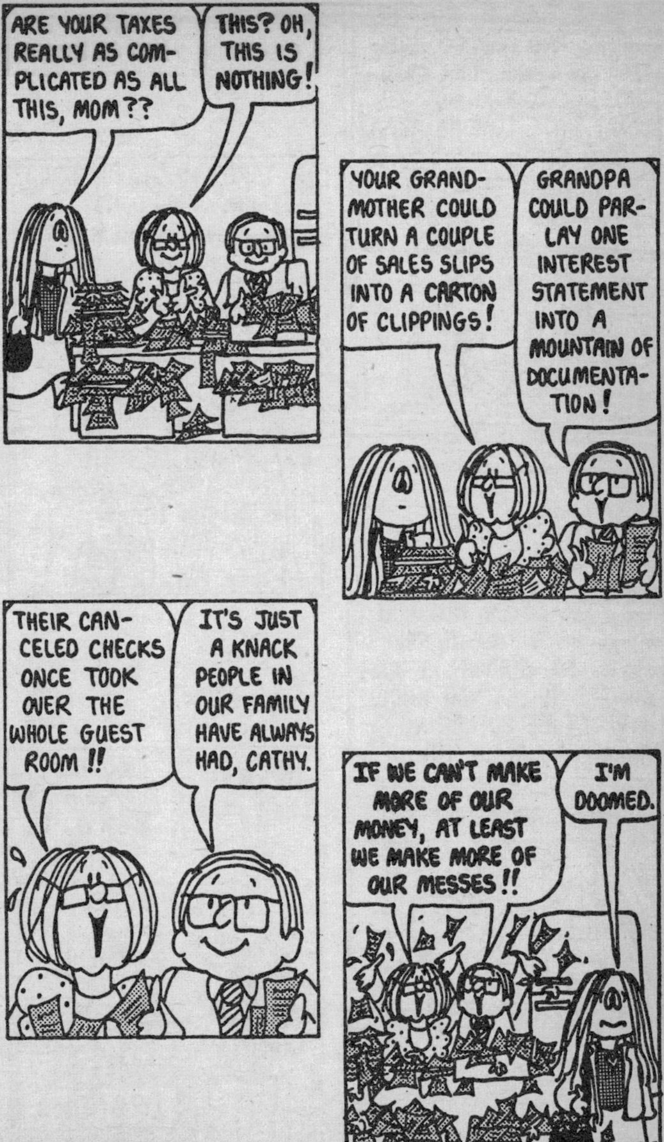
ARE YOUR TAXES REALLY AS COM-PLICATED AS ALL THIS, MOM??
THIS? OH, THIS IS NOTHING!
YOUR GRAND-MOTHER COULD TURN A COUPLE OF SALES SLIPS INTO A CARTON OF CLIPPINGS!
GRANDPA COULD PAR-LAY ONE INTEREST STATEMENT INTO A MOUNTAIN OF DOCUMENTA-TION!
THEIR CAN-CELED CHECKS ONCE TOOK OVER THE WHOLE GUEST ROOM!!
IT'S JUST A KNACK PEOPLE IN OUR FAMILY HAVE ALWAYS HAD, CATHY.
IF WE CAN'T MAKE MORE OF OUR MONEY, AT LEAST WE MAKE MORE OF OUR MESSES!!
I'M DOOMED.

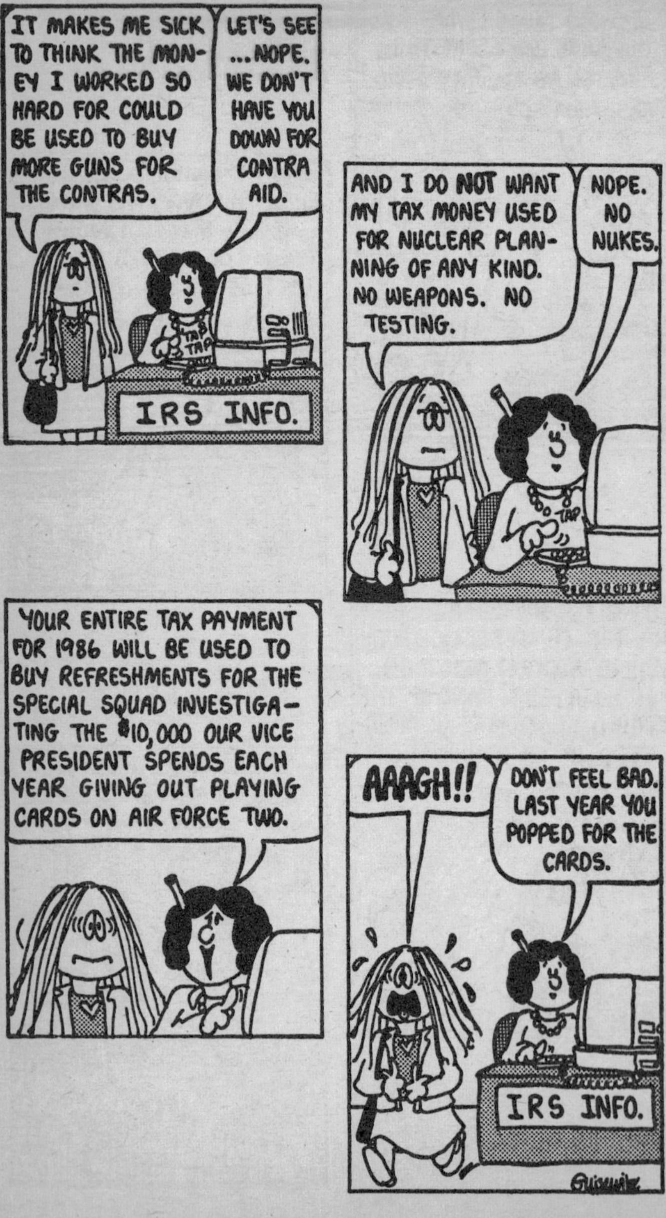
IT MAKES ME SICK TO THINK THE MONEY I WORKED SO HARD FOR COULD BE USED TO BUY MORE GUNS FOR THE CONTRAS.
LET'S SEE ...NOPE. WE DON'T HAVE YOU DOWN FOR CONTRA AID.
TAP TAP
IRS INFO.
AND I DO NOT WANT MY TAX MONEY USED FOR NUCLEAR PLANNING OF ANY KIND. NO WEAPONS. NO TESTING.
NOPE. NO NUKES.
TAP
YOUR ENTIRE TAX PAYMENT FOR 1986 WILL BE USED TO BUY REFRESHMENTS FOR THE SPECIAL SQUAD INVESTIGATING THE $10,000 OUR VICE PRESIDENT SPENDS EACH YEAR GIVING OUT PLAYING CARDS ON AIR FORCE TWO.
AAAGH!!
DON'T FEEL BAD. LAST YEAR YOU POPPED FOR THE CARDS.
IRS INFO.

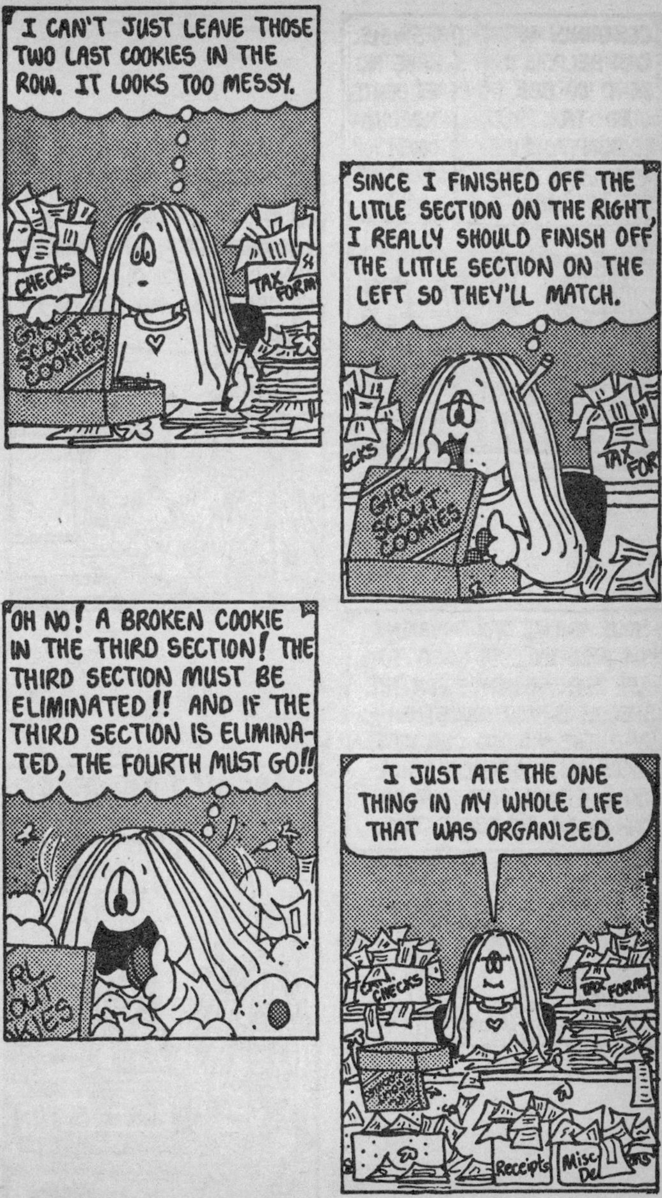
I CAN'T JUST LEAVE THOSE TWO LAST COOKIES IN THE ROW. IT LOOKS TOO MESSY.
CHECKS
GIRL SCOUT COOKIES
SINCE I FINISHED OFF THE LITTLE SECTION ON THE RIGHT, I REALLY SHOULD FINISH OFF THE LITTLE SECTION ON THE LEFT SO THEY'LL MATCH.
GIRL SCOUT COOKIES
OH NO! A BROKEN COOKIE IN THE THIRD SECTION! THE THIRD SECTION MUST BE ELIMINATED!! AND IF THE THIRD SECTION IS ELIMINATED, THE FOURTH MUST GO!!
I JUST ATE THE ONE THING IN MY WHOLE LIFE THAT WAS ORGANIZED.
CHECKS
TAX FORMS
Receipts
Misc

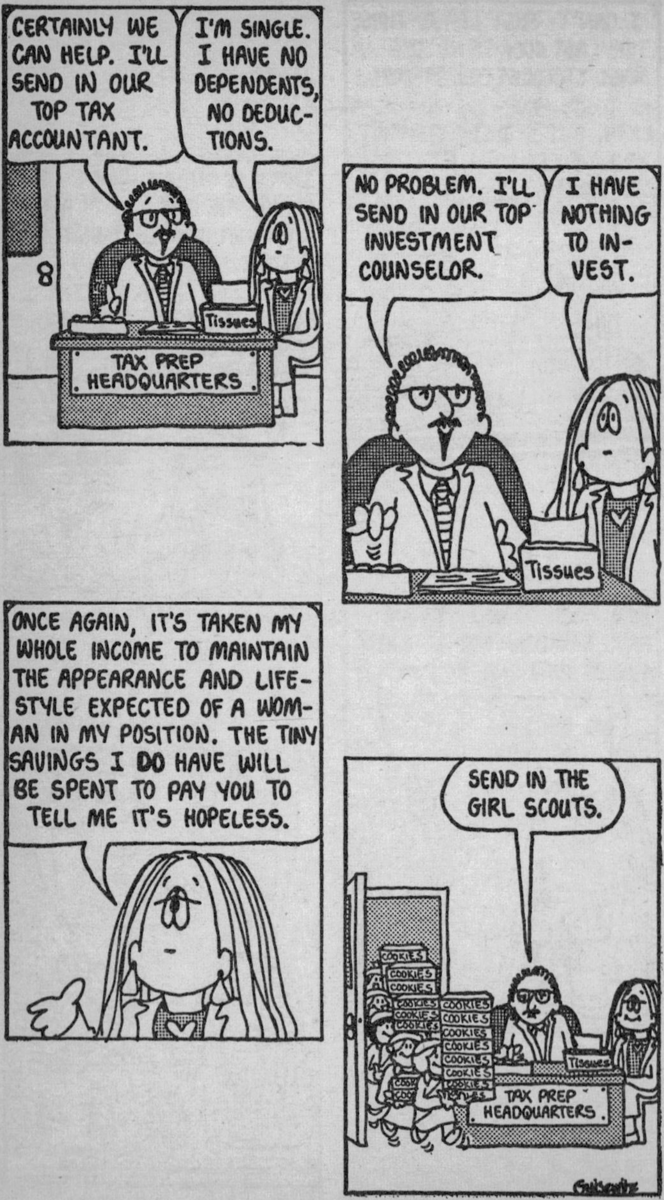
CERTAINLY WE CAN HELP. I'LL SEND IN OUR TOP TAX ACCOUNTANT.
I'M SINGLE. I HAVE NO DEPENDENTS, NO DEDUCTIONS.
8
Tissues
TAX PREP HEADQUARTERS
NO PROBLEM. I'LL SEND IN OUR TOP INVESTMENT COUNSELOR.
I HAVE NOTHING TO INVEST.
Tissues
ONCE AGAIN, IT'S TAKEN MY WHOLE INCOME TO MAINTAIN THE APPEARANCE AND LIFESTYLE EXPECTED OF A WOMAN IN MY POSITION. THE TINY SAVINGS I DO HAVE WILL BE SPENT TO PAY YOU TO TELL ME IT'S HOPELESS.
SEND IN THE GIRL SCOUTS.
COOKIES
TAX PREP HEADQUARTERS

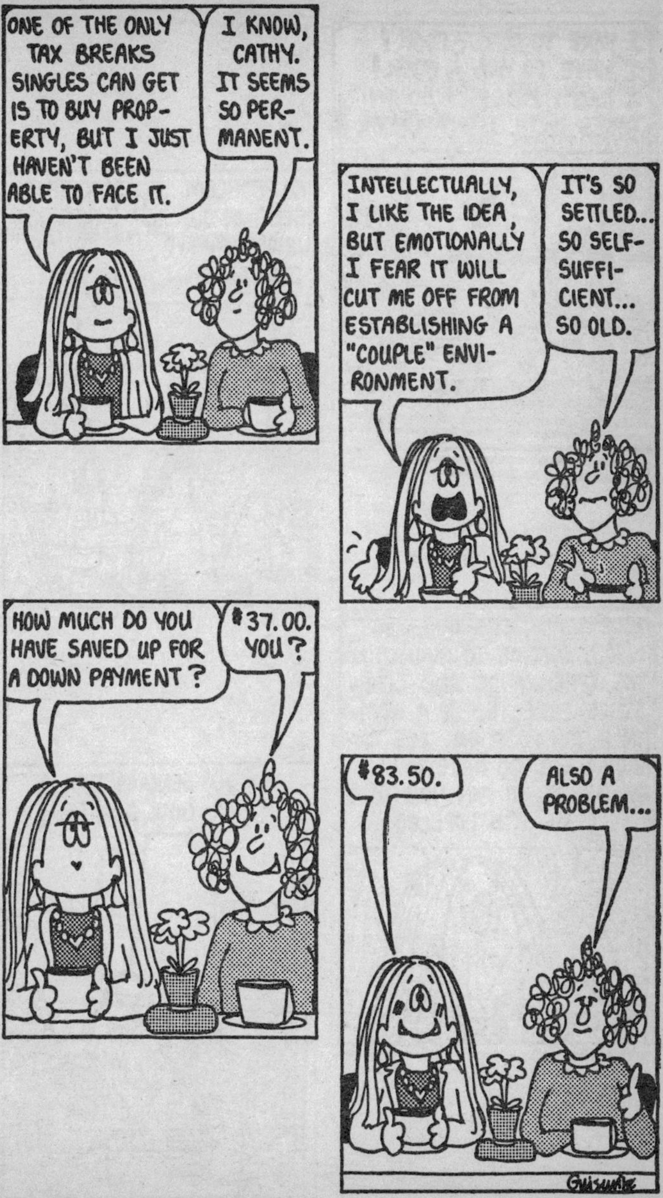
ONE OF THE ONLY TAX BREAKS SINGLES CAN GET IS TO BUY PROPERTY, BUT I JUST HAVEN'T BEEN ABLE TO FACE IT.
I KNOW, CATHY. IT SEEMS SO PERMANENT.
INTELLECTUALLY, I LIKE THE IDEA, BUT EMOTIONALLY I FEAR IT WILL CUT ME OFF FROM ESTABLISHING A "COUPLE" ENVIRONMENT.
IT'S SO SETTLED... SO SELF-SUFFICIENT... SO OLD.
HOW MUCH DO YOU HAVE SAVED UP FOR A DOWN PAYMENT?
$37.00. YOU?
$83.50.
ALSO A PROBLEM...
Guisewite

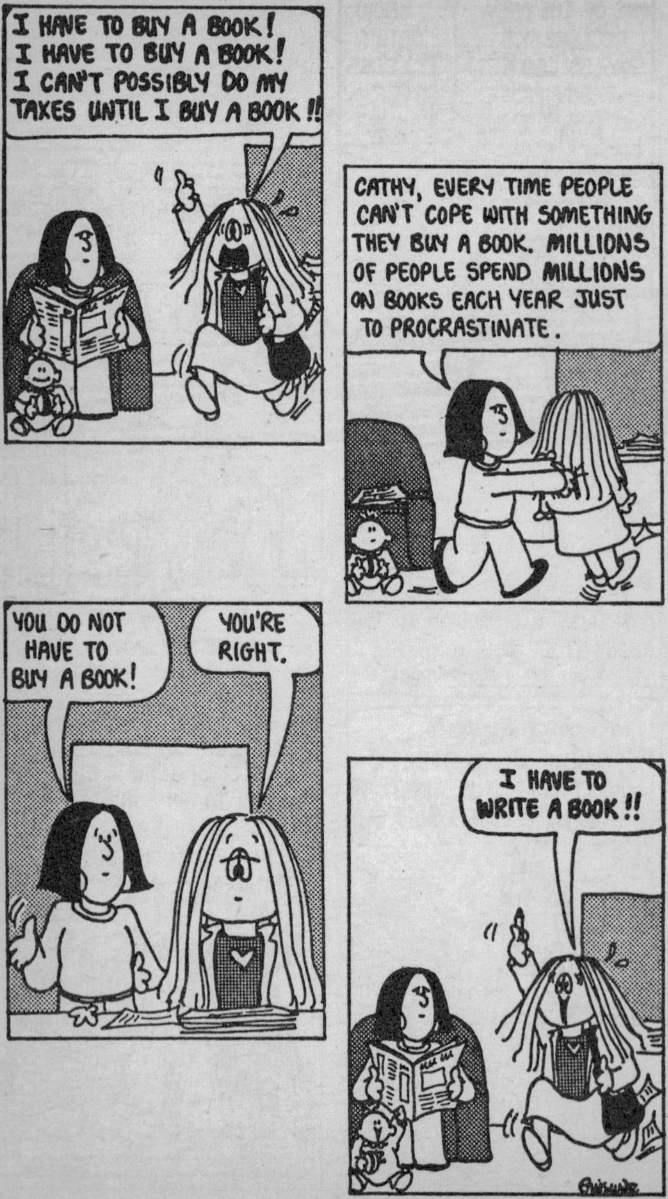
I HAVE TO BUY A BOOK! I HAVE TO BUY A BOOK! I CAN'T POSSIBLY DO MY TAXES UNTIL I BUY A BOOK!!
CATHY, EVERY TIME PEOPLE CAN'T COPE WITH SOMETHING THEY BUY A BOOK. MILLIONS OF PEOPLE SPEND MILLIONS ON BOOKS EACH YEAR JUST TO PROCRASTINATE.
YOU DO NOT HAVE TO BUY A BOOK!
YOU'RE RIGHT.
I HAVE TO WRITE A BOOK!!

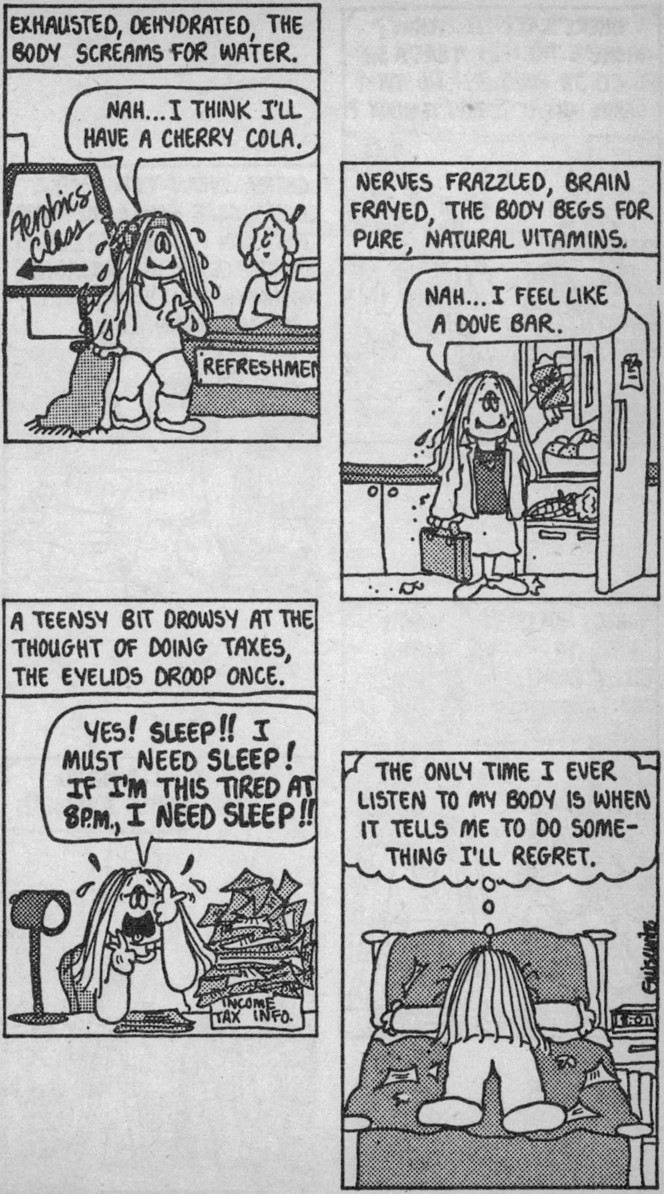
EXHAUSTED, DEHYDRATED, THE BODY SCREAMS FOR WATER.
NAH... I THINK I'LL HAVE A CHERRY COLA.
Aerobics Class
REFRESHMEN
NERVES FRAZZLED, BRAIN FRAYED, THE BODY BEGS FOR PURE, NATURAL VITAMINS.
NAH... I FEEL LIKE A DOVE BAR.
A TEENSY BIT DROWSY AT THE THOUGHT OF DOING TAXES, THE EYELIDS DROOP ONCE.
YES! SLEEP!! I MUST NEED SLEEP! IF I'M THIS TIRED AT 8P.M., I NEED SLEEP!!
INCOME TAX INFO.
THE ONLY TIME I EVER LISTEN TO MY BODY IS WHEN IT TELLS ME TO DO SOMETHING I'LL REGRET.

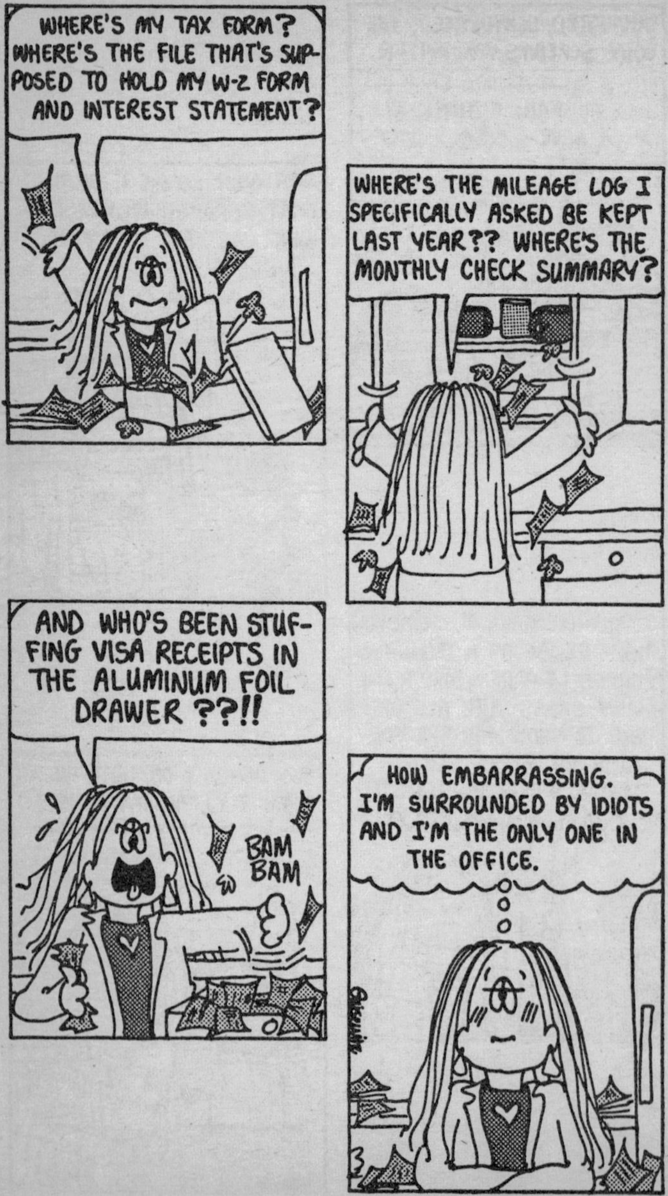
WHERE'S MY TAX FORM? WHERE'S THE FILE THAT'S SUPPOSED TO HOLD MY W-2 FORM AND INTEREST STATEMENT?
WHERE'S THE MILEAGE LOG I SPECIFICALLY ASKED BE KEPT LAST YEAR?? WHERE'S THE MONTHLY CHECK SUMMARY?
AND WHO'S BEEN STUFFING VISA RECEIPTS IN THE ALUMINUM FOIL DRAWER??!!
BAM BAM
HOW EMBARRASSING. I'M SURROUNDED BY IDIOTS AND I'M THE ONLY ONE IN THE OFFICE.

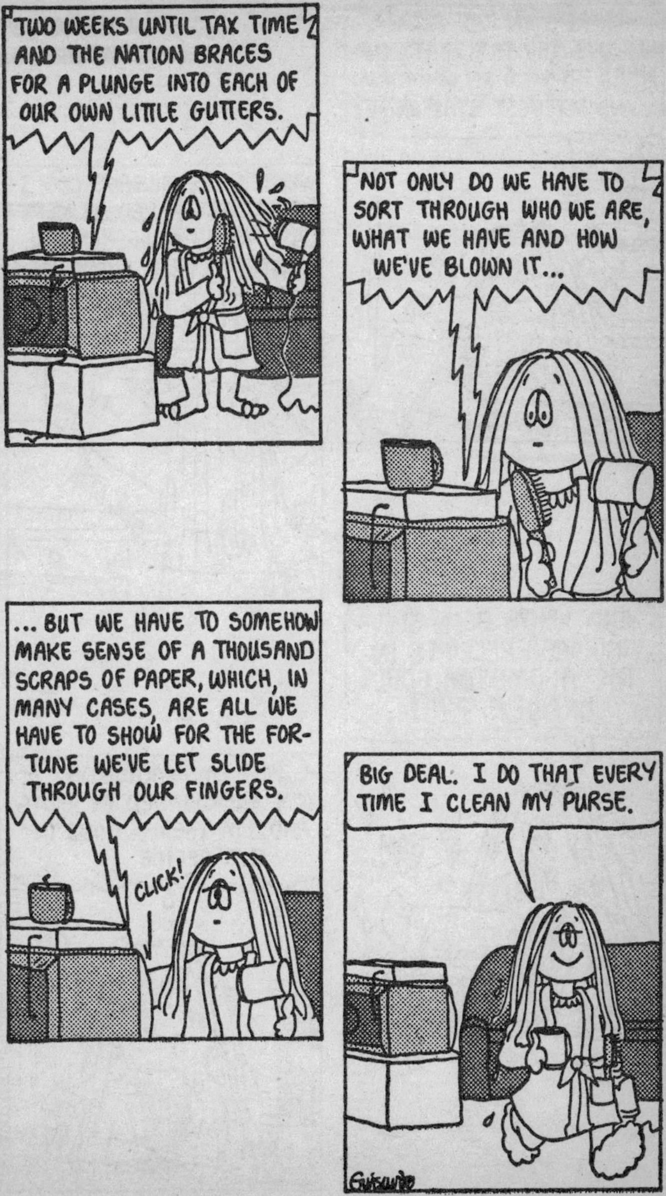
TWO WEEKS UNTIL TAX TIME AND THE NATION BRACES FOR A PLUNGE INTO EACH OF OUR OWN LITTLE GUTTERS.
NOT ONLY DO WE HAVE TO SORT THROUGH WHO WE ARE, WHAT WE HAVE AND HOW WE'VE BLOWN IT...
... BUT WE HAVE TO SOMEHOW MAKE SENSE OF A THOUSAND SCRAPS OF PAPER, WHICH, IN MANY CASES, ARE ALL WE HAVE TO SHOW FOR THE FOR-TUNE WE'VE LET SLIDE THROUGH OUR FINGERS.
CLICK!
BIG DEAL. I DO THAT EVERY TIME I CLEAN MY PURSE.

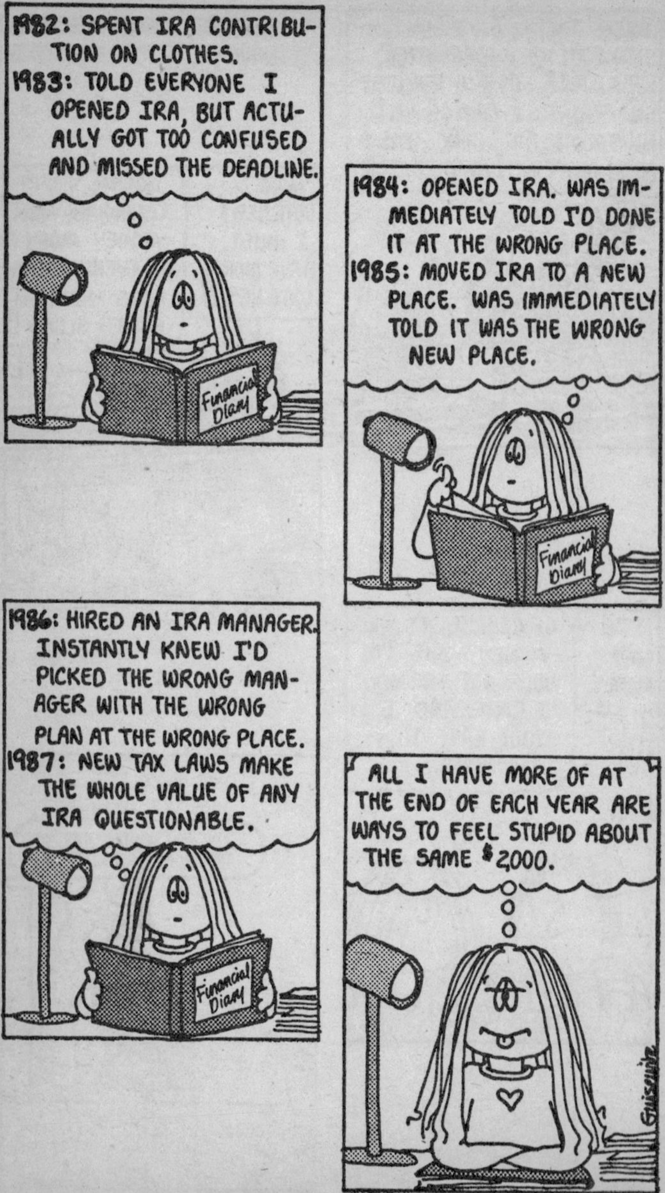
1982: SPENT IRA CONTRIBUTION ON CLOTHES.
1983: TOLD EVERYONE I OPENED IRA, BUT ACTUALLY GOT TOO CONFUSED AND MISSED THE DEADLINE.
Financial Diary
1984: OPENED IRA. WAS IMMEDIATELY TOLD I'D DONE IT AT THE WRONG PLACE.
1985: MOVED IRA TO A NEW PLACE. WAS IMMEDIATELY TOLD IT WAS THE WRONG NEW PLACE.
Financial Diary
1986: HIRED AN IRA MANAGER. INSTANTLY KNEW I'D PICKED THE WRONG MANAGER WITH THE WRONG PLAN AT THE WRONG PLACE.
1987: NEW TAX LAWS MAKE THE WHOLE VALUE OF ANY IRA QUESTIONABLE.
Financial Diary
ALL I HAVE MORE OF AT THE END OF EACH YEAR ARE WAYS TO FEEL STUPID ABOUT THE SAME $2,000.

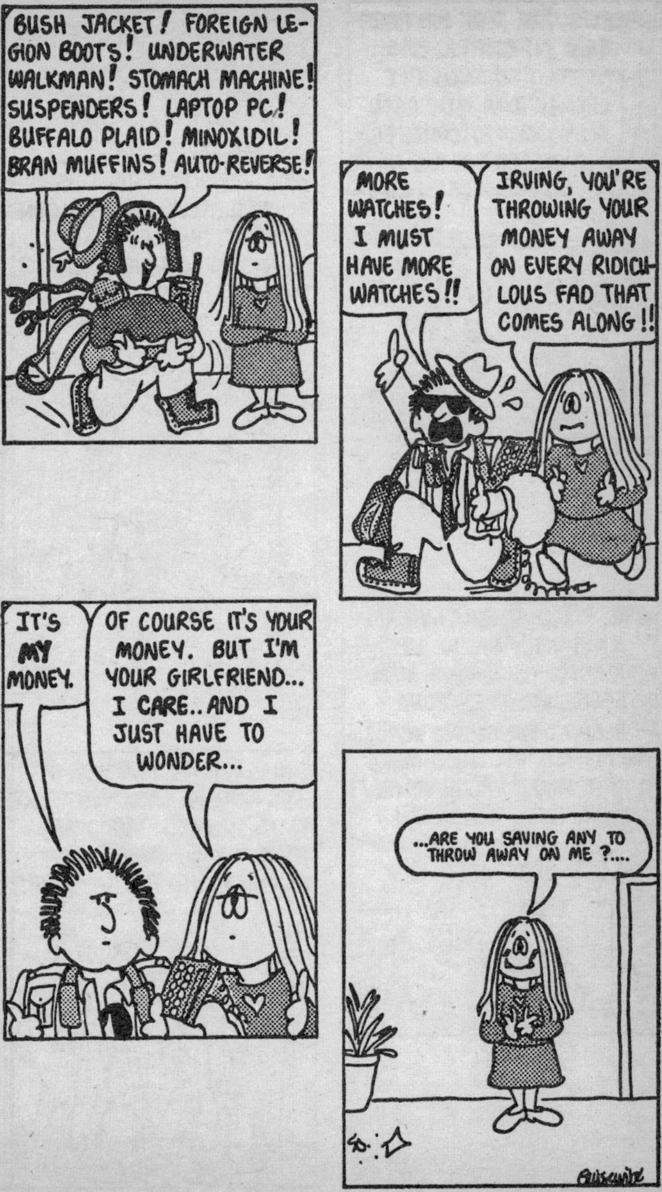
BUSH JACKET! FOREIGN LEGION BOOTS! UNDERWATER WALKMAN! STOMACH MACHINE! SUSPENDERS! LAPTOP PC! BUFFALO PLAID! MINOXIDIL! BRAN MUFFINS! AUTO-REVERSE!
MORE WATCHES! I MUST HAVE MORE WATCHES!!
IRVING, YOU'RE THROWING YOUR MONEY AWAY ON EVERY RIDICULOUS FAD THAT COMES ALONG!!
IT'S **MY** MONEY.
OF COURSE IT'S YOUR MONEY. BUT I'M YOUR GIRLFRIEND... I CARE.. AND I JUST HAVE TO WONDER...
...ARE YOU SAVING ANY TO THROW AWAY ON ME ?....
Guisewite

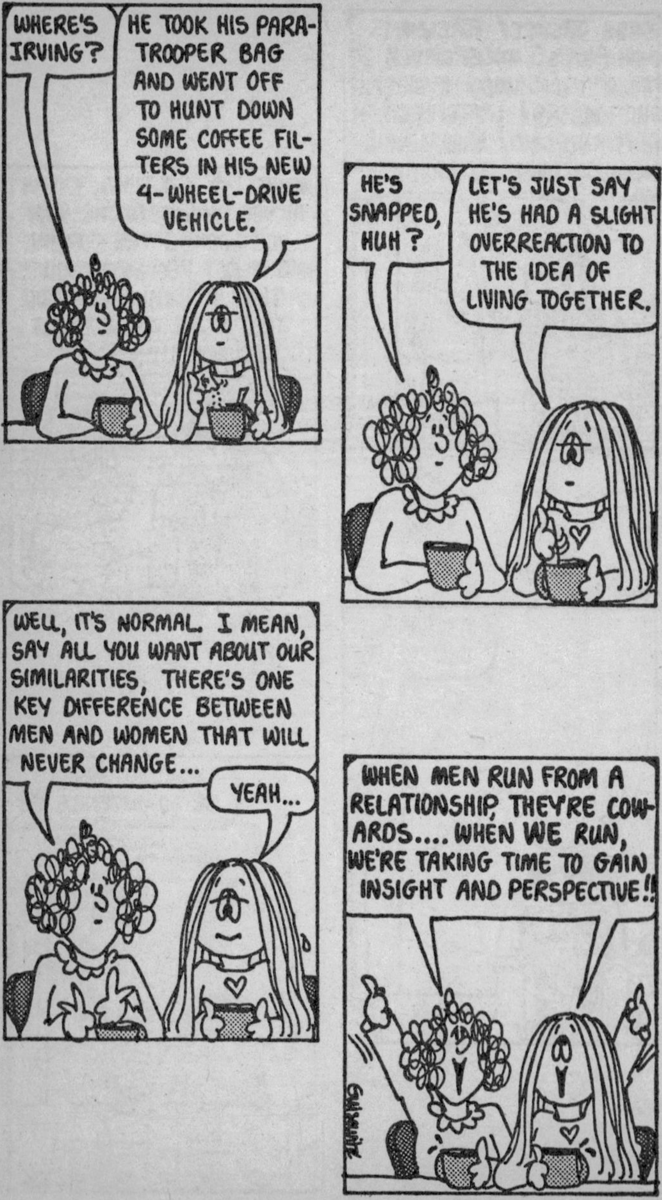
WHERE'S IRVING?
HE TOOK HIS PARA-TROOPER BAG AND WENT OFF TO HUNT DOWN SOME COFFEE FIL-TERS IN HIS NEW 4-WHEEL-DRIVE VEHICLE.
HE'S SNAPPED, HUH?
LET'S JUST SAY HE'S HAD A SLIGHT OVERREACTION TO THE IDEA OF LIVING TOGETHER.
WELL, IT'S NORMAL. I MEAN, SAY ALL YOU WANT ABOUT OUR SIMILARITIES, THERE'S ONE KEY DIFFERENCE BETWEEN MEN AND WOMEN THAT WILL NEVER CHANGE...
YEAH...
WHEN MEN RUN FROM A RELATIONSHIP, THEY'RE COW-ARDS.... WHEN WE RUN, WE'RE TAKING TIME TO GAIN INSIGHT AND PERSPECTIVE!!
Guisewite

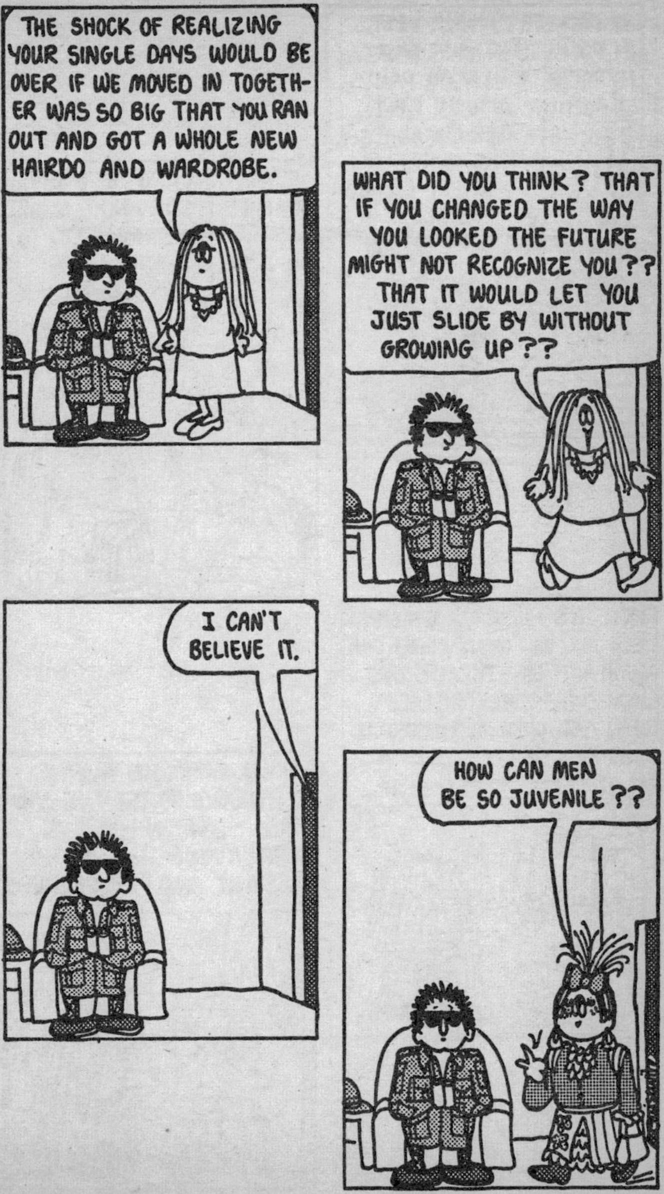
THE SHOCK OF REALIZING YOUR SINGLE DAYS WOULD BE OVER IF WE MOVED IN TOGETHER WAS SO BIG THAT YOU RAN OUT AND GOT A WHOLE NEW HAIRDO AND WARDROBE.
WHAT DID YOU THINK? THAT IF YOU CHANGED THE WAY YOU LOOKED THE FUTURE MIGHT NOT RECOGNIZE YOU?? THAT IT WOULD LET YOU JUST SLIDE BY WITHOUT GROWING UP??
I CAN'T BELIEVE IT.
HOW CAN MEN BE SO JUVENILE??

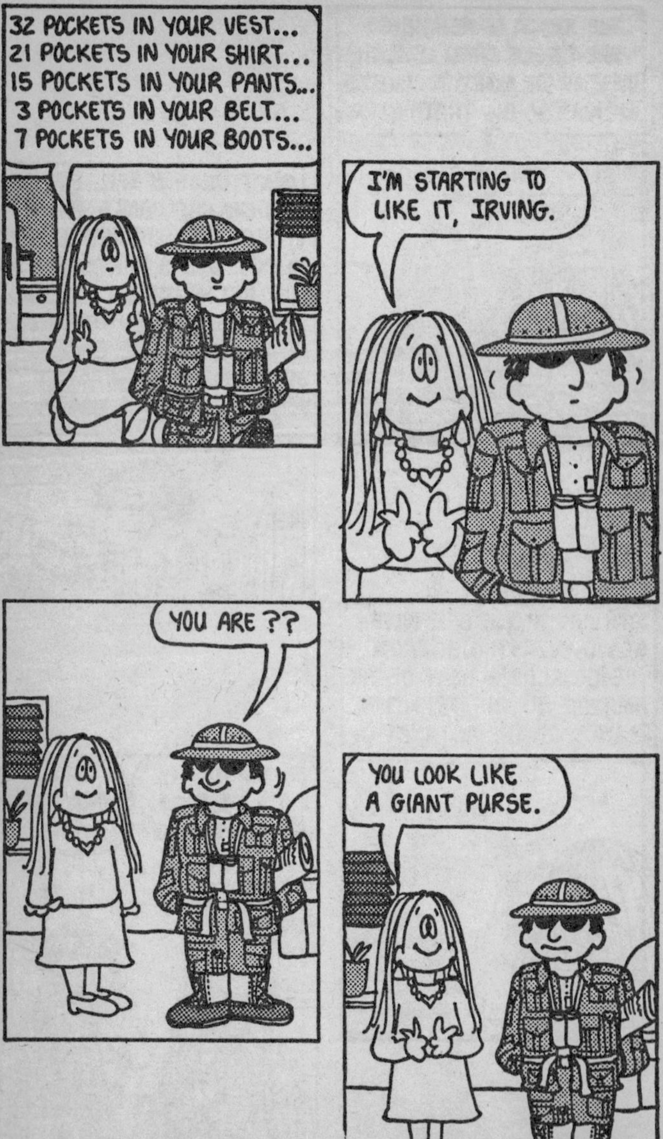
32 POCKETS IN YOUR VEST... 21 POCKETS IN YOUR SHIRT... 15 POCKETS IN YOUR PANTS... 3 POCKETS IN YOUR BELT... 7 POCKETS IN YOUR BOOTS...
I'M STARTING TO LIKE IT, IRVING.
YOU ARE??
YOU LOOK LIKE A GIANT PURSE.
Guisewite

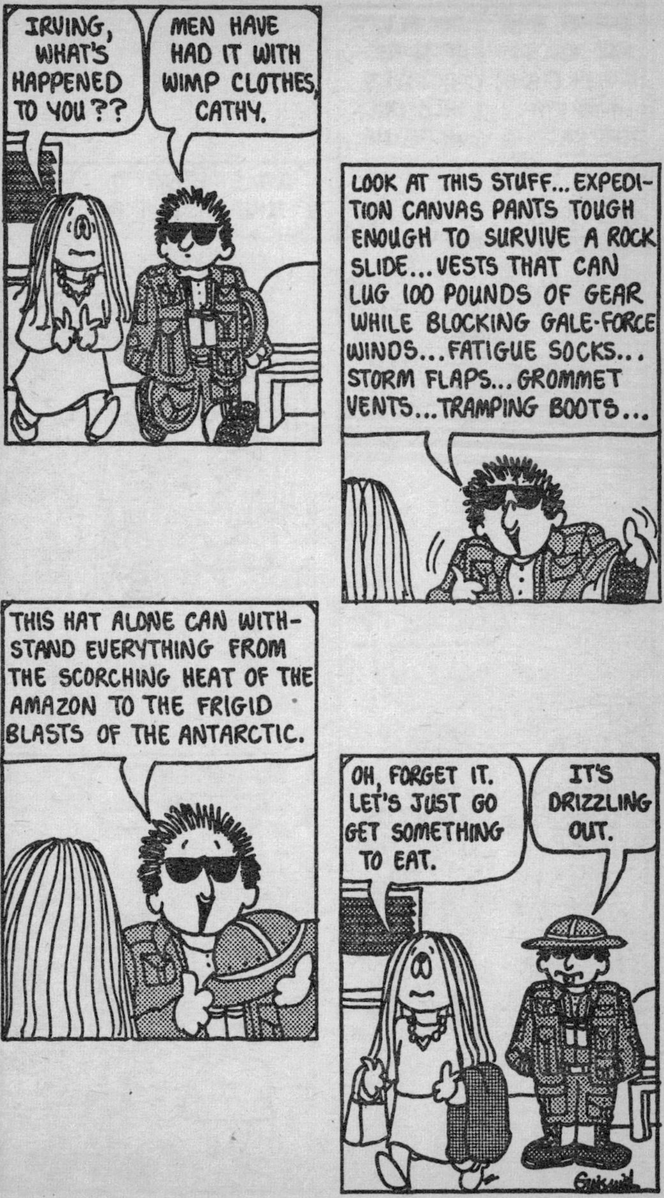
IRVING, WHAT'S HAPPENED TO YOU??
MEN HAVE HAD IT WITH WIMP CLOTHES, CATHY.
LOOK AT THIS STUFF... EXPEDITION CANVAS PANTS TOUGH ENOUGH TO SURVIVE A ROCK SLIDE... VESTS THAT CAN LUG 100 POUNDS OF GEAR WHILE BLOCKING GALE-FORCE WINDS... FATIGUE SOCKS... STORM FLAPS... GROMMET VENTS... TRAMPING BOOTS...
THIS HAT ALONE CAN WITHSTAND EVERYTHING FROM THE SCORCHING HEAT OF THE AMAZON TO THE FRIGID BLASTS OF THE ANTARCTIC.
OH, FORGET IT. LET'S JUST GO GET SOMETHING TO EAT.
IT'S DRIZZLING OUT.

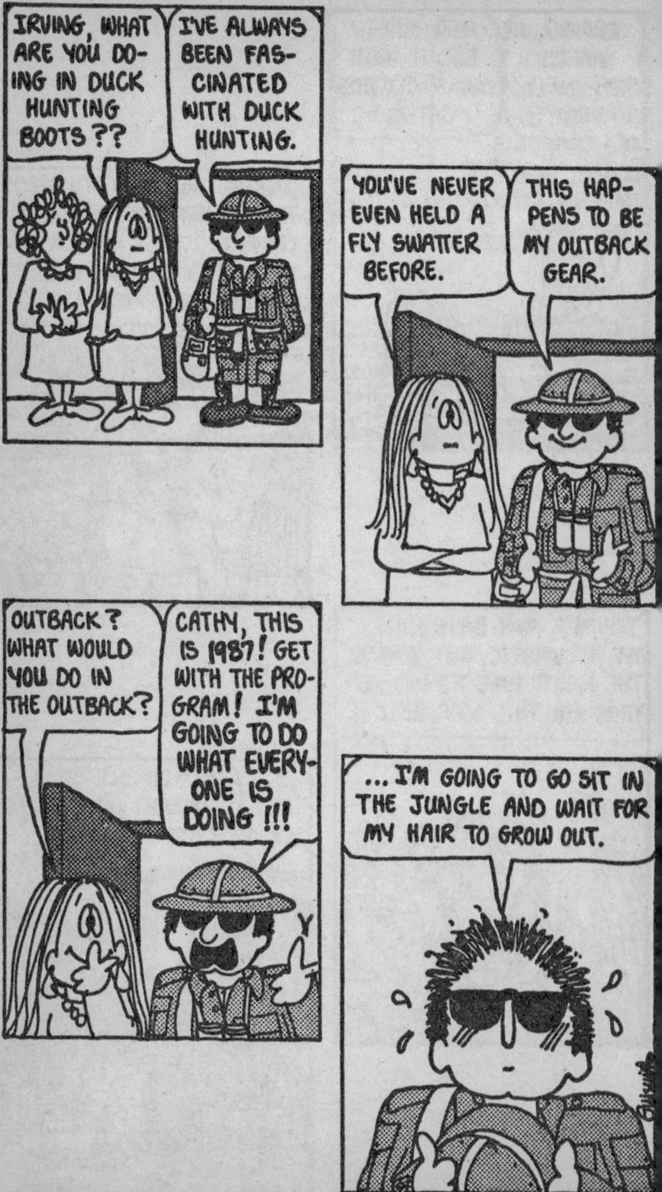

IRVING, WHAT ARE YOU DO-ING IN DUCK HUNTING BOOTS ??
I'VE ALWAYS BEEN FAS-CINATED WITH DUCK HUNTING.
YOU'VE NEVER EVEN HELD A FLY SWATTER BEFORE.
THIS HAP-PENS TO BE MY OUTBACK GEAR.
OUTBACK ? WHAT WOULD YOU DO IN THE OUTBACK?
CATHY, THIS IS 1987! GET WITH THE PRO-GRAM! I'M GOING TO DO WHAT EVERY-ONE IS DOING !!!
... I'M GOING TO GO SIT IN THE JUNGLE AND WAIT FOR MY HAIR TO GROW OUT.

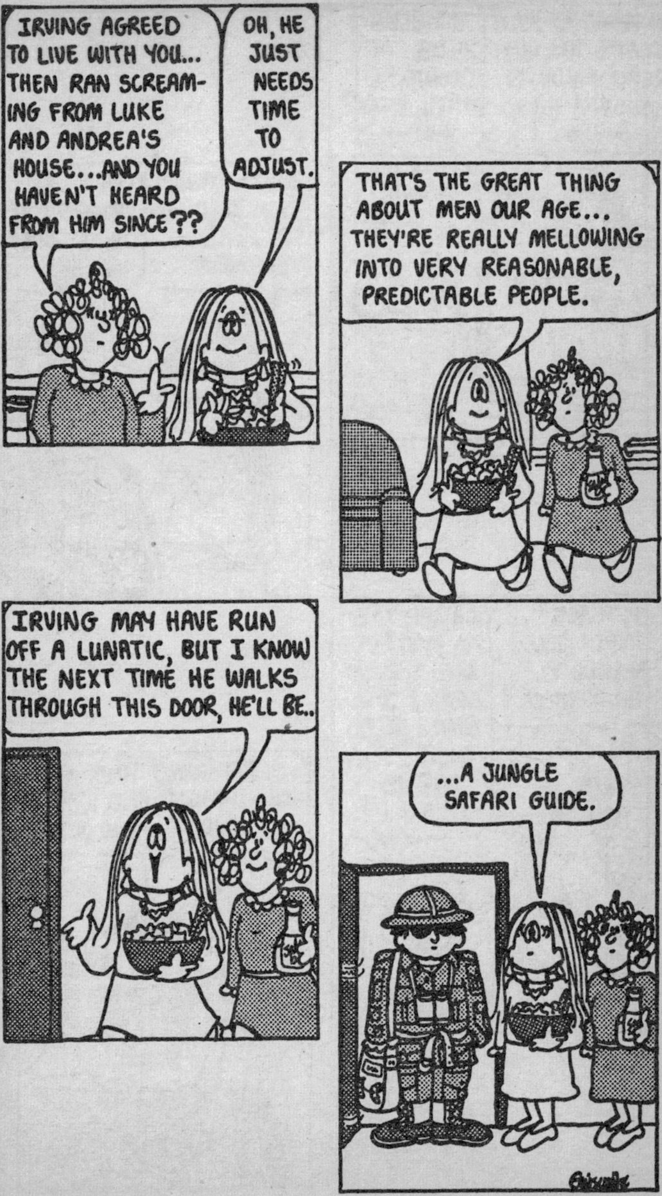
IRVING AGREED TO LIVE WITH YOU... THEN RAN SCREAMING FROM LUKE AND ANDREA'S HOUSE...AND YOU HAVEN'T HEARD FROM HIM SINCE??
OH, HE JUST NEEDS TIME TO ADJUST.
THAT'S THE GREAT THING ABOUT MEN OUR AGE... THEY'RE REALLY MELLOWING INTO VERY REASONABLE, PREDICTABLE PEOPLE.
IRVING MAY HAVE RUN OFF A LUNATIC, BUT I KNOW THE NEXT TIME HE WALKS THROUGH THIS DOOR, HE'LL BE..
...A JUNGLE SAFARI GUIDE.

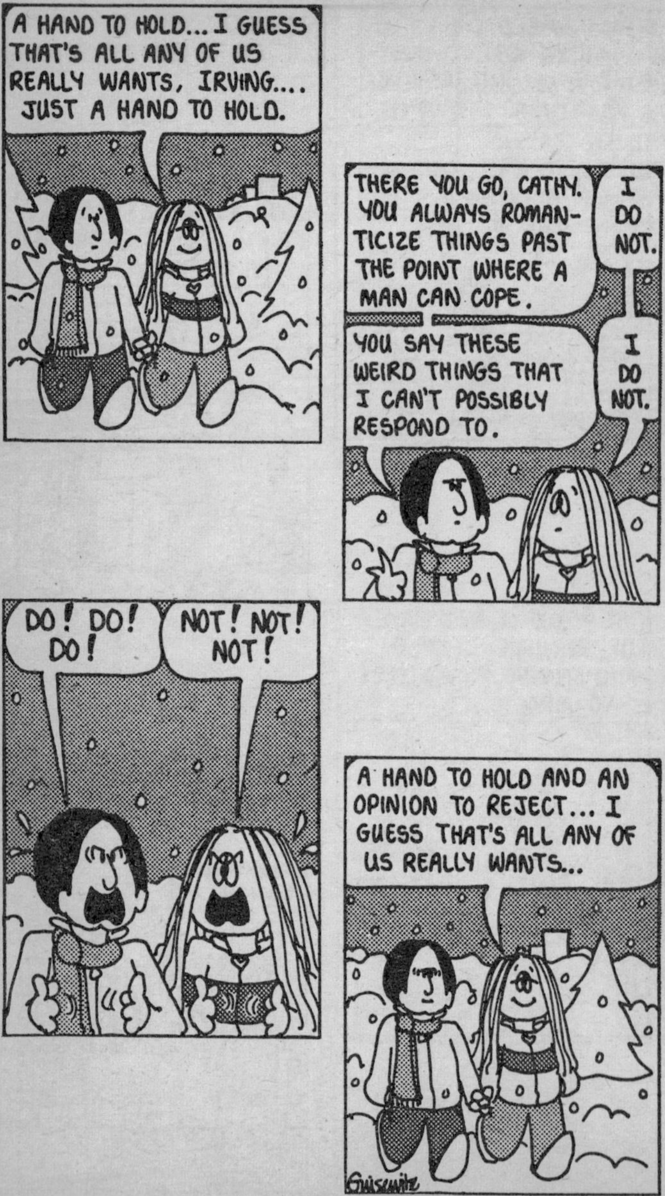
A HAND TO HOLD... I GUESS THAT'S ALL ANY OF US REALLY WANTS, IRVING.... JUST A HAND TO HOLD.
THERE YOU GO, CATHY. YOU ALWAYS ROMANTICIZE THINGS PAST THE POINT WHERE A MAN CAN COPE.
I DO NOT.
YOU SAY THESE WEIRD THINGS THAT I CAN'T POSSIBLY RESPOND TO.
I DO NOT.
DO! DO! DO!
NOT! NOT! NOT!
A HAND TO HOLD AND AN OPINION TO REJECT... I GUESS THAT'S ALL ANY OF US REALLY WANTS...
Guisewite

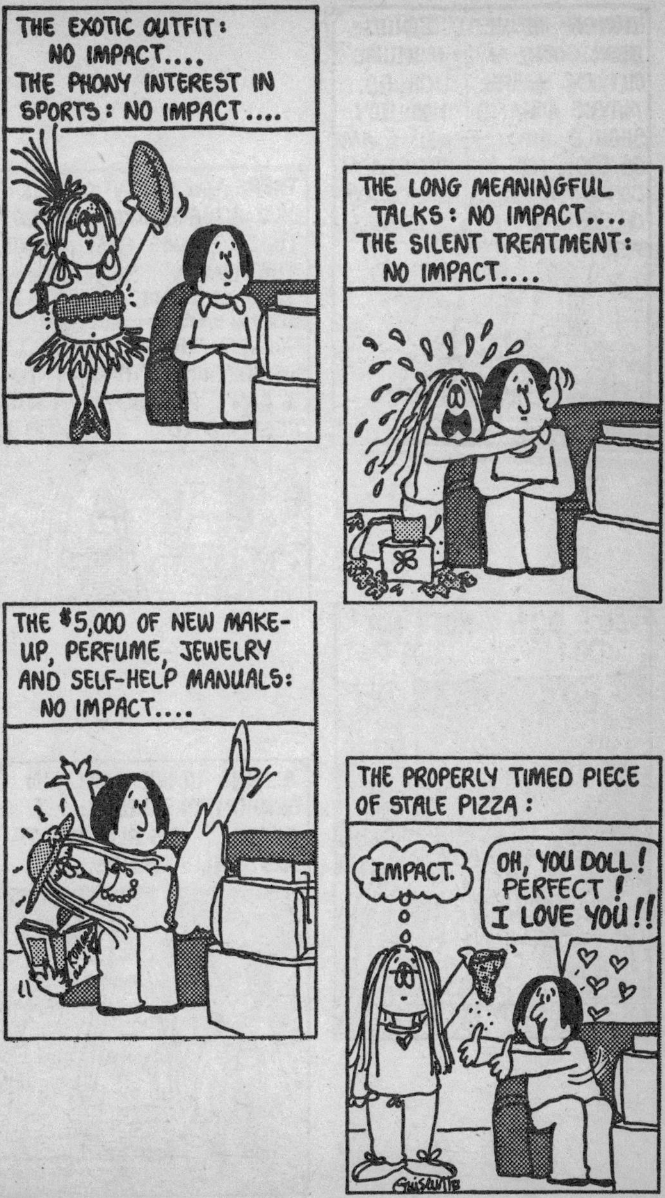
THE EXOTIC OUTFIT: NO IMPACT.... THE PHONY INTEREST IN SPORTS: NO IMPACT....
THE LONG MEANINGFUL TALKS: NO IMPACT.... THE SILENT TREATMENT: NO IMPACT....
THE $5,000 OF NEW MAKE-UP, PERFUME, JEWELRY AND SELF-HELP MANUALS: NO IMPACT....
THE PROPERLY TIMED PIECE OF STALE PIZZA:
IMPACT.
OH, YOU DOLL! PERFECT! I LOVE YOU!!

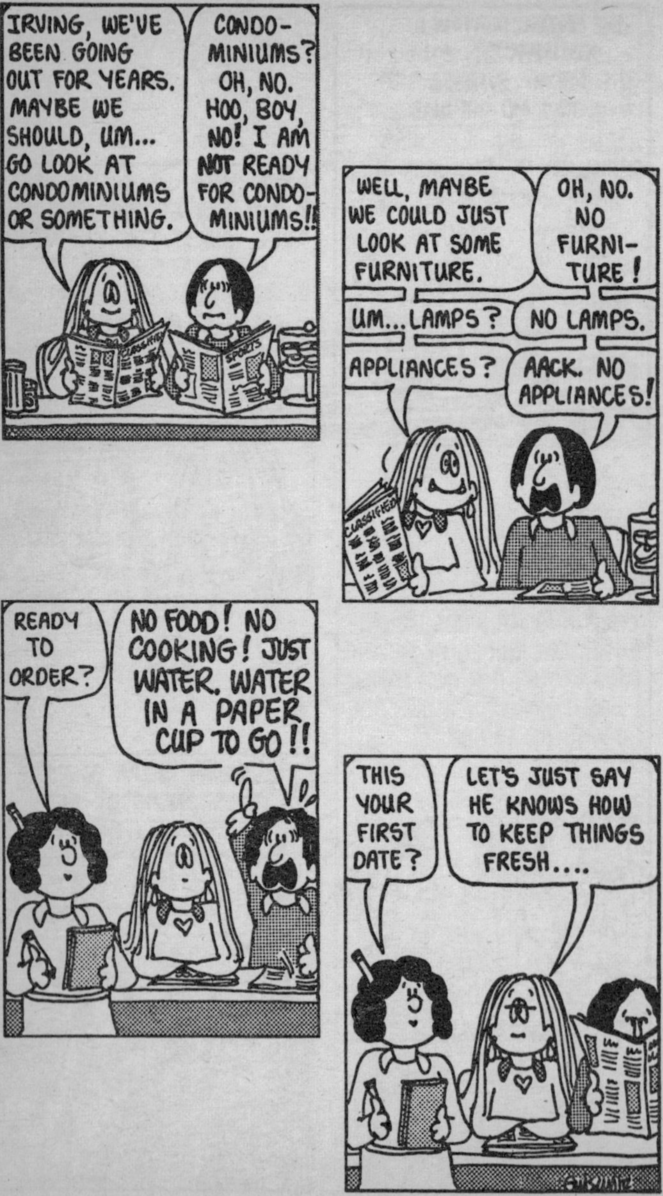
IRVING, WE'VE BEEN GOING OUT FOR YEARS. MAYBE WE SHOULD, UM... GO LOOK AT CONDOMINIUMS OR SOMETHING.
CONDO-MINIUMS? OH, NO. HOO, BOY, NO! I AM NOT READY FOR CONDO-MINIUMS!!
WELL, MAYBE WE COULD JUST LOOK AT SOME FURNITURE.
OH, NO. NO FURNI-TURE!
UM... LAMPS?
NO LAMPS.
APPLIANCES?
AACK. NO APPLIANCES!
READY TO ORDER?
NO FOOD! NO COOKING! JUST WATER. WATER IN A PAPER CUP TO GO!!
THIS YOUR FIRST DATE?
LET'S JUST SAY HE KNOWS HOW TO KEEP THINGS FRESH....

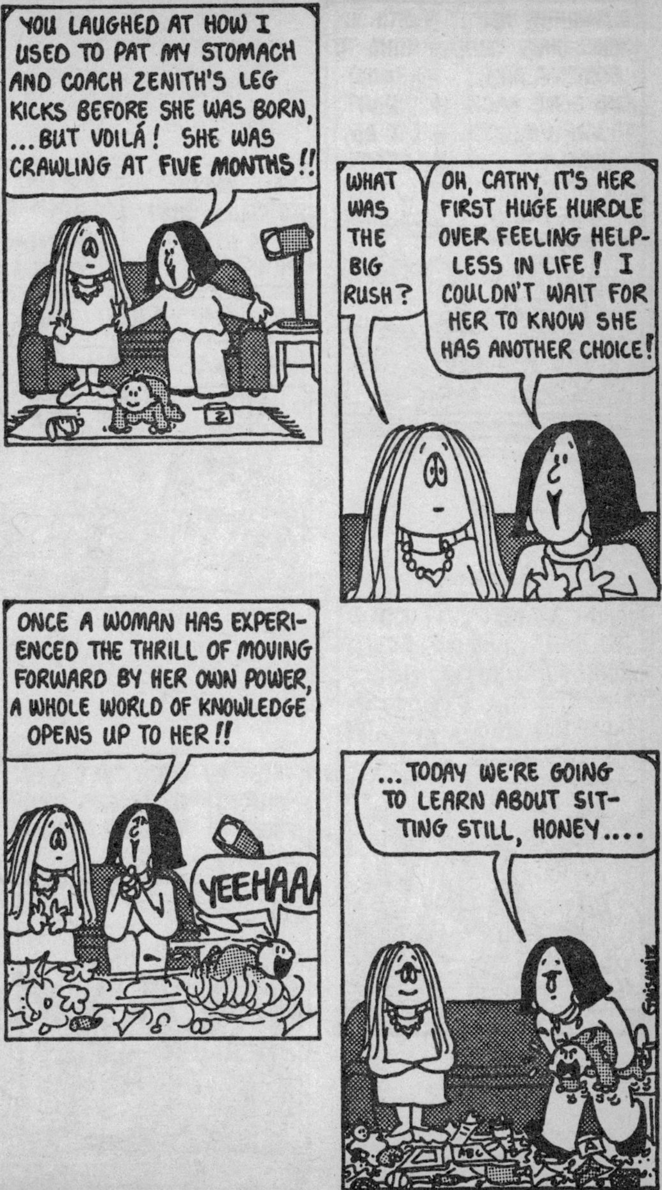

YOU LAUGHED AT HOW I USED TO PAT MY STOMACH AND COACH ZENITH'S LEG KICKS BEFORE SHE WAS BORN, ...BUT VOILÁ! SHE WAS CRAWLING AT FIVE MONTHS!!
WHAT WAS THE BIG RUSH?
OH, CATHY, IT'S HER FIRST HUGE HURDLE OVER FEELING HELP-LESS IN LIFE! I COULDN'T WAIT FOR HER TO KNOW SHE HAS ANOTHER CHOICE!
ONCE A WOMAN HAS EXPERI-ENCED THE THRILL OF MOVING FORWARD BY HER OWN POWER, A WHOLE WORLD OF KNOWLEDGE OPENS UP TO HER!!
YEEHAA
...TODAY WE'RE GOING TO LEARN ABOUT SIT-TING STILL, HONEY....

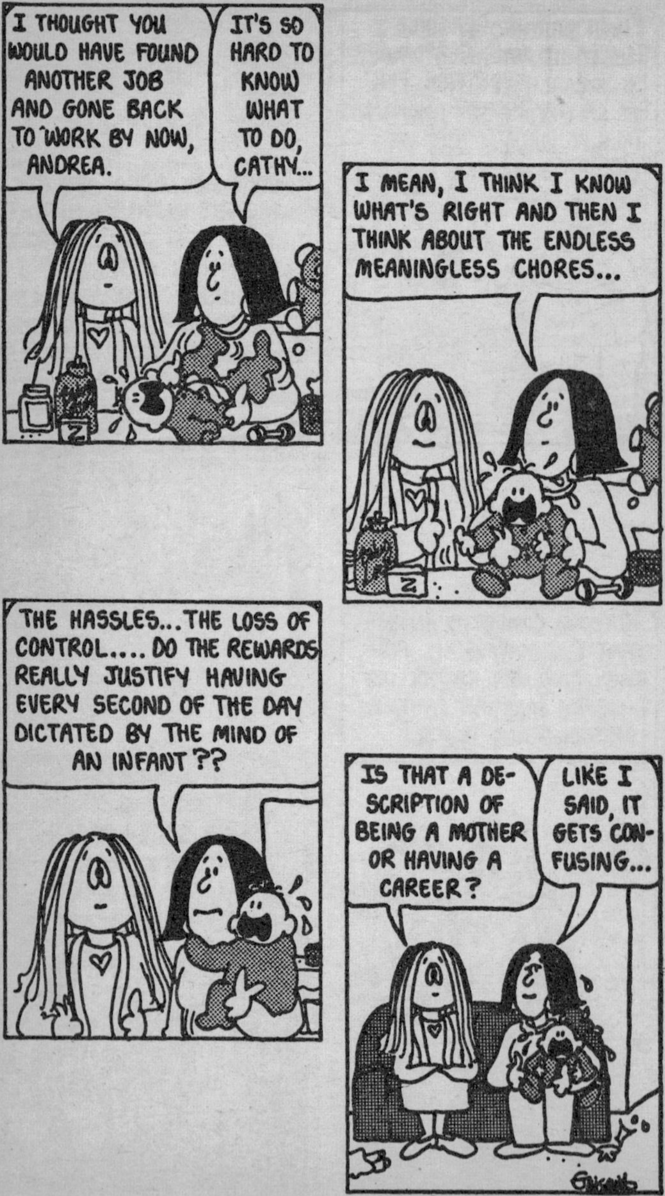
I THOUGHT YOU WOULD HAVE FOUND ANOTHER JOB AND GONE BACK TO WORK BY NOW, ANDREA.
IT'S SO HARD TO KNOW WHAT TO DO, CATHY...
I MEAN, I THINK I KNOW WHAT'S RIGHT AND THEN I THINK ABOUT THE ENDLESS MEANINGLESS CHORES...
THE HASSLES...THE LOSS OF CONTROL.... DO THE REWARDS REALLY JUSTIFY HAVING EVERY SECOND OF THE DAY DICTATED BY THE MIND OF AN INFANT??
IS THAT A DE-SCRIPTION OF BEING A MOTHER OR HAVING A CAREER?
LIKE I SAID, IT GETS CON-FUSING...

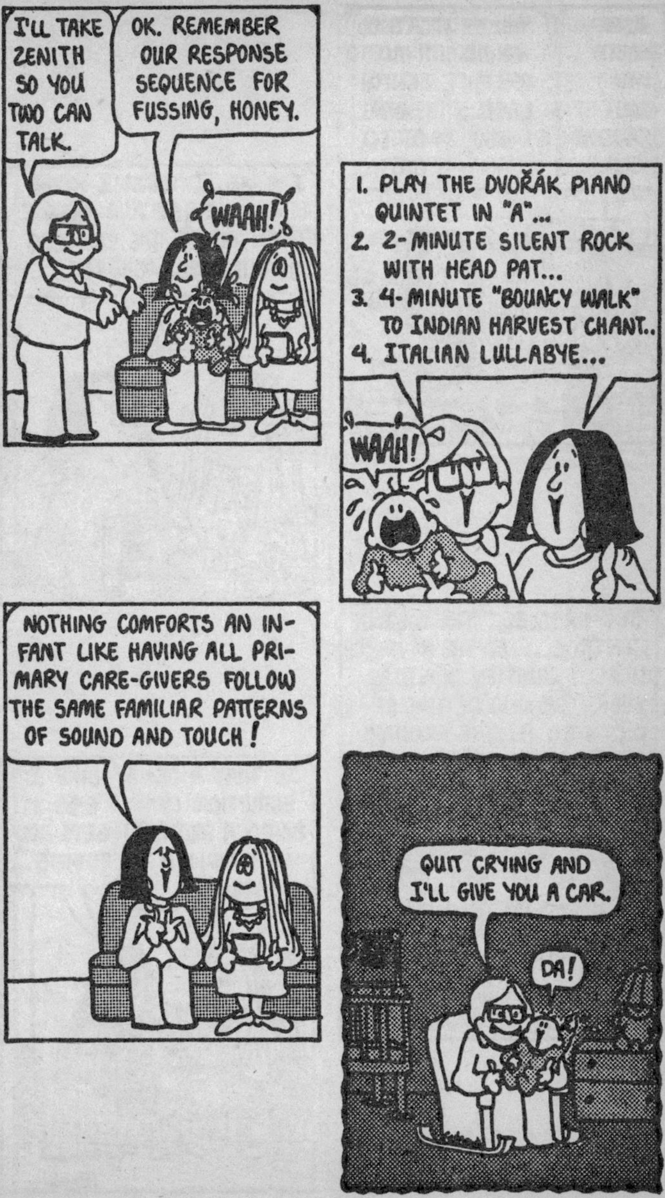
I'LL TAKE ZENITH SO YOU TWO CAN TALK.
OK. REMEMBER OUR RESPONSE SEQUENCE FOR FUSSING, HONEY.
WAAH!
1. PLAY THE DVOŘÁK PIANO QUINTET IN "A"...
2. 2-MINUTE SILENT ROCK WITH HEAD PAT...
3. 4-MINUTE "BOUNCY WALK" TO INDIAN HARVEST CHANT..
4. ITALIAN LULLABYE...
WAAH!
NOTHING COMFORTS AN INFANT LIKE HAVING ALL PRIMARY CARE-GIVERS FOLLOW THE SAME FAMILIAR PATTERNS OF SOUND AND TOUCH!
QUIT CRYING AND I'LL GIVE YOU A CAR.
DA!

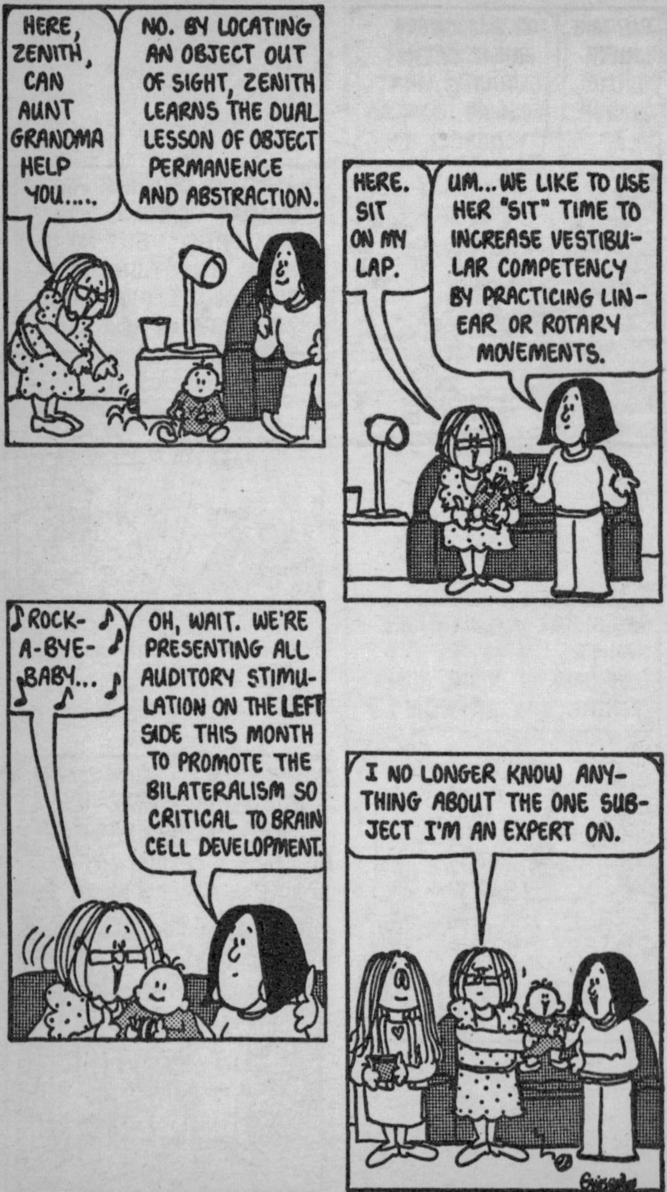

HERE, ZENITH, CAN AUNT GRANDMA HELP YOU.....
NO. BY LOCATING AN OBJECT OUT OF SIGHT, ZENITH LEARNS THE DUAL LESSON OF OBJECT PERMANENCE AND ABSTRACTION.
HERE. SIT ON MY LAP.
UM... WE LIKE TO USE HER "SIT" TIME TO INCREASE VESTIBU-LAR COMPETENCY BY PRACTICING LIN-EAR OR ROTARY MOVEMENTS.
♪ ROCK-A-BYE-BABY... ♪
OH, WAIT. WE'RE PRESENTING ALL AUDITORY STIMU-LATION ON THE LEFT SIDE THIS MONTH TO PROMOTE THE BILATERALISM SO CRITICAL TO BRAIN CELL DEVELOPMENT.
I NO LONGER KNOW ANY-THING ABOUT THE ONE SUB-JECT I'M AN EXPERT ON.

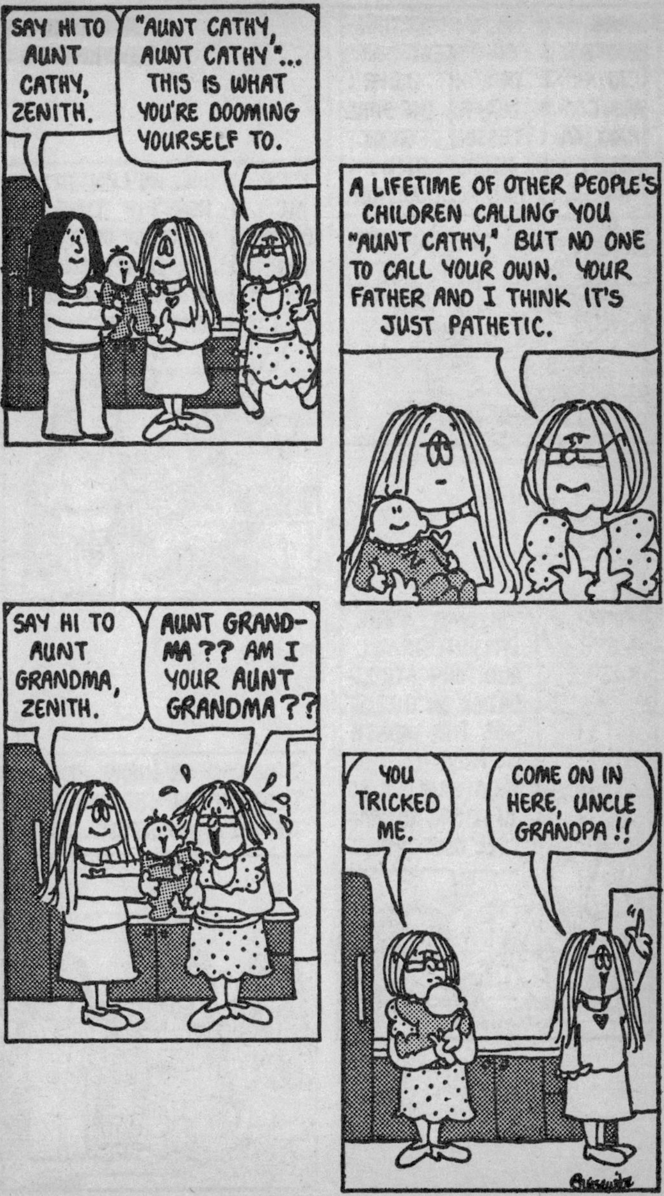
SAY HI TO AUNT CATHY, ZENITH.
"AUNT CATHY, AUNT CATHY"... THIS IS WHAT YOU'RE DOOMING YOURSELF TO.
A LIFETIME OF OTHER PEOPLE'S CHILDREN CALLING YOU "AUNT CATHY," BUT NO ONE TO CALL YOUR OWN. YOUR FATHER AND I THINK IT'S JUST PATHETIC.
SAY HI TO AUNT GRANDMA, ZENITH.
AUNT GRANDMA?? AM I YOUR AUNT GRANDMA??
YOU TRICKED ME.
COME ON IN HERE, UNCLE GRANDPA!!

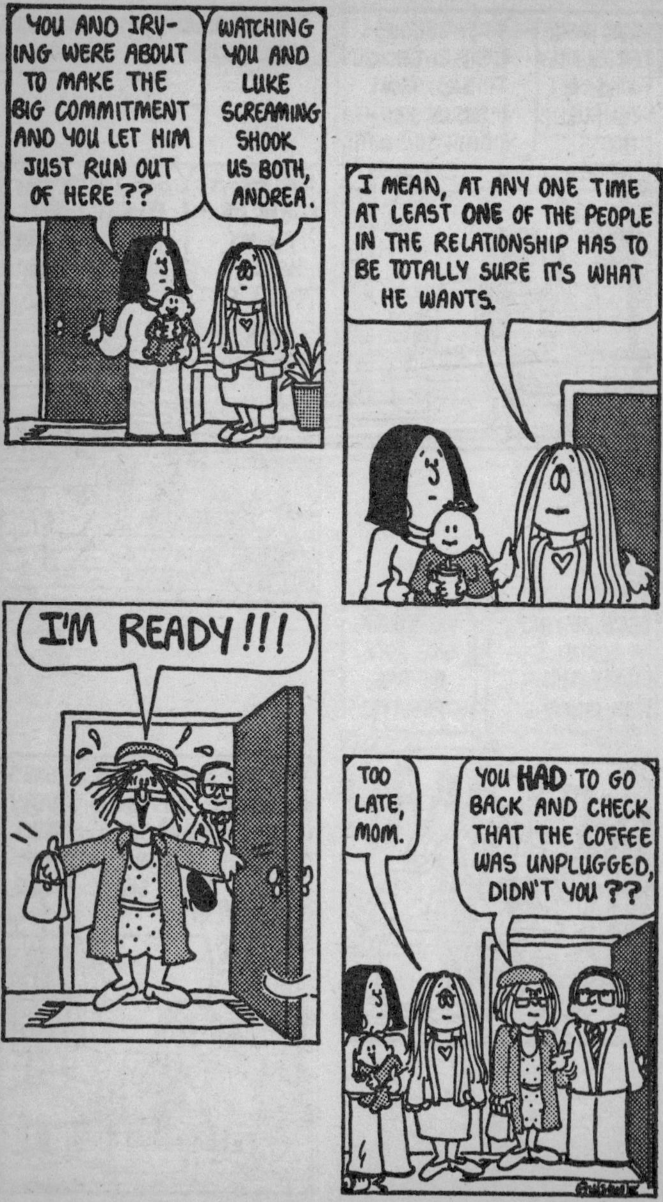
YOU AND IRV-ING WERE ABOUT TO MAKE THE BIG COMMITMENT AND YOU LET HIM JUST RUN OUT OF HERE??
WATCHING YOU AND LUKE SCREAMING SHOOK US BOTH, ANDREA.
I MEAN, AT ANY ONE TIME AT LEAST ONE OF THE PEOPLE IN THE RELATIONSHIP HAS TO BE TOTALLY SURE IT'S WHAT HE WANTS.
I'M READY!!!
TOO LATE, MOM.
YOU HAD TO GO BACK AND CHECK THAT THE COFFEE WAS UNPLUGGED, DIDN'T YOU??

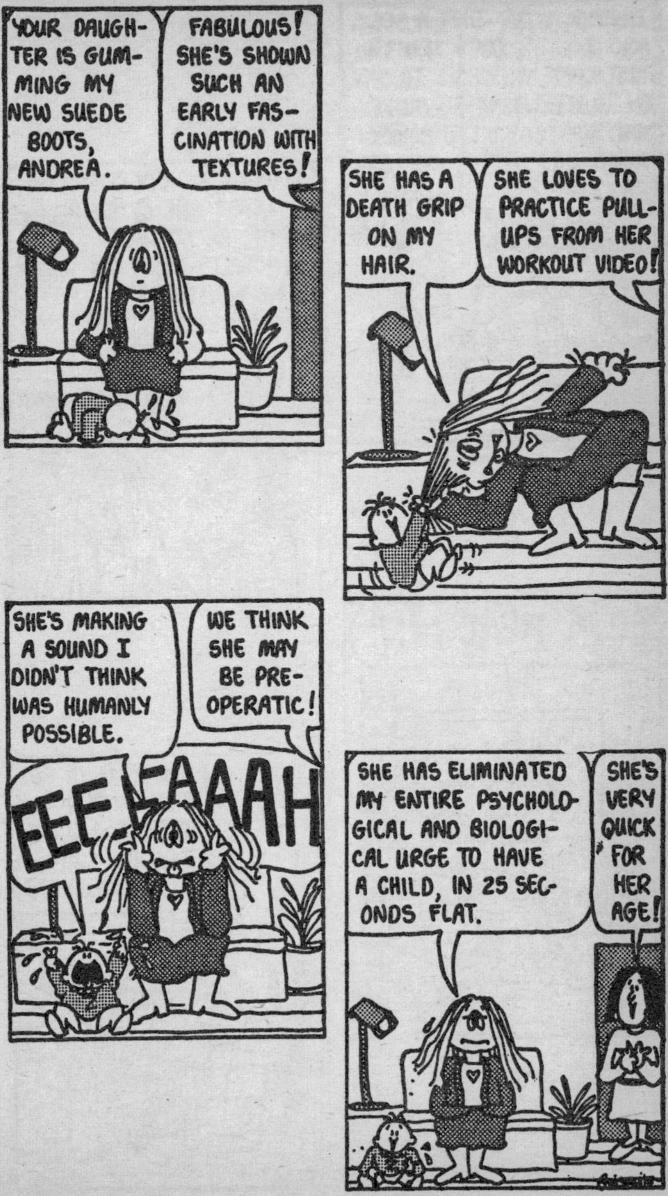
YOUR DAUGHTER IS GUMMING MY NEW SUEDE BOOTS, ANDREA.
FABULOUS! SHE'S SHOWN SUCH AN EARLY FASCINATION WITH TEXTURES!
SHE HAS A DEATH GRIP ON MY HAIR.
SHE LOVES TO PRACTICE PULL-UPS FROM HER WORKOUT VIDEO!
SHE'S MAKING A SOUND I DIDN'T THINK WAS HUMANLY POSSIBLE.
WE THINK SHE MAY BE PRE-OPERATIC!
EEEEAAAH
SHE HAS ELIMINATED MY ENTIRE PSYCHOLOGICAL AND BIOLOGICAL URGE TO HAVE A CHILD, IN 25 SECONDS FLAT.
SHE'S VERY QUICK FOR HER AGE!

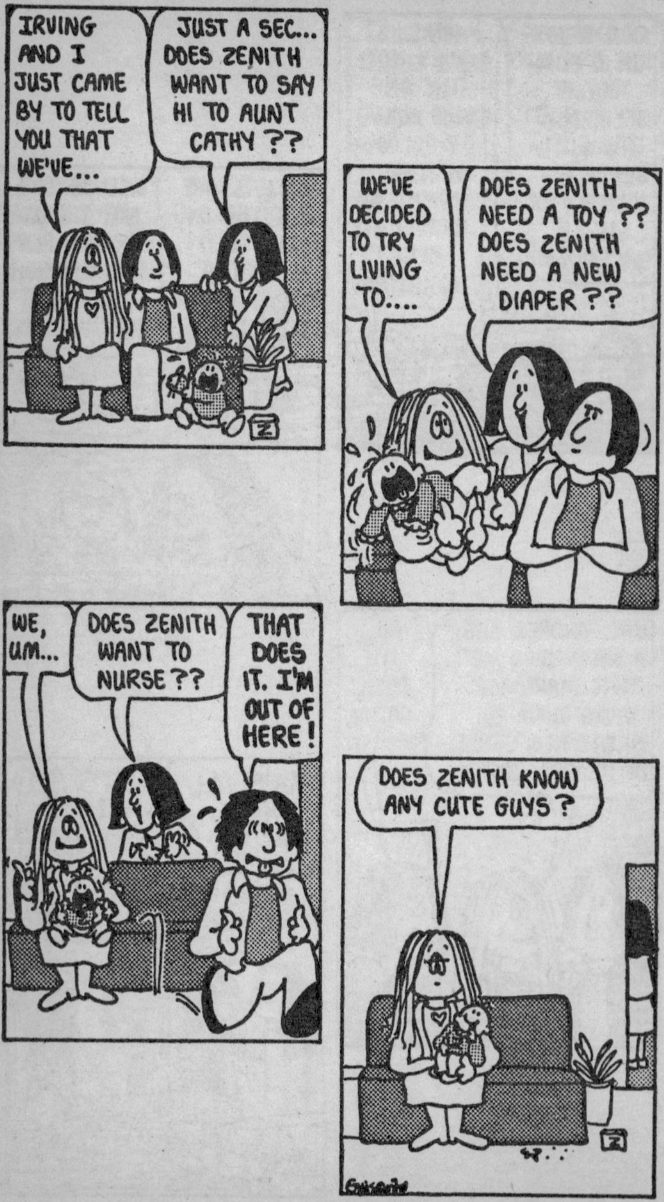
IRVING AND I JUST CAME BY TO TELL YOU THAT WE'VE...
JUST A SEC... DOES ZENITH WANT TO SAY HI TO AUNT CATHY ??
WE'VE DECIDED TO TRY LIVING TO....
DOES ZENITH NEED A TOY ?? DOES ZENITH NEED A NEW DIAPER ??
WE, UM...
DOES ZENITH WANT TO NURSE ??
THAT DOES IT. I'M OUT OF HERE !
DOES ZENITH KNOW ANY CUTE GUYS ?

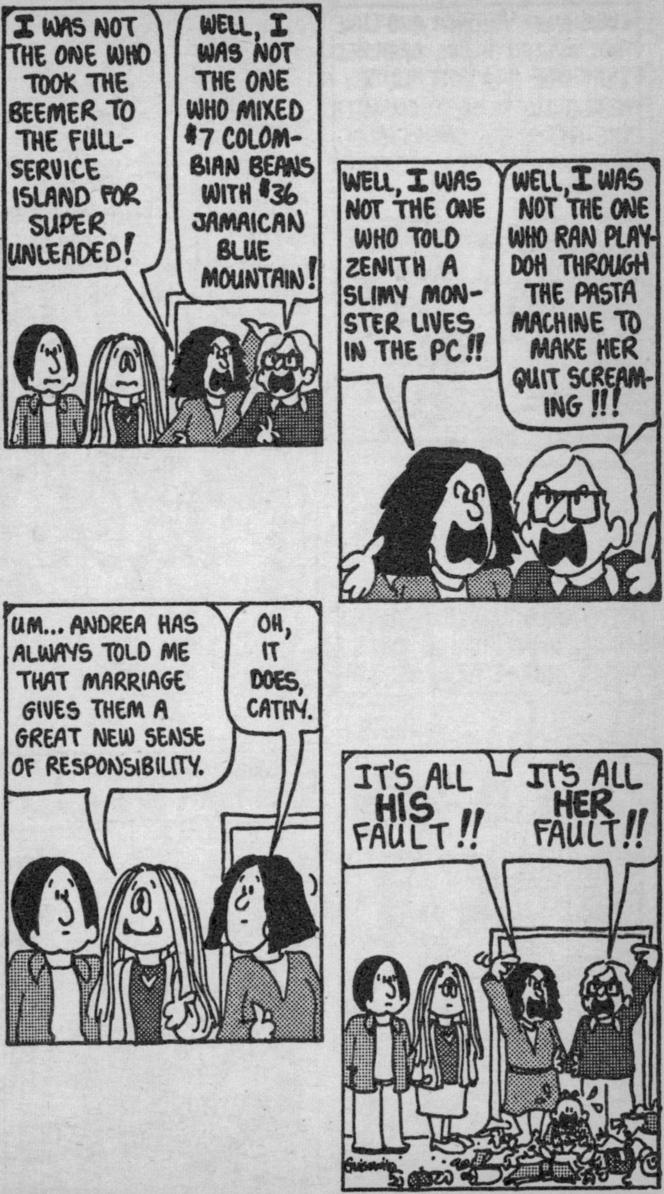
I WAS NOT THE ONE WHO TOOK THE BEEMER TO THE FULL-SERVICE ISLAND FOR SUPER UNLEADED!
WELL, I WAS NOT THE ONE WHO MIXED #7 COLOMBIAN BEANS WITH #36 JAMAICAN BLUE MOUNTAIN!
WELL, I WAS NOT THE ONE WHO TOLD ZENITH A SLIMY MONSTER LIVES IN THE PC!!
WELL, I WAS NOT THE ONE WHO RAN PLAY-DOH THROUGH THE PASTA MACHINE TO MAKE HER QUIT SCREAMING!!!
UM... ANDREA HAS ALWAYS TOLD ME THAT MARRIAGE GIVES THEM A GREAT NEW SENSE OF RESPONSIBILITY.
OH, IT DOES, CATHY.
IT'S ALL HIS FAULT!!
IT'S ALL HER FAULT!!

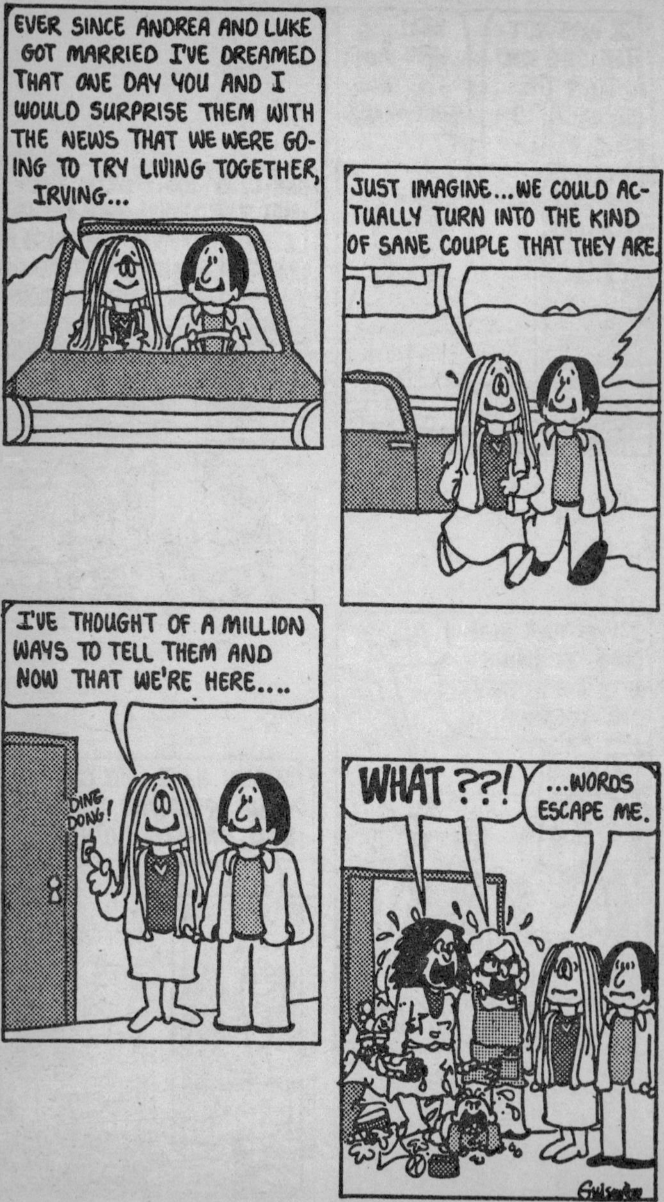
EVER SINCE ANDREA AND LUKE GOT MARRIED I'VE DREAMED THAT ONE DAY YOU AND I WOULD SURPRISE THEM WITH THE NEWS THAT WE WERE GO-ING TO TRY LIVING TOGETHER, IRVING...
JUST IMAGINE...WE COULD AC-TUALLY TURN INTO THE KIND OF SANE COUPLE THAT THEY ARE.
I'VE THOUGHT OF A MILLION WAYS TO TELL THEM AND NOW THAT WE'RE HERE....
DING DONG!
WHAT ??!
...WORDS ESCAPE ME.

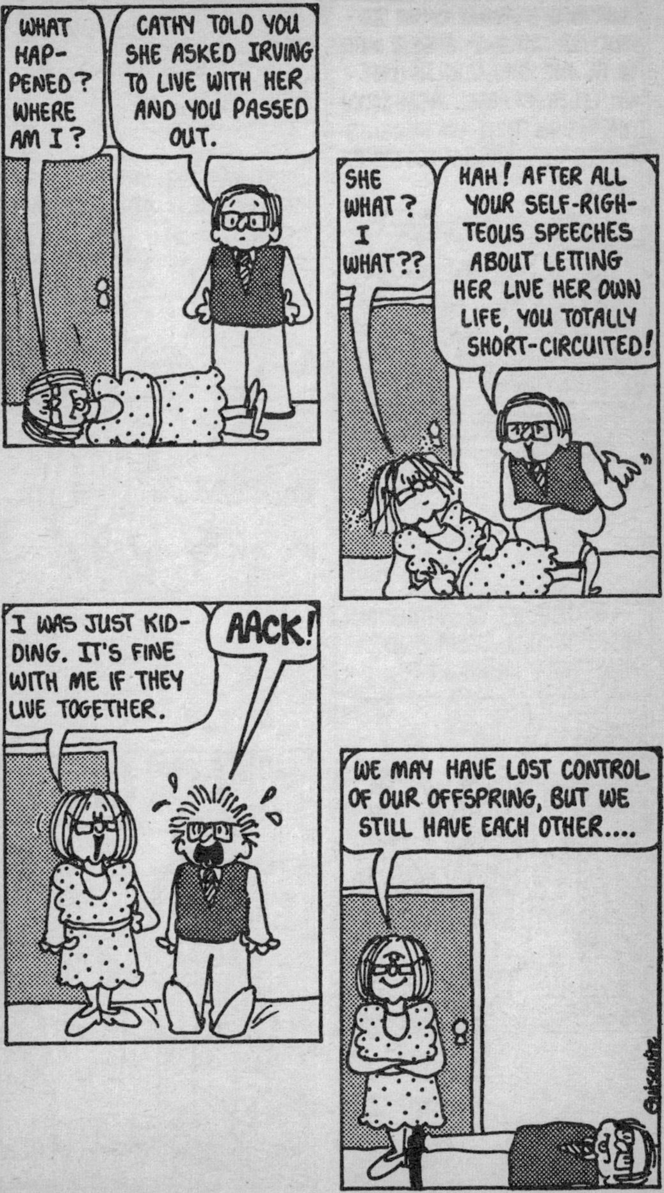
WHAT HAP-PENED? WHERE AM I?
CATHY TOLD YOU SHE ASKED IRVING TO LIVE WITH HER AND YOU PASSED OUT.
SHE WHAT? I WHAT??
HAH! AFTER ALL YOUR SELF-RIGH-TEOUS SPEECHES ABOUT LETTING HER LIVE HER OWN LIFE, YOU TOTALLY SHORT-CIRCUITED!
I WAS JUST KID-DING. IT'S FINE WITH ME IF THEY LIVE TOGETHER.
AACK!
WE MAY HAVE LOST CONTROL OF OUR OFFSPRING, BUT WE STILL HAVE EACH OTHER....

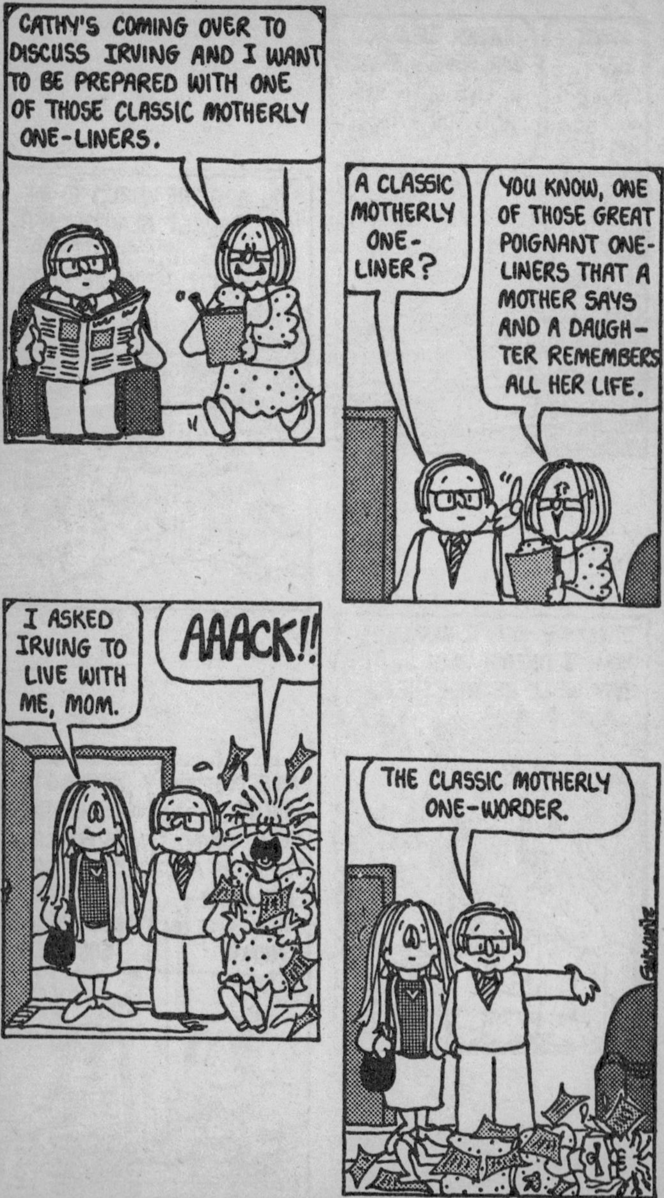
CATHY'S COMING OVER TO DISCUSS IRVING AND I WANT TO BE PREPARED WITH ONE OF THOSE CLASSIC MOTHERLY ONE-LINERS.
A CLASSIC MOTHERLY ONE-LINER?
YOU KNOW, ONE OF THOSE GREAT POIGNANT ONE-LINERS THAT A MOTHER SAYS AND A DAUGHTER REMEMBERS ALL HER LIFE.
I ASKED IRVING TO LIVE WITH ME, MOM.
AAACK!!
THE CLASSIC MOTHERLY ONE-WORDER.

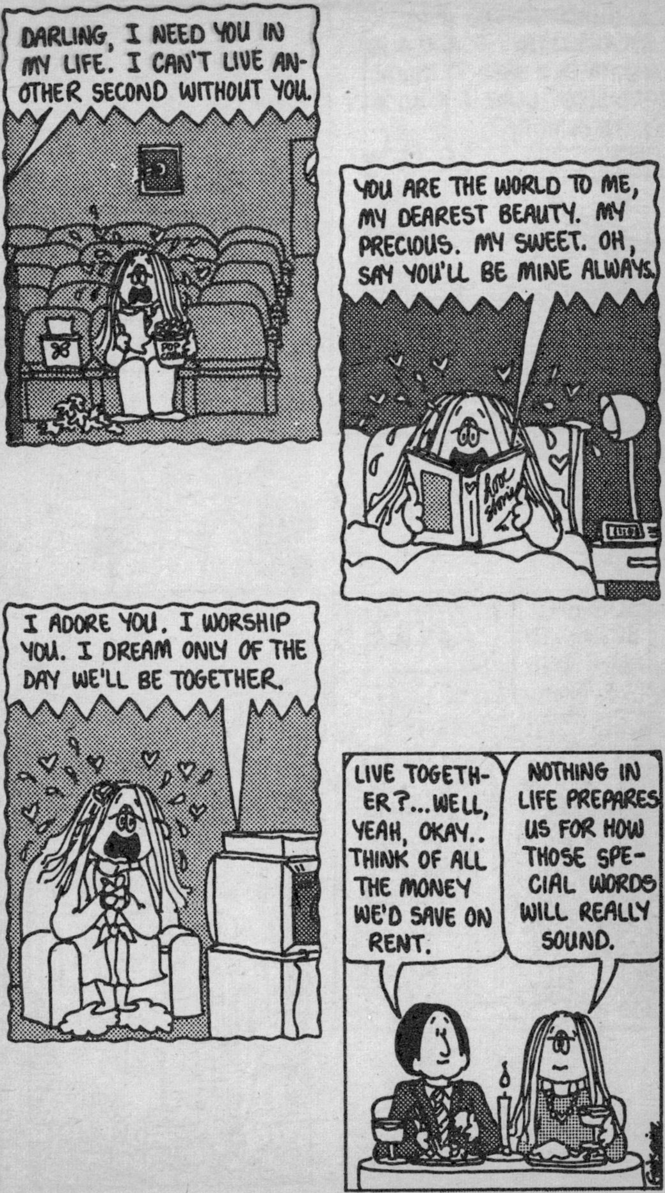
DARLING, I NEED YOU IN MY LIFE. I CAN'T LIVE AN-OTHER SECOND WITHOUT YOU.
YOU ARE THE WORLD TO ME, MY DEAREST BEAUTY. MY PRECIOUS. MY SWEET. OH, SAY YOU'LL BE MINE ALWAYS.
I ADORE YOU. I WORSHIP YOU. I DREAM ONLY OF THE DAY WE'LL BE TOGETHER.
LIVE TOGETH-ER?...WELL, YEAH, OKAY.. THINK OF ALL THE MONEY WE'D SAVE ON RENT.
NOTHING IN LIFE PREPARES US FOR HOW THOSE SPE-CIAL WORDS WILL REALLY SOUND.

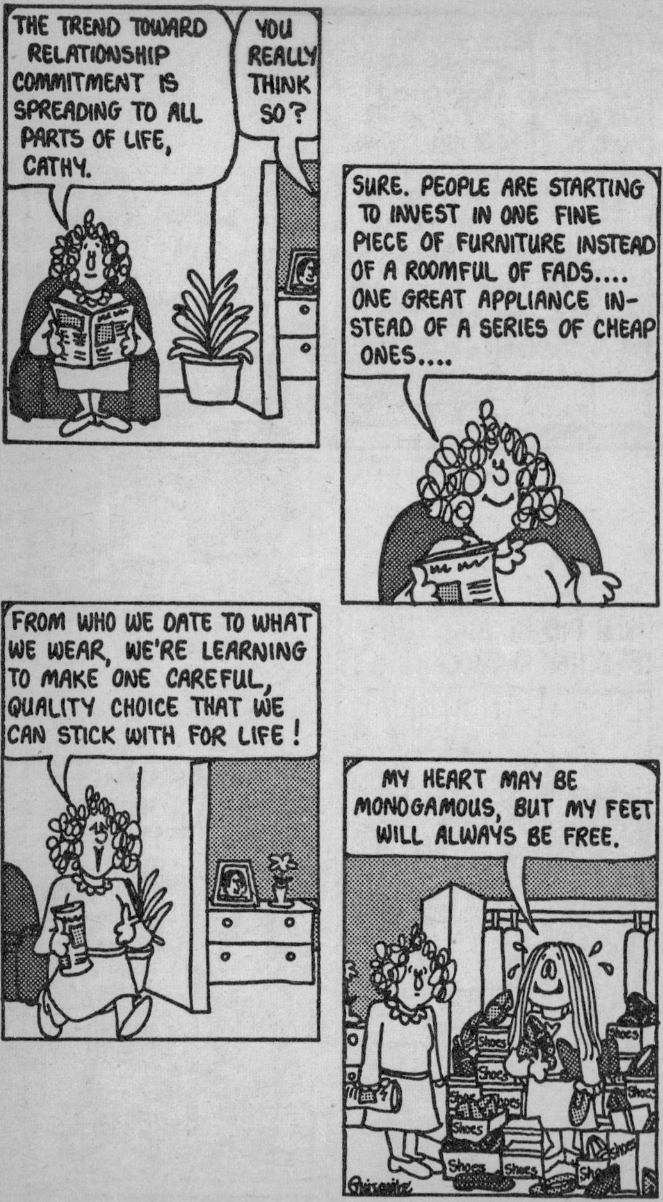
THE TREND TOWARD RELATIONSHIP COMMITMENT IS SPREADING TO ALL PARTS OF LIFE, CATHY.
YOU REALLY THINK SO?
SURE. PEOPLE ARE STARTING TO INVEST IN ONE FINE PIECE OF FURNITURE INSTEAD OF A ROOMFUL OF FADS.... ONE GREAT APPLIANCE INSTEAD OF A SERIES OF CHEAP ONES....
FROM WHO WE DATE TO WHAT WE WEAR, WE'RE LEARNING TO MAKE ONE CAREFUL, QUALITY CHOICE THAT WE CAN STICK WITH FOR LIFE!
MY HEART MAY BE MONOGAMOUS, BUT MY FEET WILL ALWAYS BE FREE.

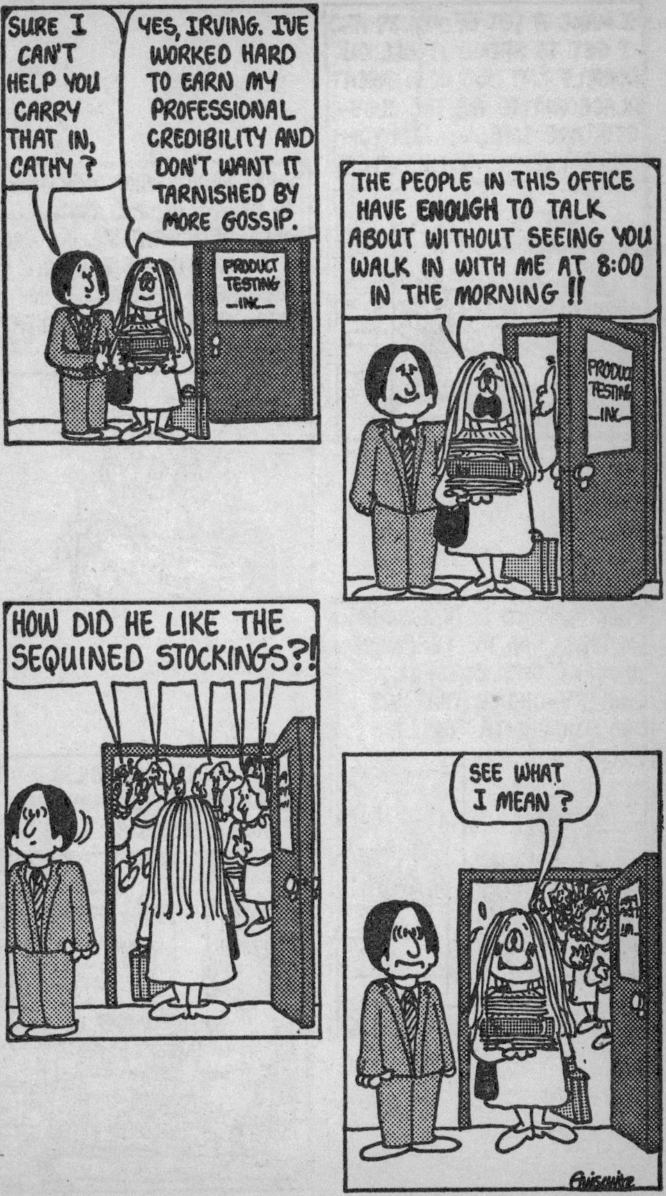
SURE I CAN'T HELP YOU CARRY THAT IN, CATHY ?
YES, IRVING. I'VE WORKED HARD TO EARN MY PROFESSIONAL CREDIBILITY AND DON'T WANT IT TARNISHED BY MORE GOSSIP.
PRODUCT TESTING —INC—
THE PEOPLE IN THIS OFFICE HAVE ENOUGH TO TALK ABOUT WITHOUT SEEING YOU WALK IN WITH ME AT 8:00 IN THE MORNING !!
HOW DID HE LIKE THE SEQUINED STOCKINGS?!
SEE WHAT I MEAN ?

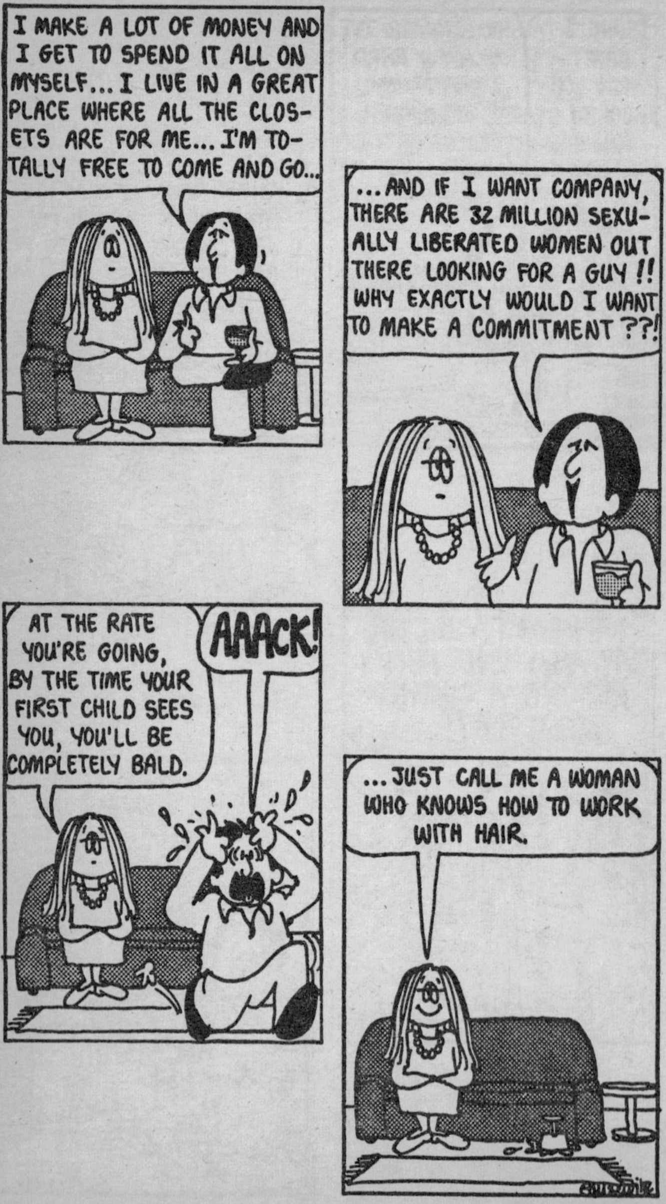
I MAKE A LOT OF MONEY AND I GET TO SPEND IT ALL ON MYSELF... I LIVE IN A GREAT PLACE WHERE ALL THE CLOSETS ARE FOR ME... I'M TOTALLY FREE TO COME AND GO...
...AND IF I WANT COMPANY, THERE ARE 32 MILLION SEXUALLY LIBERATED WOMEN OUT THERE LOOKING FOR A GUY!! WHY EXACTLY WOULD I WANT TO MAKE A COMMITMENT??!
AT THE RATE YOU'RE GOING, BY THE TIME YOUR FIRST CHILD SEES YOU, YOU'LL BE COMPLETELY BALD.
AAACK!
...JUST CALL ME A WOMAN WHO KNOWS HOW TO WORK WITH HAIR.

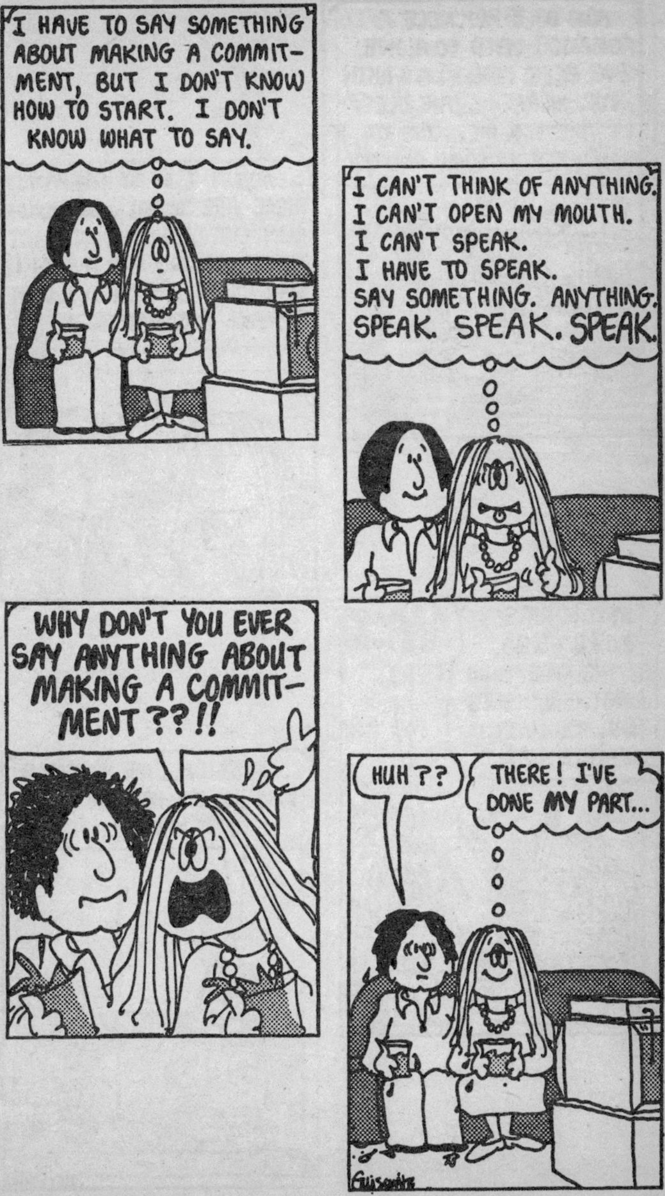
I HAVE TO SAY SOMETHING ABOUT MAKING A COMMITMENT, BUT I DON'T KNOW HOW TO START. I DON'T KNOW WHAT TO SAY.
I CAN'T THINK OF ANYTHING. I CAN'T OPEN MY MOUTH. I CAN'T SPEAK. I HAVE TO SPEAK. SAY SOMETHING. ANYTHING. SPEAK. SPEAK. SPEAK.
WHY DON'T YOU EVER SAY ANYTHING ABOUT MAKING A COMMITMENT??!!
HUH??
THERE! I'VE DONE MY PART...

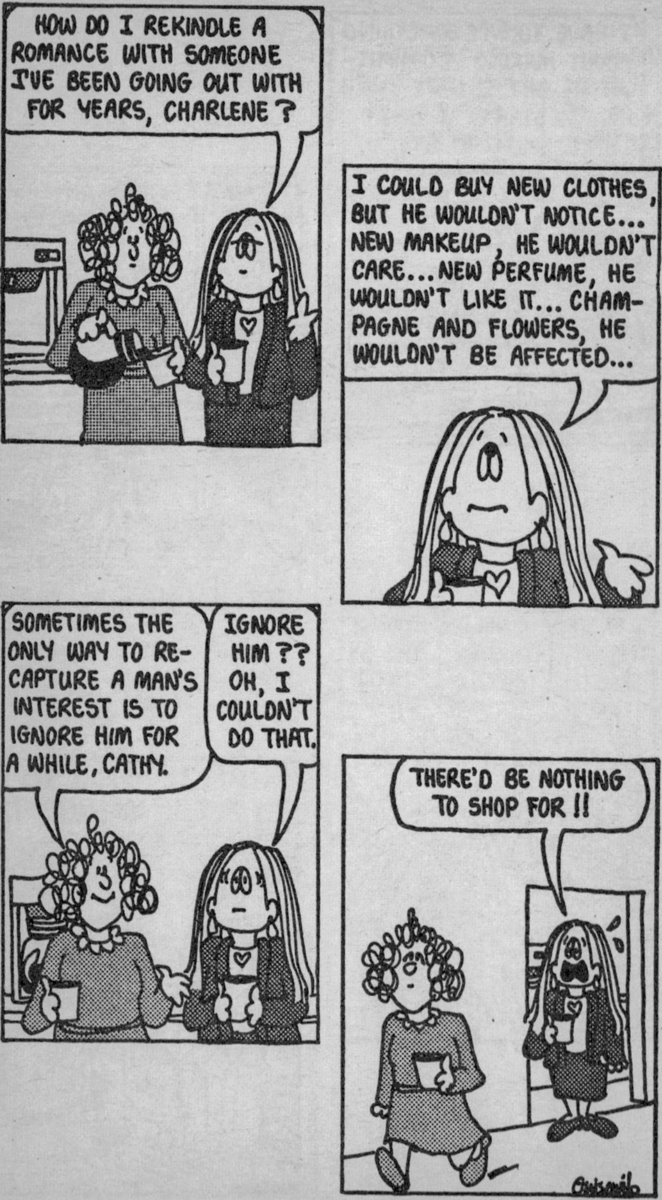
HOW DO I REKINDLE A ROMANCE WITH SOMEONE I'VE BEEN GOING OUT WITH FOR YEARS, CHARLENE?
I COULD BUY NEW CLOTHES, BUT HE WOULDN'T NOTICE... NEW MAKEUP, HE WOULDN'T CARE... NEW PERFUME, HE WOULDN'T LIKE IT... CHAMPAGNE AND FLOWERS, HE WOULDN'T BE AFFECTED...
SOMETIMES THE ONLY WAY TO RECAPTURE A MAN'S INTEREST IS TO IGNORE HIM FOR A WHILE, CATHY.
IGNORE HIM?? OH, I COULDN'T DO THAT.
THERE'D BE NOTHING TO SHOP FOR!!

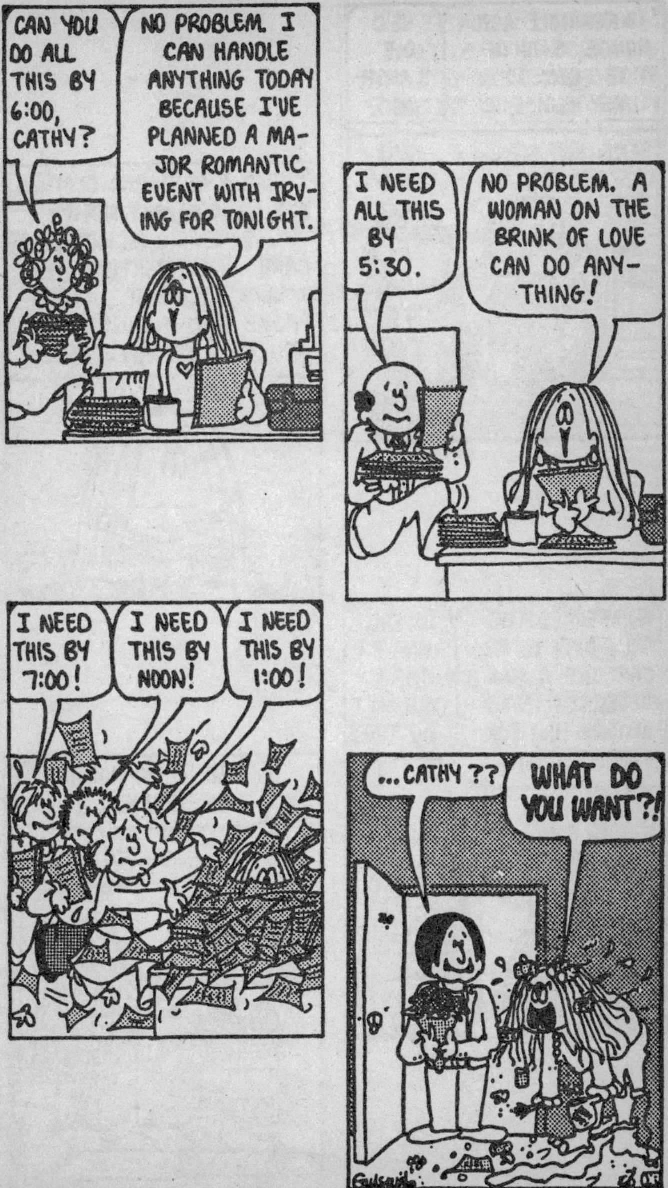
CAN YOU DO ALL THIS BY 6:00, CATHY?
NO PROBLEM. I CAN HANDLE ANYTHING TODAY BECAUSE I'VE PLANNED A MAJOR ROMANTIC EVENT WITH IRVING FOR TONIGHT.
I NEED ALL THIS BY 5:30.
NO PROBLEM. A WOMAN ON THE BRINK OF LOVE CAN DO ANYTHING!
I NEED THIS BY 7:00!
I NEED THIS BY NOON!
I NEED THIS BY 1:00!
...CATHY??
WHAT DO YOU WANT?!

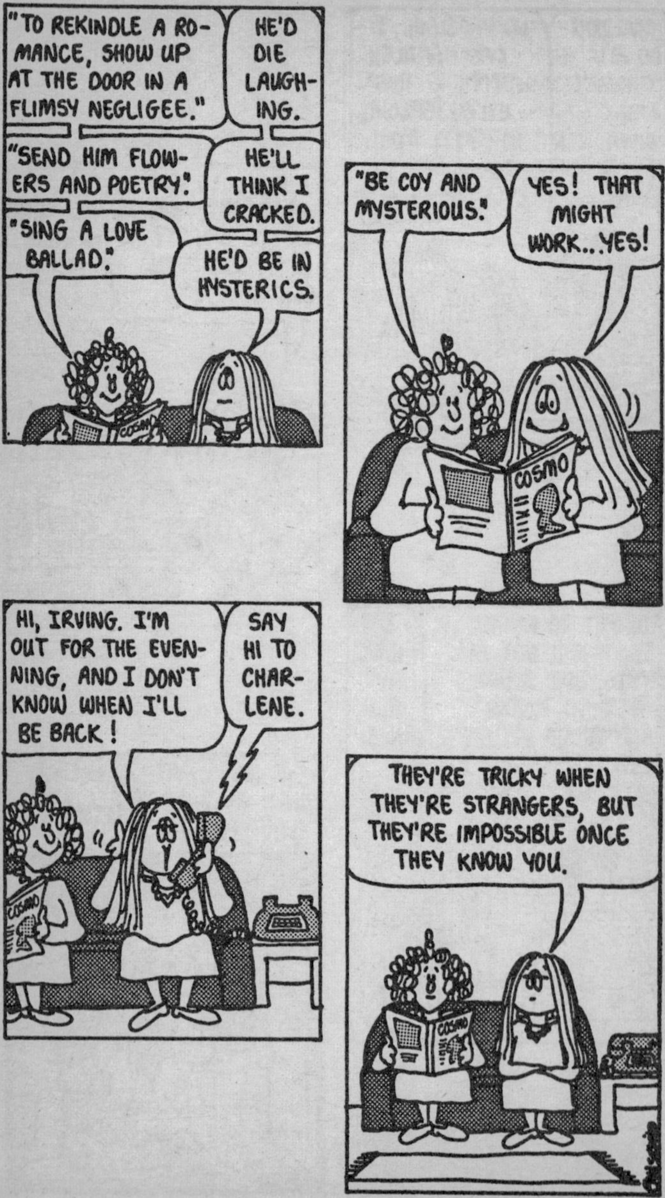
"TO REKINDLE A ROMANCE, SHOW UP AT THE DOOR IN A FLIMSY NEGLIGEE."
HE'D DIE LAUGHING.
"SEND HIM FLOWERS AND POETRY."
HE'LL THINK I CRACKED.
"SING A LOVE BALLAD."
HE'D BE IN HYSTERICS.
COSMO
"BE COY AND MYSTERIOUS."
YES! THAT MIGHT WORK... YES!
COSMO
HI, IRVING. I'M OUT FOR THE EVENING, AND I DON'T KNOW WHEN I'LL BE BACK!
SAY HI TO CHARLENE.
COSMO
THEY'RE TRICKY WHEN THEY'RE STRANGERS, BUT THEY'RE IMPOSSIBLE ONCE THEY KNOW YOU.
COSMO

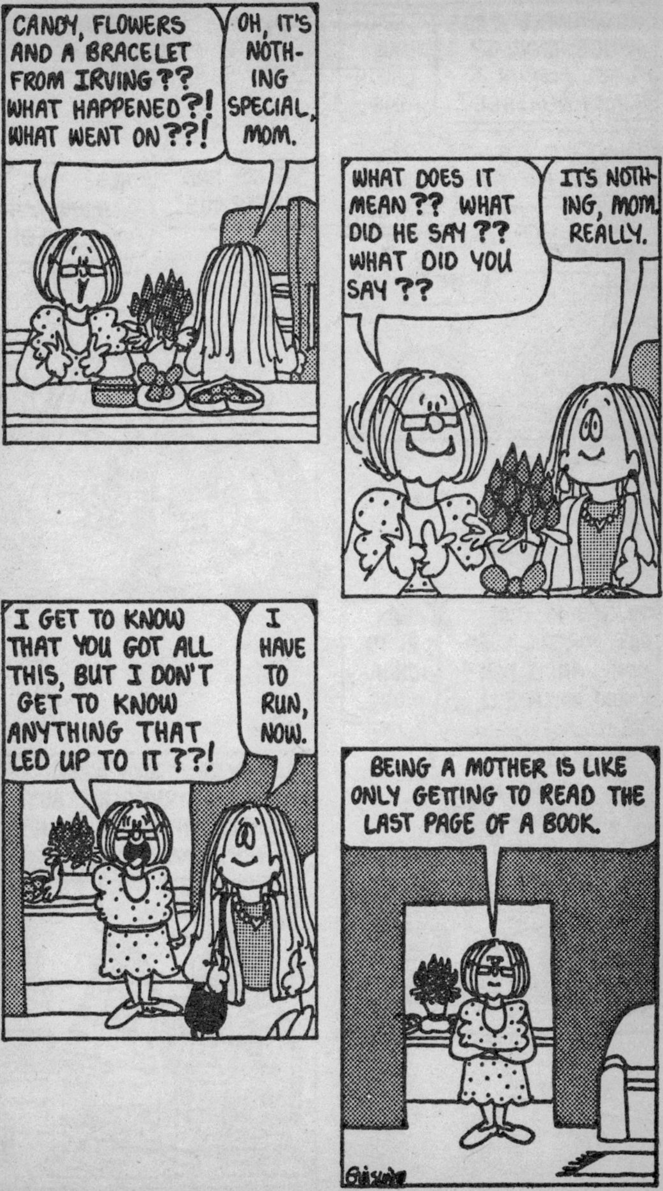
CANDY, FLOWERS AND A BRACELET FROM IRVING?? WHAT HAPPENED?! WHAT WENT ON??!
OH, IT'S NOTHING SPECIAL, MOM.
WHAT DOES IT MEAN?? WHAT DID HE SAY?? WHAT DID YOU SAY??
IT'S NOTHING, MOM. REALLY.
I GET TO KNOW THAT YOU GOT ALL THIS, BUT I DON'T GET TO KNOW ANYTHING THAT LED UP TO IT??!
I HAVE TO RUN, NOW.
BEING A MOTHER IS LIKE ONLY GETTING TO READ THE LAST PAGE OF A BOOK.

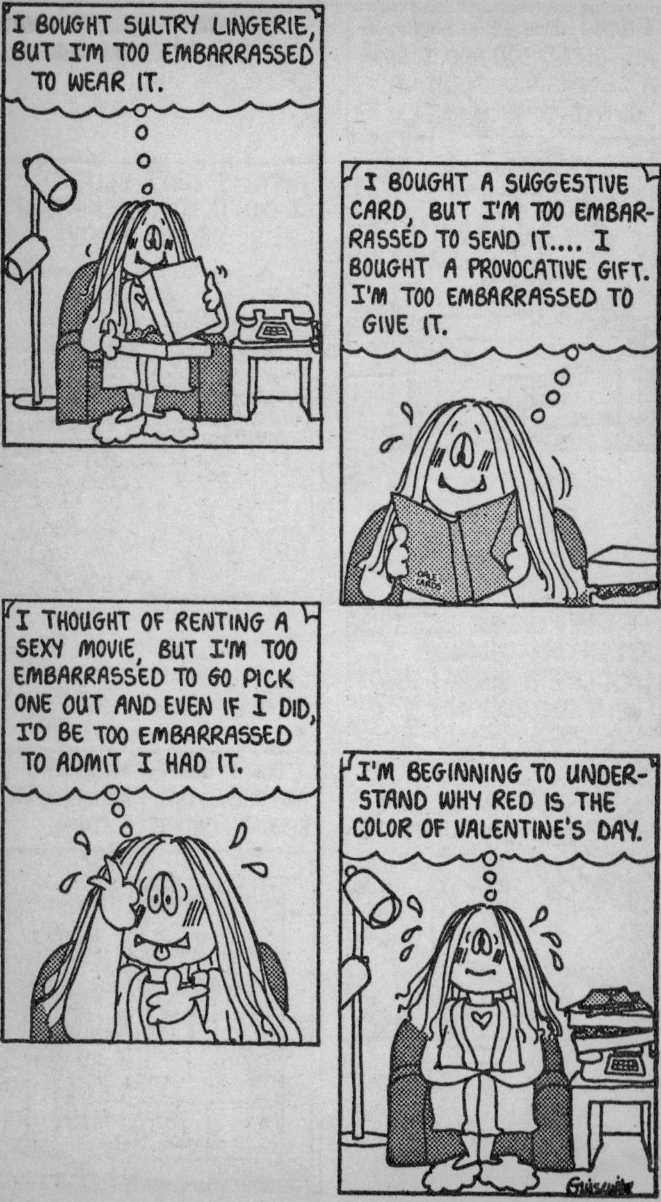
I BOUGHT SULTRY LINGERIE, BUT I'M TOO EMBARRASSED TO WEAR IT.
I BOUGHT A SUGGESTIVE CARD, BUT I'M TOO EMBARRASSED TO SEND IT.... I BOUGHT A PROVOCATIVE GIFT. I'M TOO EMBARRASSED TO GIVE IT.
I THOUGHT OF RENTING A SEXY MOVIE, BUT I'M TOO EMBARRASSED TO GO PICK ONE OUT AND EVEN IF I DID, I'D BE TOO EMBARRASSED TO ADMIT I HAD IT.
I'M BEGINNING TO UNDERSTAND WHY RED IS THE COLOR OF VALENTINE'S DAY.

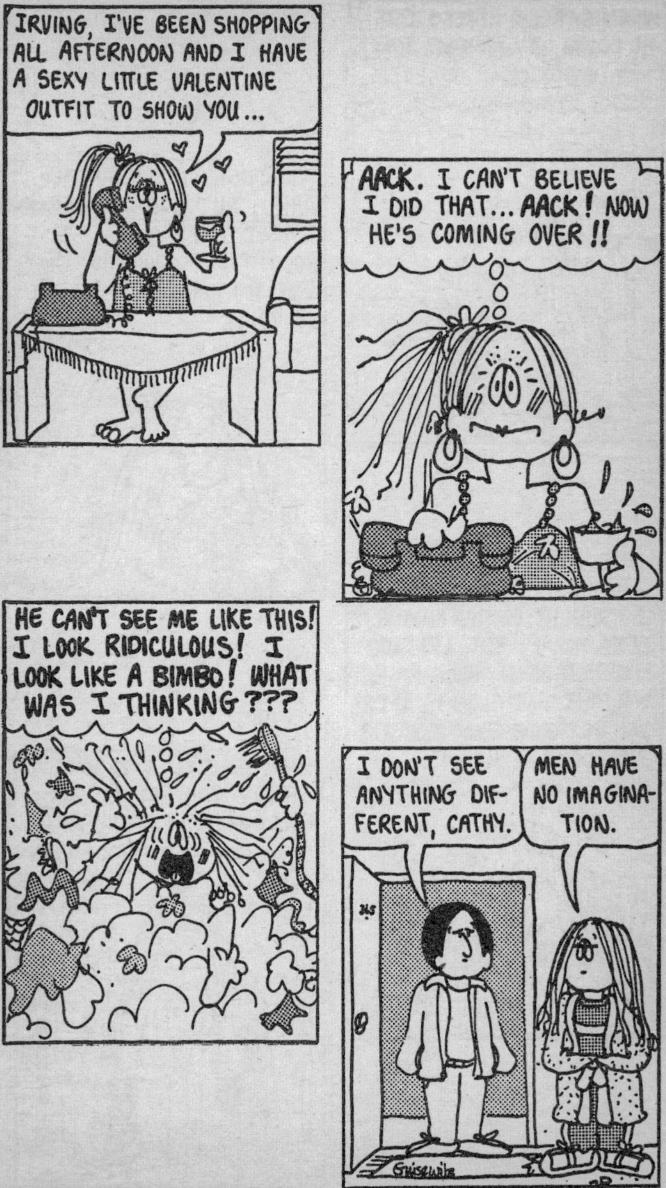
IRVING, I'VE BEEN SHOPPING ALL AFTERNOON AND I HAVE A SEXY LITTLE VALENTINE OUTFIT TO SHOW YOU...
AACK. I CAN'T BELIEVE I DID THAT... AACK! NOW HE'S COMING OVER!!
HE CAN'T SEE ME LIKE THIS! I LOOK RIDICULOUS! I LOOK LIKE A BIMBO! WHAT WAS I THINKING???
I DON'T SEE ANYTHING DIF-FERENT, CATHY.
MEN HAVE NO IMAGINA-TION.

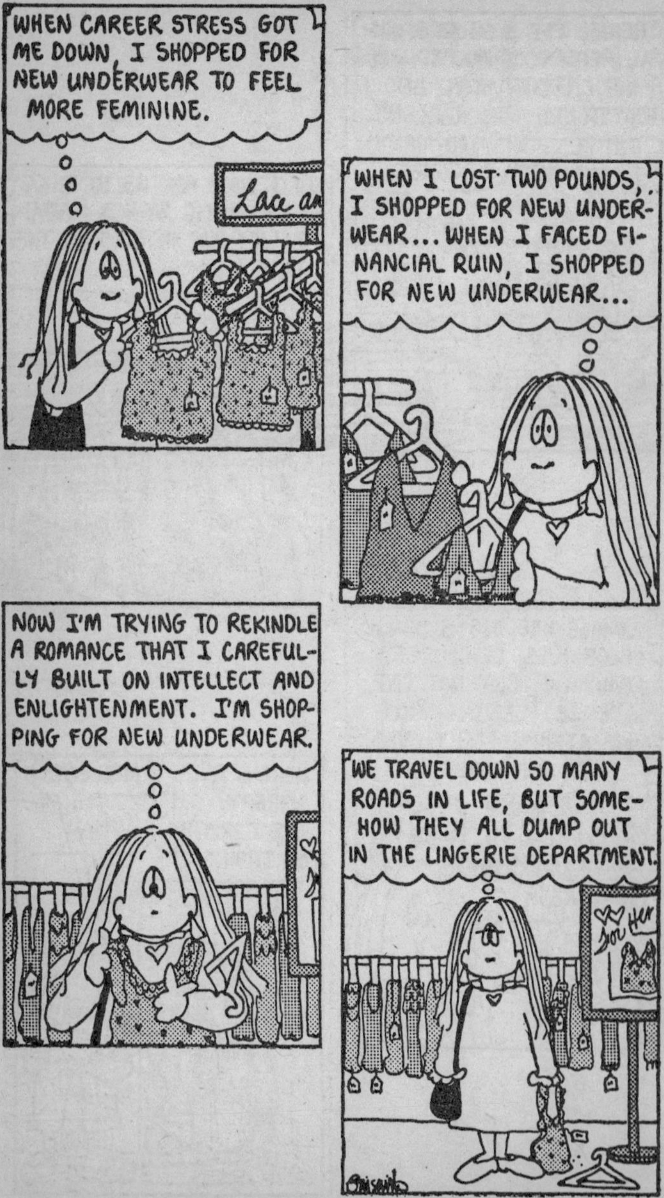
WHEN CAREER STRESS GOT ME DOWN, I SHOPPED FOR NEW UNDERWEAR TO FEEL MORE FEMININE.
WHEN I LOST TWO POUNDS, I SHOPPED FOR NEW UNDER-WEAR... WHEN I FACED FI-NANCIAL RUIN, I SHOPPED FOR NEW UNDERWEAR...
NOW I'M TRYING TO REKINDLE A ROMANCE THAT I CAREFUL-LY BUILT ON INTELLECT AND ENLIGHTENMENT. I'M SHOP-PING FOR NEW UNDERWEAR.
WE TRAVEL DOWN SO MANY ROADS IN LIFE, BUT SOME-HOW THEY ALL DUMP OUT IN THE LINGERIE DEPARTMENT.

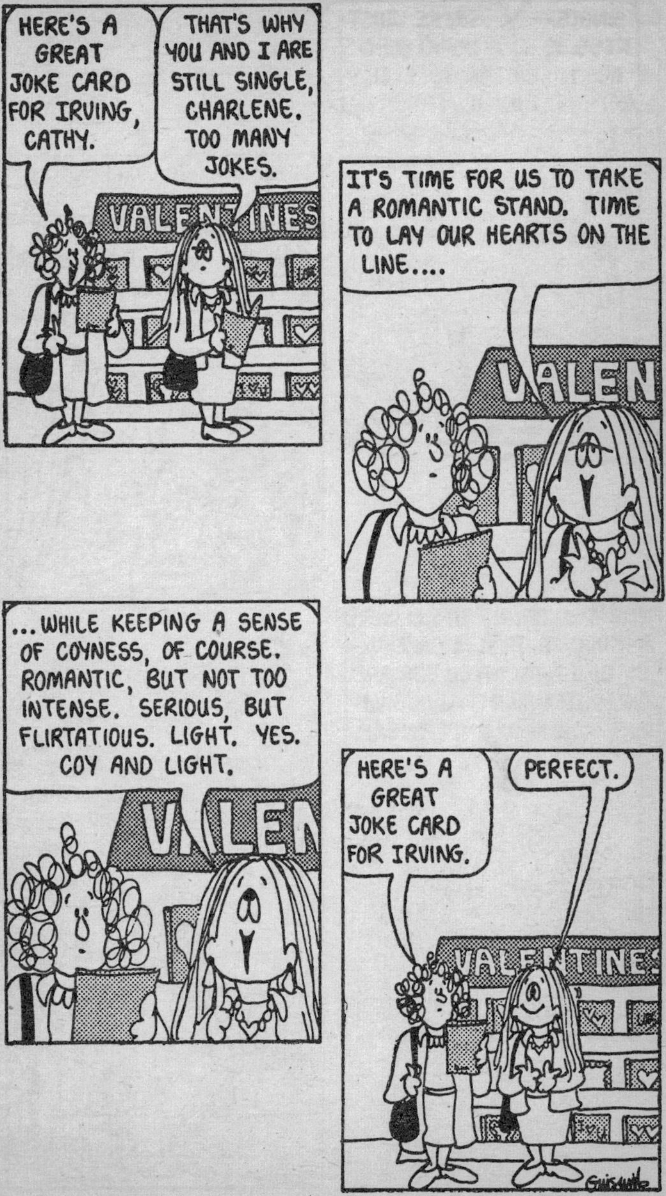
HERE'S A GREAT JOKE CARD FOR IRVING, CATHY.
THAT'S WHY YOU AND I ARE STILL SINGLE, CHARLENE. TOO MANY JOKES.
VALENTINES
IT'S TIME FOR US TO TAKE A ROMANTIC STAND. TIME TO LAY OUR HEARTS ON THE LINE....
...WHILE KEEPING A SENSE OF COYNESS, OF COURSE. ROMANTIC, BUT NOT TOO INTENSE. SERIOUS, BUT FLIRTATIOUS. LIGHT. YES. COY AND LIGHT.
HERE'S A GREAT JOKE CARD FOR IRVING.
PERFECT.
VALENTINES

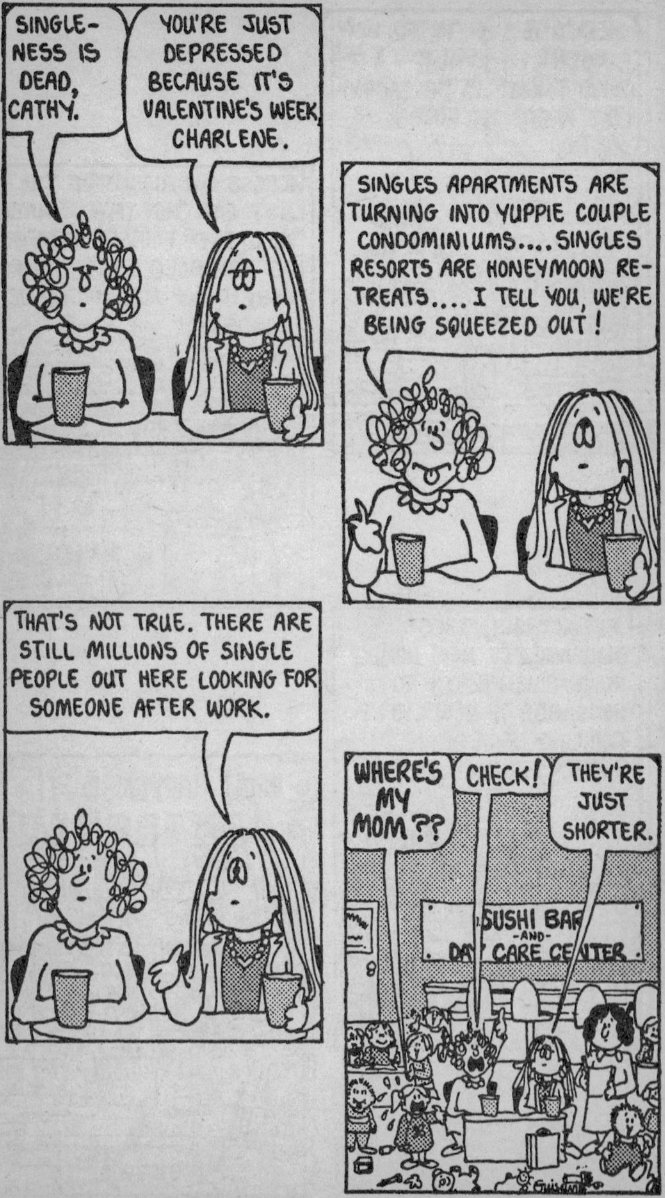
SINGLE-NESS IS DEAD, CATHY.
YOU'RE JUST DEPRESSED BECAUSE IT'S VALENTINE'S WEEK, CHARLENE.
SINGLES APARTMENTS ARE TURNING INTO YUPPIE COUPLE CONDOMINIUMS.... SINGLES RESORTS ARE HONEYMOON RETREATS.... I TELL YOU, WE'RE BEING SQUEEZED OUT!
THAT'S NOT TRUE. THERE ARE STILL MILLIONS OF SINGLE PEOPLE OUT HERE LOOKING FOR SOMEONE AFTER WORK.
WHERE'S MY MOM??
CHECK!
THEY'RE JUST SHORTER.
SUSHI BA
-AND-
CARE

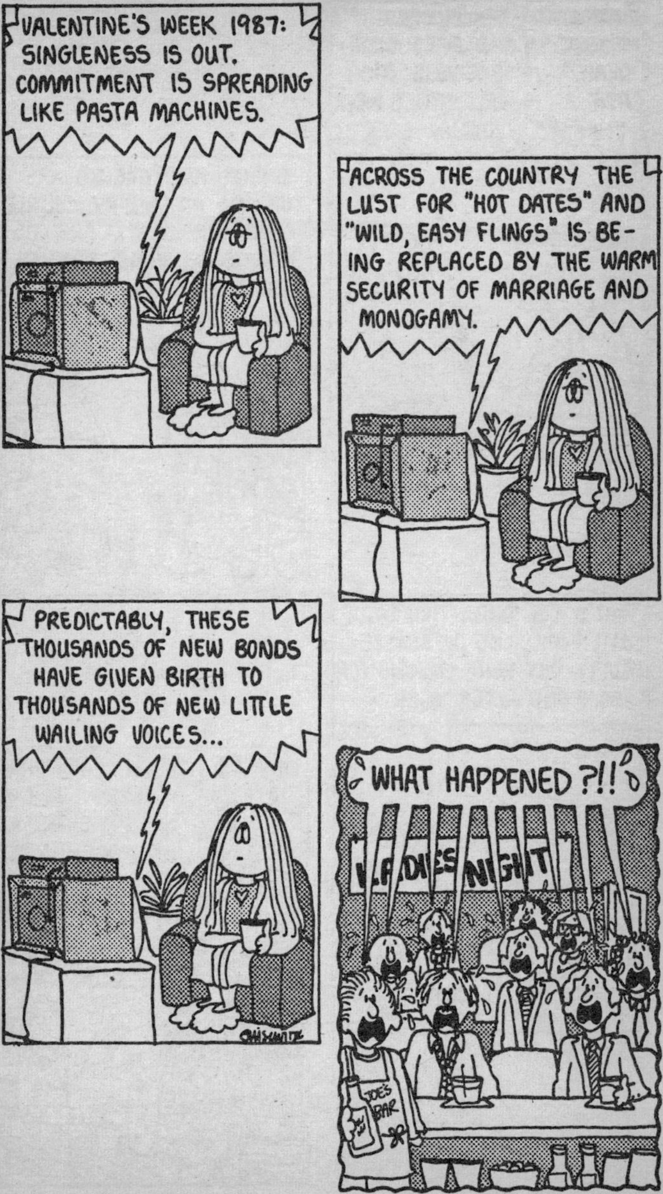
VALENTINE'S WEEK 1987: SINGLENESS IS OUT. COMMITMENT IS SPREADING LIKE PASTA MACHINES.
ACROSS THE COUNTRY THE LUST FOR "HOT DATES" AND "WILD, EASY FLINGS" IS BEING REPLACED BY THE WARM SECURITY OF MARRIAGE AND MONOGAMY.
PREDICTABLY, THESE THOUSANDS OF NEW BONDS HAVE GIVEN BIRTH TO THOUSANDS OF NEW LITTLE WAILING VOICES...
WHAT HAPPENED ?!!
JOE'S BAR

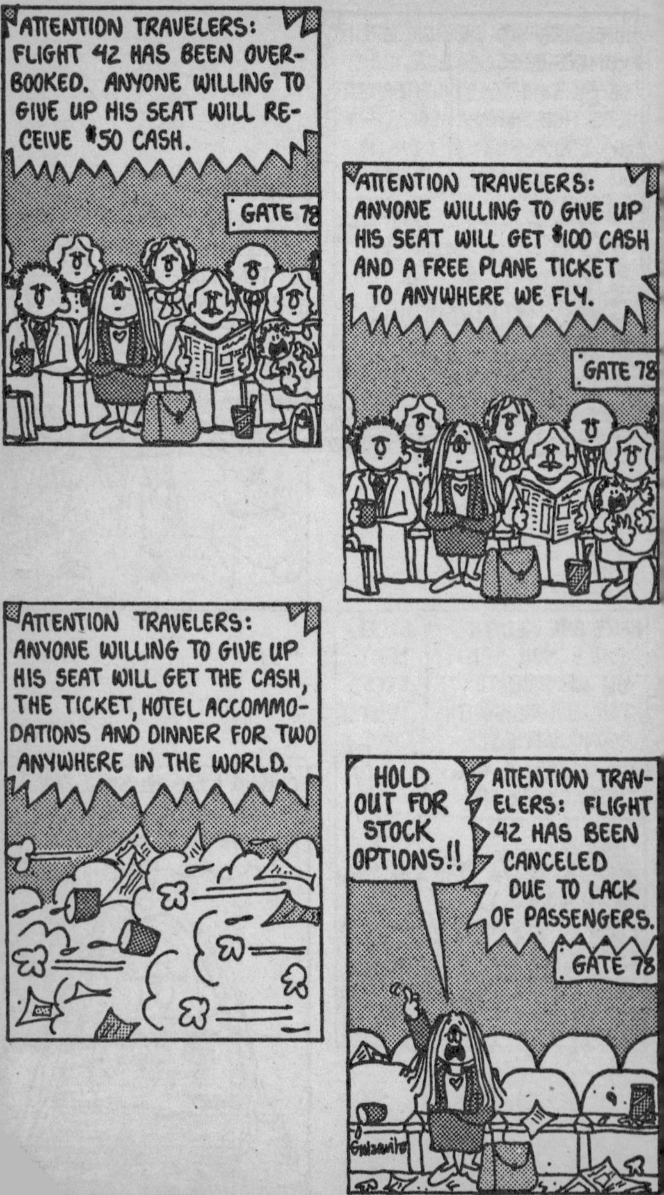
ATTENTION TRAVELERS: FLIGHT 42 HAS BEEN OVER-BOOKED. ANYONE WILLING TO GIVE UP HIS SEAT WILL RECEIVE $50 CASH.
GATE 78
ATTENTION TRAVELERS: ANYONE WILLING TO GIVE UP HIS SEAT WILL GET $100 CASH AND A FREE PLANE TICKET TO ANYWHERE WE FLY.
GATE 78
ATTENTION TRAVELERS: ANYONE WILLING TO GIVE UP HIS SEAT WILL GET THE CASH, THE TICKET, HOTEL ACCOMMODATIONS AND DINNER FOR TWO ANYWHERE IN THE WORLD.
HOLD OUT FOR STOCK OPTIONS!!
ATTENTION TRAVELERS: FLIGHT 42 HAS BEEN CANCELED DUE TO LACK OF PASSENGERS.
GATE 78

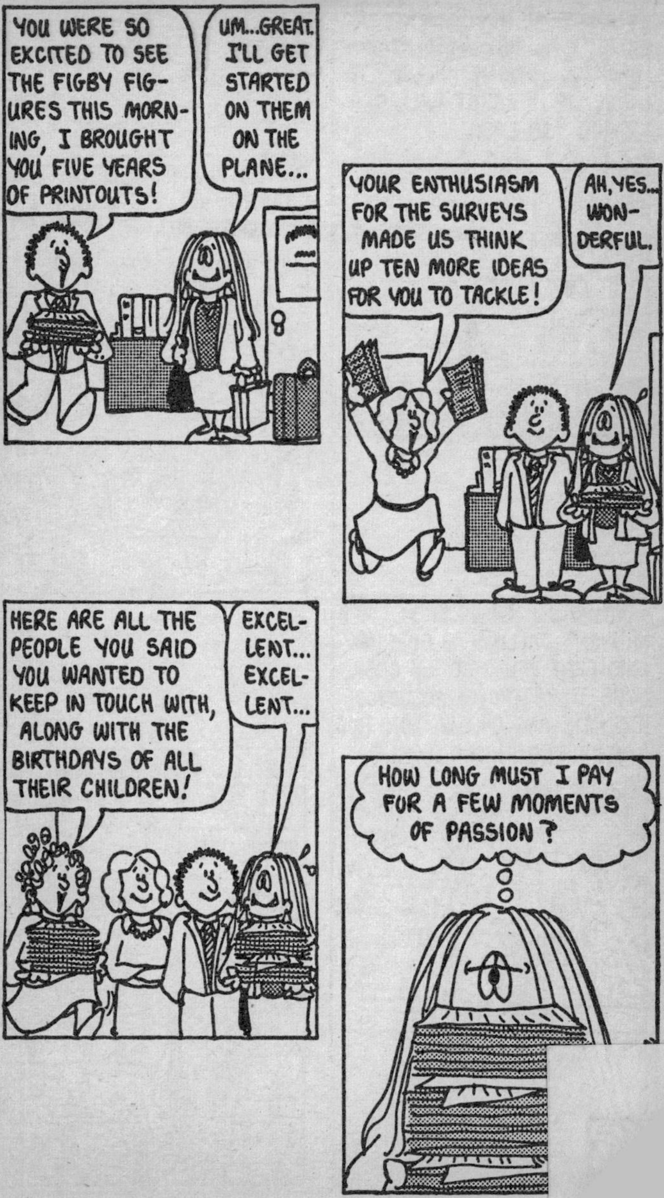

YOU WERE SO EXCITED TO SEE THE FIGBY FIGURES THIS MORNING, I BROUGHT YOU FIVE YEARS OF PRINTOUTS!
UM...GREAT. I'LL GET STARTED ON THEM ON THE PLANE...
YOUR ENTHUSIASM FOR THE SURVEYS MADE US THINK UP TEN MORE IDEAS FOR YOU TO TACKLE!
AH, YES... WONDERFUL.
HERE ARE ALL THE PEOPLE YOU SAID YOU WANTED TO KEEP IN TOUCH WITH, ALONG WITH THE BIRTHDAYS OF ALL THEIR CHILDREN!
EXCELLENT... EXCELLENT...
HOW LONG MUST I PAY FOR A FEW MOMENTS OF PASSION?

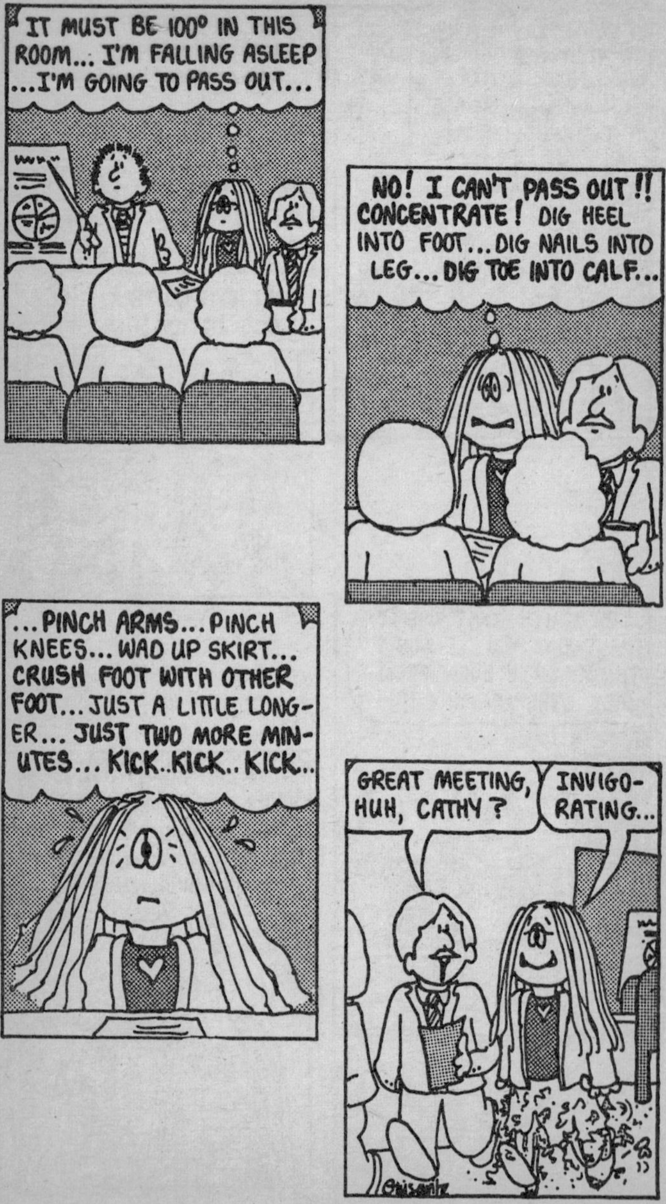
IT MUST BE 100° IN THIS ROOM... I'M FALLING ASLEEP ...I'M GOING TO PASS OUT...
NO! I CAN'T PASS OUT!! CONCENTRATE! DIG HEEL INTO FOOT... DIG NAILS INTO LEG... DIG TOE INTO CALF...
...PINCH ARMS...PINCH KNEES...WAD UP SKIRT... CRUSH FOOT WITH OTHER FOOT... JUST A LITTLE LONG-ER... JUST TWO MORE MIN-UTES... KICK..KICK..KICK..
GREAT MEETING, HUH, CATHY?
INVIGO-RATING...

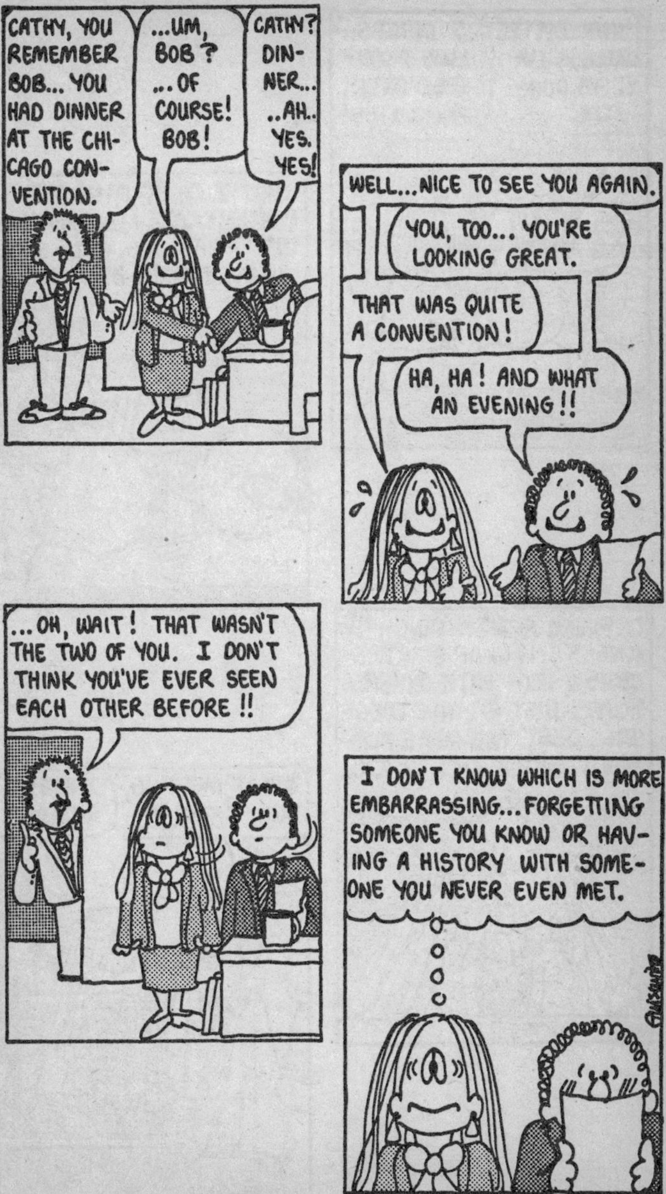
CATHY, YOU REMEMBER BOB... YOU HAD DINNER AT THE CHICAGO CONVENTION.
...UM, BOB? ...OF COURSE! BOB!
CATHY? DINNER... ..AH.. YES. YES!
WELL...NICE TO SEE YOU AGAIN.
YOU, TOO... YOU'RE LOOKING GREAT.
THAT WAS QUITE A CONVENTION!
HA, HA! AND WHAT AN EVENING!!
...OH, WAIT! THAT WASN'T THE TWO OF YOU. I DON'T THINK YOU'VE EVER SEEN EACH OTHER BEFORE!!
I DON'T KNOW WHICH IS MORE EMBARRASSING... FORGETTING SOMEONE YOU KNOW OR HAVING A HISTORY WITH SOMEONE YOU NEVER EVEN MET.

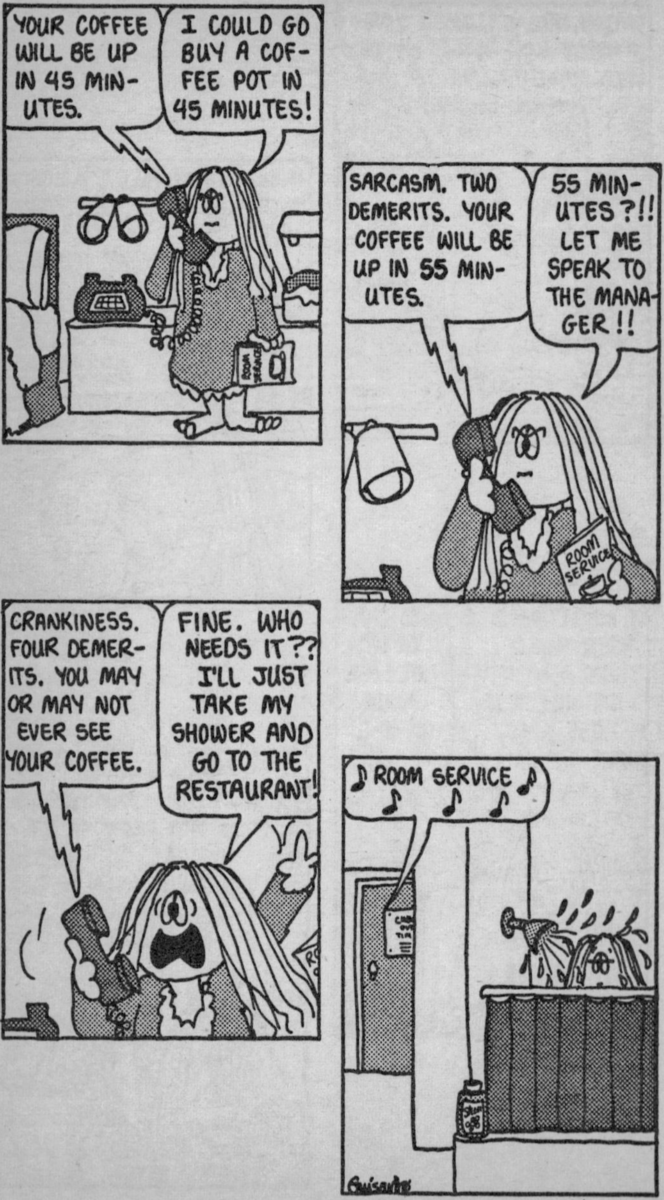
YOUR COFFEE WILL BE UP IN 45 MIN-UTES.
I COULD GO BUY A COF-FEE POT IN 45 MINUTES!
ROOM SERVICE
SARCASM. TWO DEMERITS. YOUR COFFEE WILL BE UP IN 55 MIN-UTES.
55 MIN-UTES?!! LET ME SPEAK TO THE MANA-GER!!
ROOM SERVICE
CRANKINESS. FOUR DEMER-ITS. YOU MAY OR MAY NOT EVER SEE YOUR COFFEE.
FINE. WHO NEEDS IT?? I'LL JUST TAKE MY SHOWER AND GO TO THE RESTAURANT!
♪ ROOM SERVICE ♪ ♪ ♪ ♪ ♪

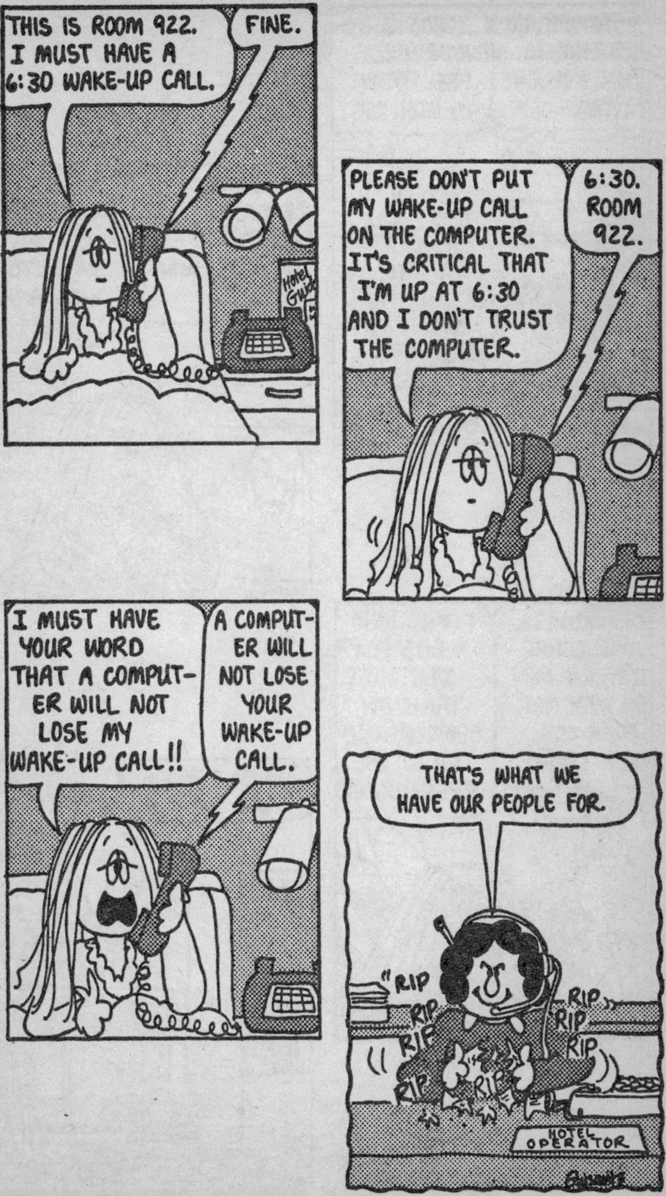
THIS IS ROOM 922. I MUST HAVE A 6:30 WAKE-UP CALL.
FINE.
PLEASE DON'T PUT MY WAKE-UP CALL ON THE COMPUTER. IT'S CRITICAL THAT I'M UP AT 6:30 AND I DON'T TRUST THE COMPUTER.
6:30. ROOM 922.
I MUST HAVE YOUR WORD THAT A COMPUTER WILL NOT LOSE MY WAKE-UP CALL!!
A COMPUTER WILL NOT LOSE YOUR WAKE-UP CALL.
THAT'S WHAT WE HAVE OUR PEOPLE FOR.
"RIP
RIP
RIP
RIP
RIP
RIP"
RIP
RIP
HOTEL OPERATOR

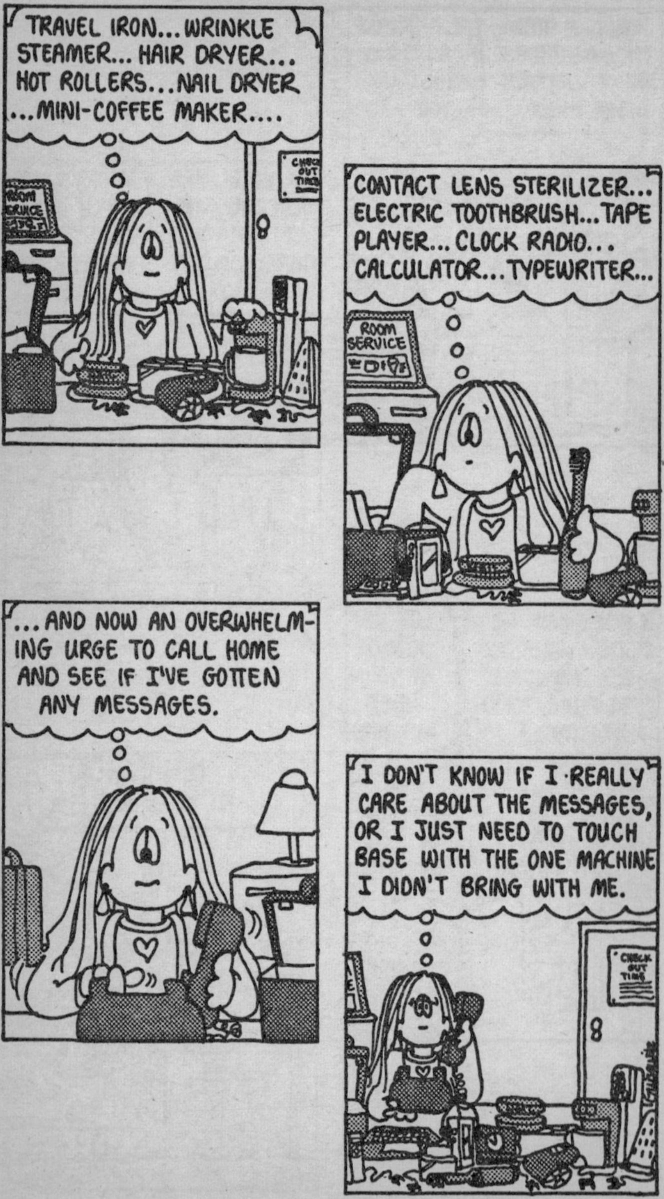
TRAVEL IRON... WRINKLE STEAMER... HAIR DRYER... HOT ROLLERS... NAIL DRYER ...MINI-COFFEE MAKER....
CONTACT LENS STERILIZER... ELECTRIC TOOTHBRUSH... TAPE PLAYER... CLOCK RADIO... CALCULATOR... TYPEWRITER...
ROOM SERVICE
... AND NOW AN OVERWHELMING URGE TO CALL HOME AND SEE IF I'VE GOTTEN ANY MESSAGES.
I DON'T KNOW IF I REALLY CARE ABOUT THE MESSAGES, OR I JUST NEED TO TOUCH BASE WITH THE ONE MACHINE I DIDN'T BRING WITH ME.
CHECK OUT TIME

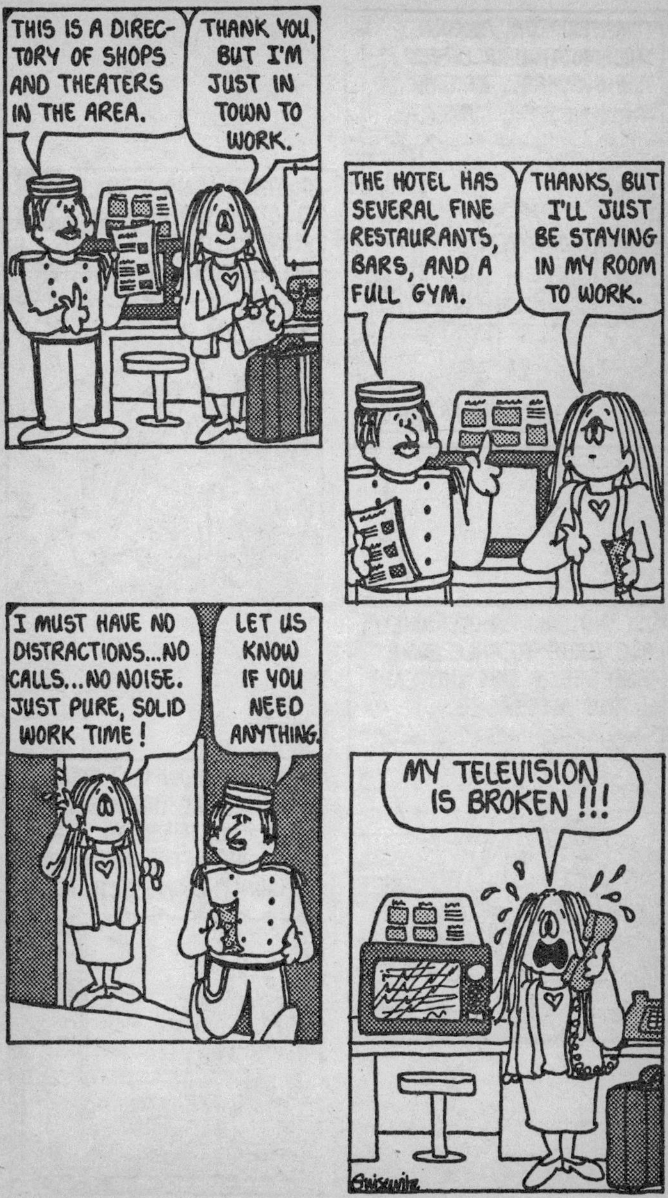
THIS IS A DIRECTORY OF SHOPS AND THEATERS IN THE AREA.
THANK YOU, BUT I'M JUST IN TOWN TO WORK.
THE HOTEL HAS SEVERAL FINE RESTAURANTS, BARS, AND A FULL GYM.
THANKS, BUT I'LL JUST BE STAYING IN MY ROOM TO WORK.
I MUST HAVE NO DISTRACTIONS...NO CALLS...NO NOISE. JUST PURE, SOLID WORK TIME!
LET US KNOW IF YOU NEED ANYTHING.
MY TELEVISION IS BROKEN!!!

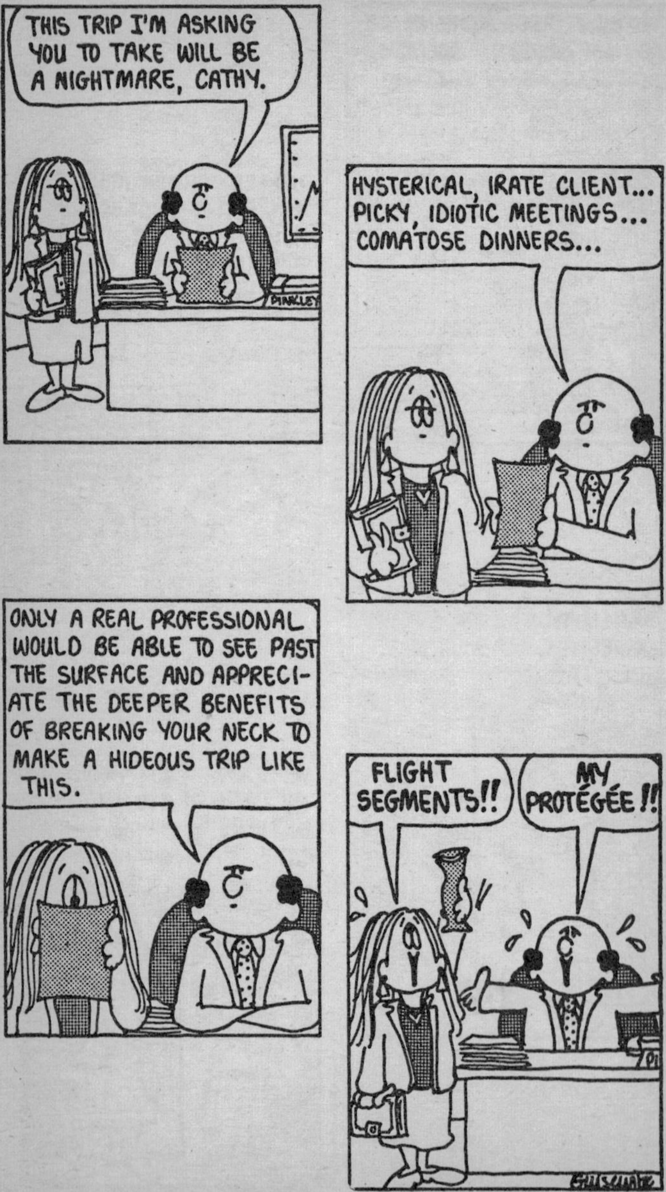
THIS TRIP I'M ASKING YOU TO TAKE WILL BE A NIGHTMARE, CATHY.
HYSTERICAL, IRATE CLIENT... PICKY, IDIOTIC MEETINGS... COMATOSE DINNERS...
ONLY A REAL PROFESSIONAL WOULD BE ABLE TO SEE PAST THE SURFACE AND APPRECIATE THE DEEPER BENEFITS OF BREAKING YOUR NECK TO MAKE A HIDEOUS TRIP LIKE THIS.
FLIGHT SEGMENTS!!
MY PROTÉGÉE!!

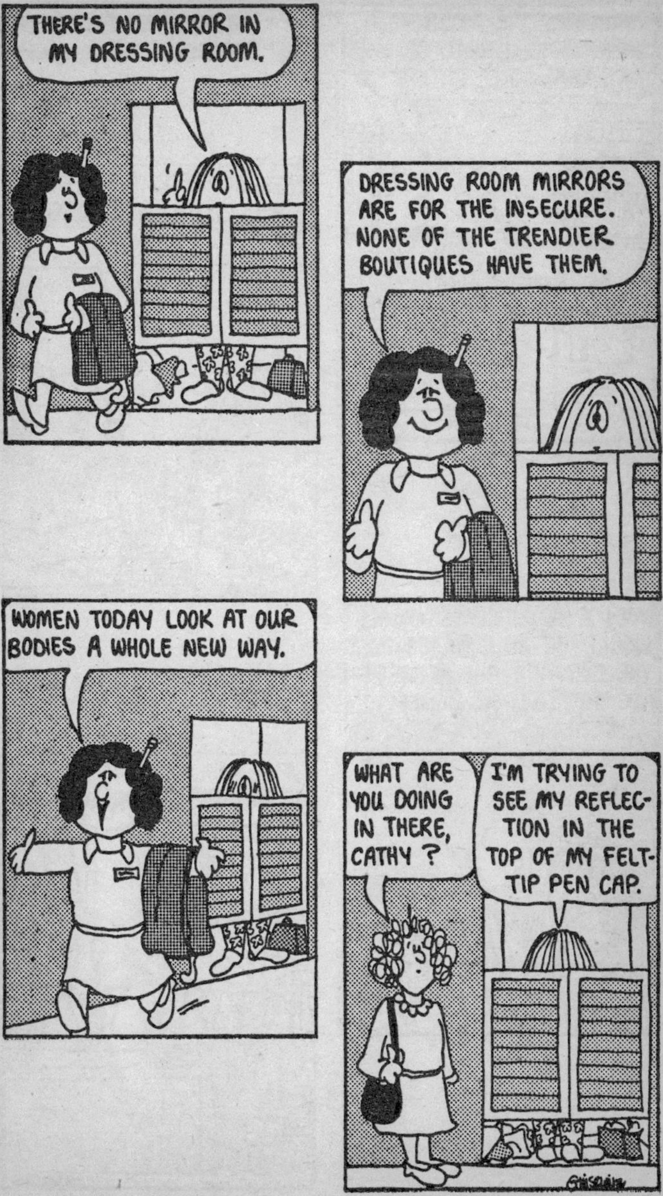
THERE'S NO MIRROR IN MY DRESSING ROOM.
DRESSING ROOM MIRRORS ARE FOR THE INSECURE. NONE OF THE TRENDIER BOUTIQUES HAVE THEM.
WOMEN TODAY LOOK AT OUR BODIES A WHOLE NEW WAY.
WHAT ARE YOU DOING IN THERE, CATHY?
I'M TRYING TO SEE MY REFLECTION IN THE TOP OF MY FELT-TIP PEN CAP.

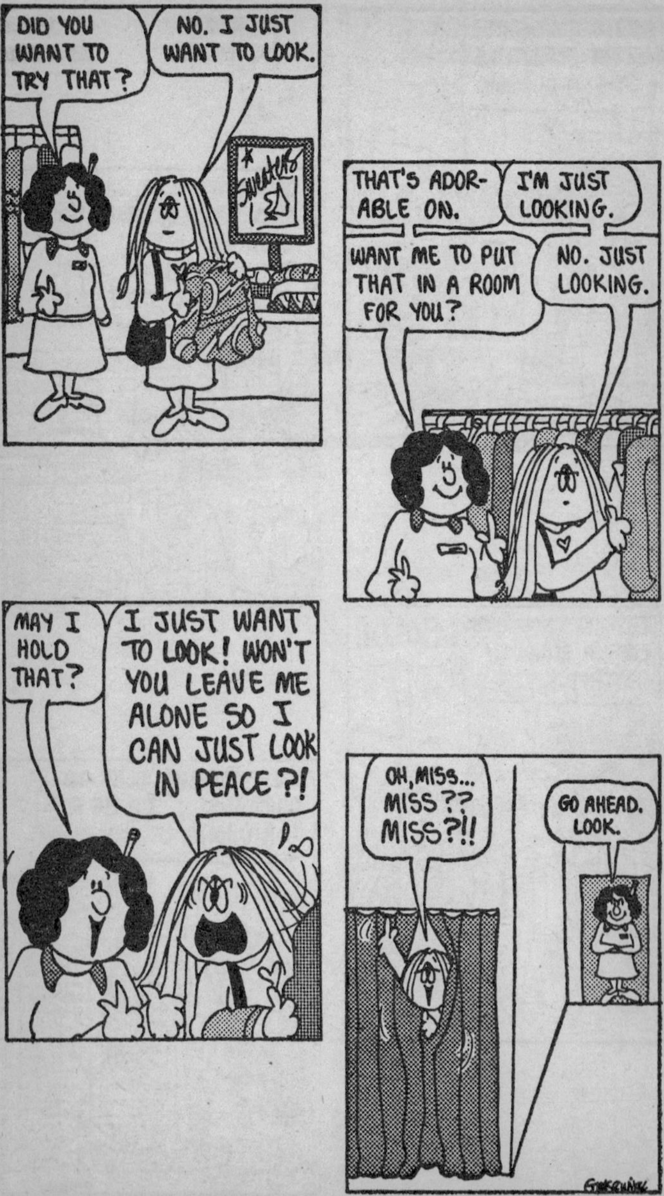
DID YOU WANT TO TRY THAT?
NO. I JUST WANT TO LOOK.
Sweaters
THAT'S ADORABLE ON.
I'M JUST LOOKING.
WANT ME TO PUT THAT IN A ROOM FOR YOU?
NO. JUST LOOKING.
MAY I HOLD THAT?
I JUST WANT TO LOOK! WON'T YOU LEAVE ME ALONE SO I CAN JUST LOOK IN PEACE?!
OH, MISS... MISS?? MISS?!!
GO AHEAD. LOOK.

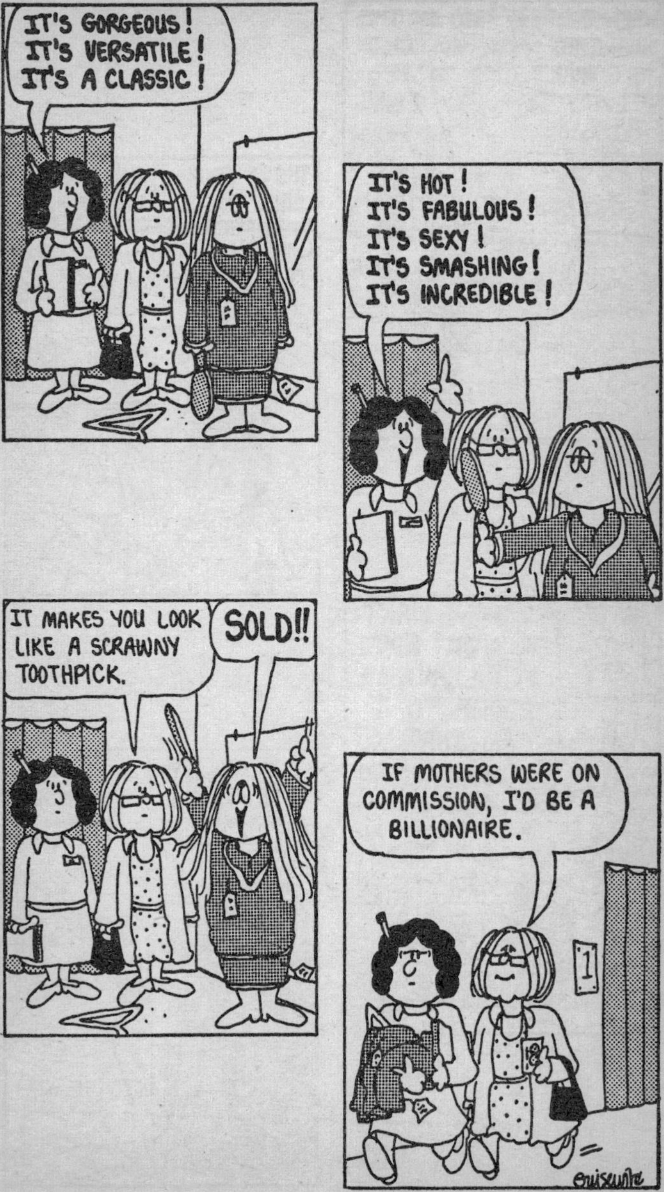
IT'S GORGEOUS! IT'S VERSATILE! IT'S A CLASSIC!
IT'S HOT! IT'S FABULOUS! IT'S SEXY! IT'S SMASHING! IT'S INCREDIBLE!
IT MAKES YOU LOOK LIKE A SCRAWNY TOOTHPICK.
SOLD!!
IF MOTHERS WERE ON COMMISSION, I'D BE A BILLIONAIRE.
1

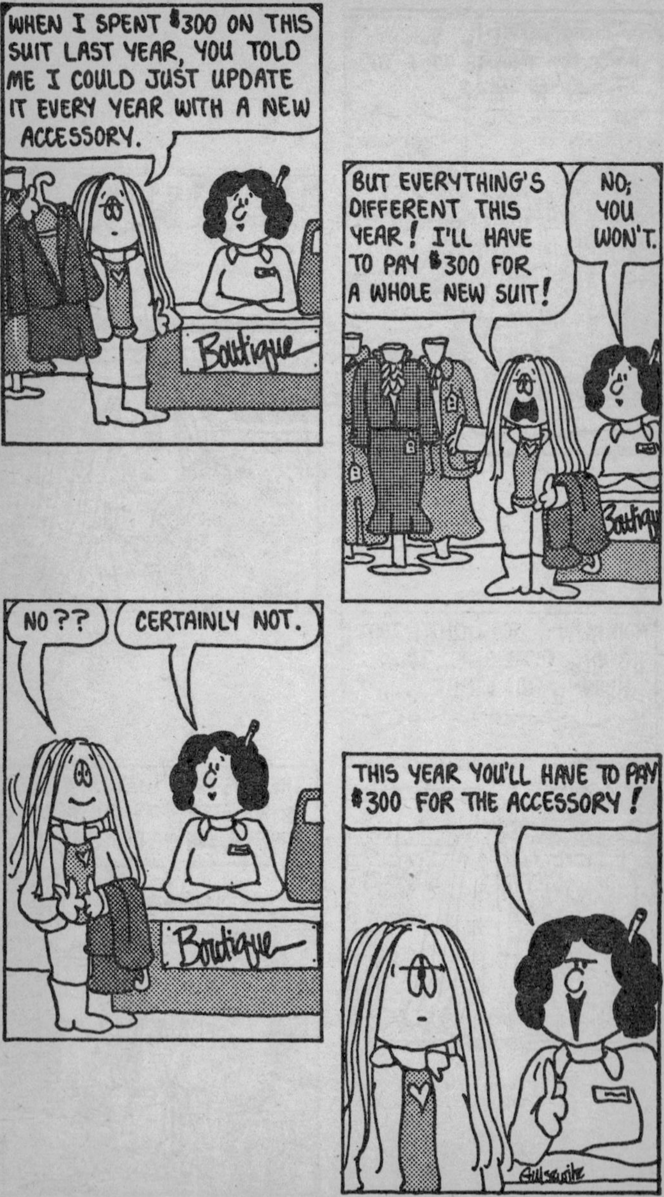
WHEN I SPENT $300 ON THIS SUIT LAST YEAR, YOU TOLD ME I COULD JUST UPDATE IT EVERY YEAR WITH A NEW ACCESSORY.
Boutique
BUT EVERYTHING'S DIFFERENT THIS YEAR! I'LL HAVE TO PAY $300 FOR A WHOLE NEW SUIT!
NO; YOU WON'T.
NO??
CERTAINLY NOT.
Boutique
THIS YEAR YOU'LL HAVE TO PAY $300 FOR THE ACCESSORY!
Guisewite

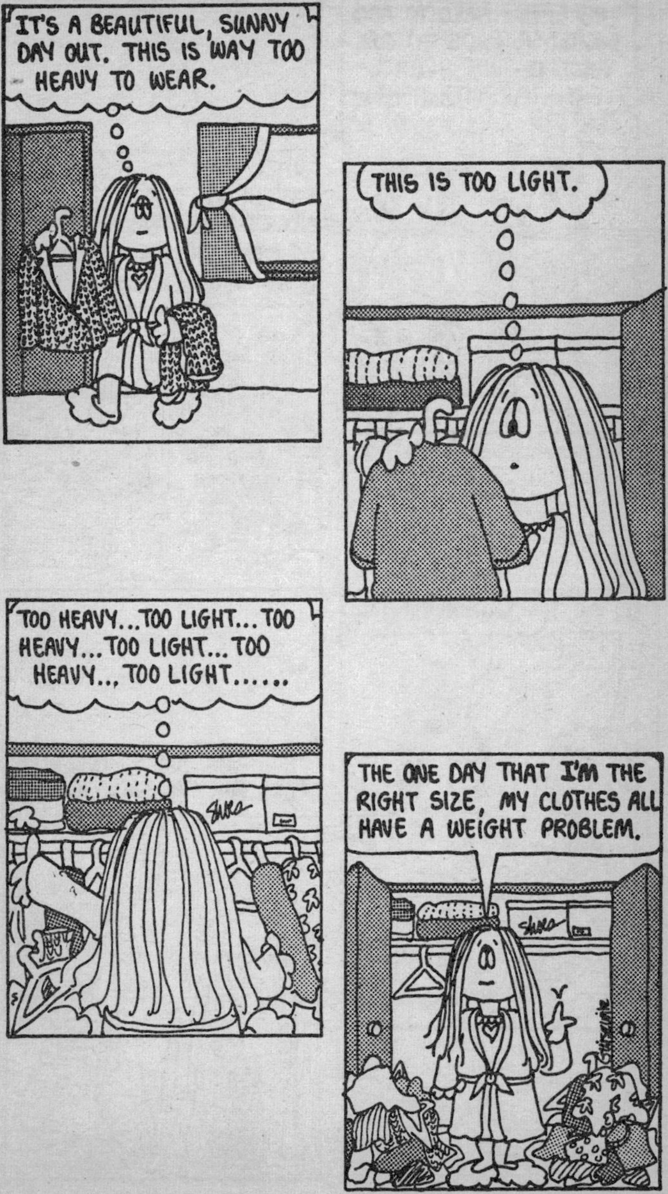
IT'S A BEAUTIFUL, SUNNY DAY OUT. THIS IS WAY TOO HEAVY TO WEAR.
THIS IS TOO LIGHT.
TOO HEAVY...TOO LIGHT... TOO HEAVY... TOO LIGHT... TOO HEAVY..., TOO LIGHT......
THE ONE DAY THAT I'M THE RIGHT SIZE, MY CLOTHES ALL HAVE A WEIGHT PROBLEM.

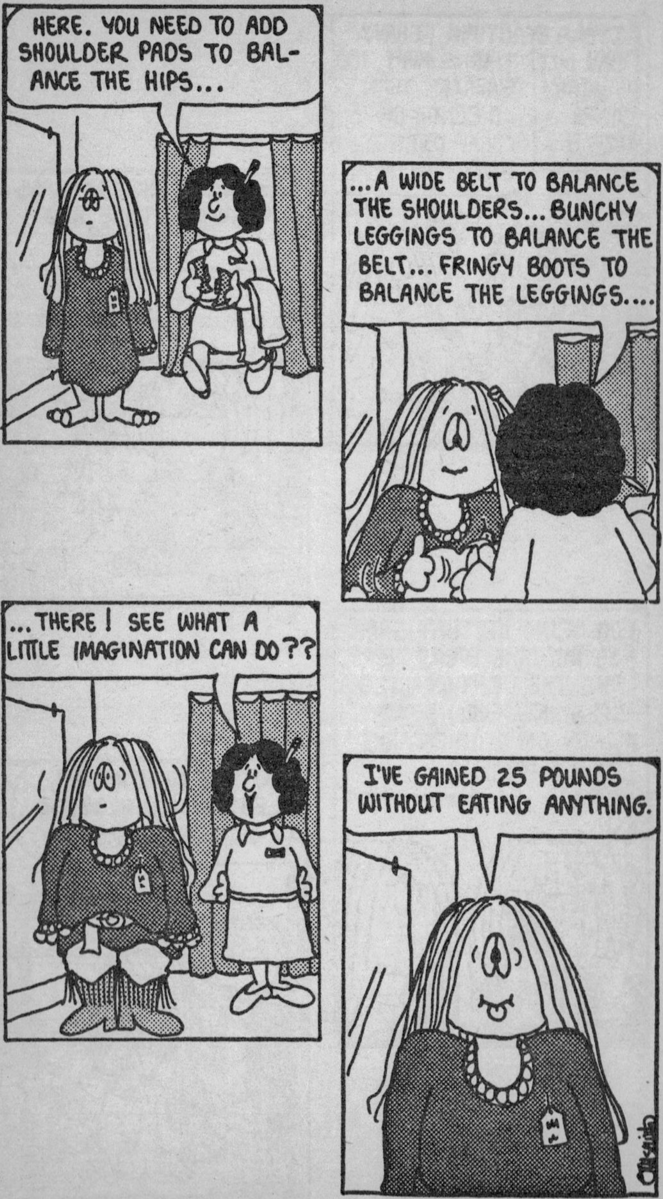
HERE. YOU NEED TO ADD SHOULDER PADS TO BAL- ANCE THE HIPS...
...A WIDE BELT TO BALANCE THE SHOULDERS... BUNCHY LEGGINGS TO BALANCE THE BELT... FRINGY BOOTS TO BALANCE THE LEGGINGS....
...THERE! SEE WHAT A LITTLE IMAGINATION CAN DO??
I'VE GAINED 25 POUNDS WITHOUT EATING ANYTHING.

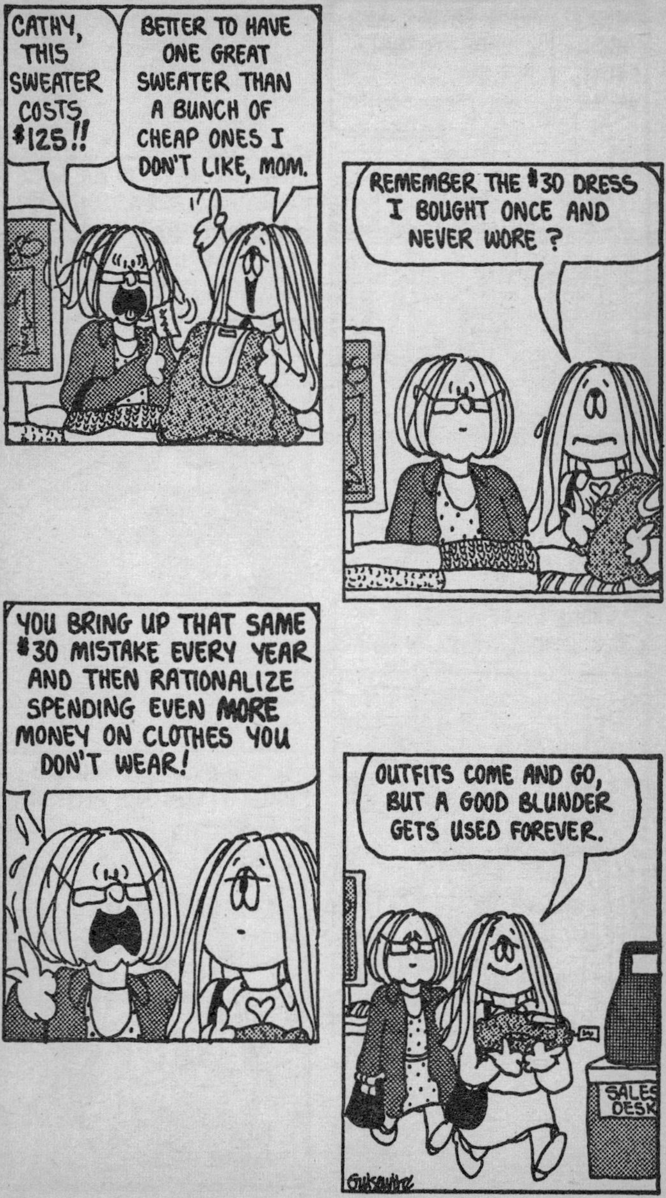
CATHY, THIS SWEATER COSTS $125!!
BETTER TO HAVE ONE GREAT SWEATER THAN A BUNCH OF CHEAP ONES I DON'T LIKE, MOM.
REMEMBER THE $30 DRESS I BOUGHT ONCE AND NEVER WORE ?
YOU BRING UP THAT SAME $30 MISTAKE EVERY YEAR AND THEN RATIONALIZE SPENDING EVEN MORE MONEY ON CLOTHES YOU DON'T WEAR!
OUTFITS COME AND GO, BUT A GOOD BLUNDER GETS USED FOREVER.
SALES DESK

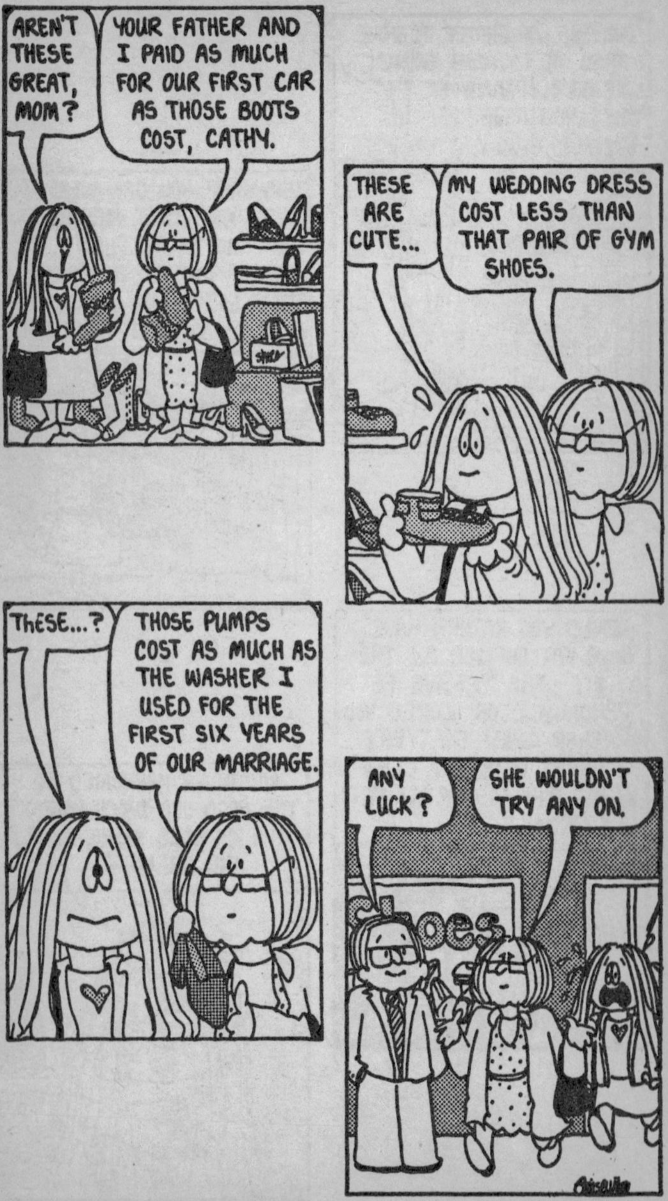
AREN'T THESE GREAT, MOM?
YOUR FATHER AND I PAID AS MUCH FOR OUR FIRST CAR AS THOSE BOOTS COST, CATHY.
THESE ARE CUTE...
MY WEDDING DRESS COST LESS THAN THAT PAIR OF GYM SHOES.
THESE...?
THOSE PUMPS COST AS MUCH AS THE WASHER I USED FOR THE FIRST SIX YEARS OF OUR MARRIAGE.
ANY LUCK?
SHE WOULDN'T TRY ANY ON.

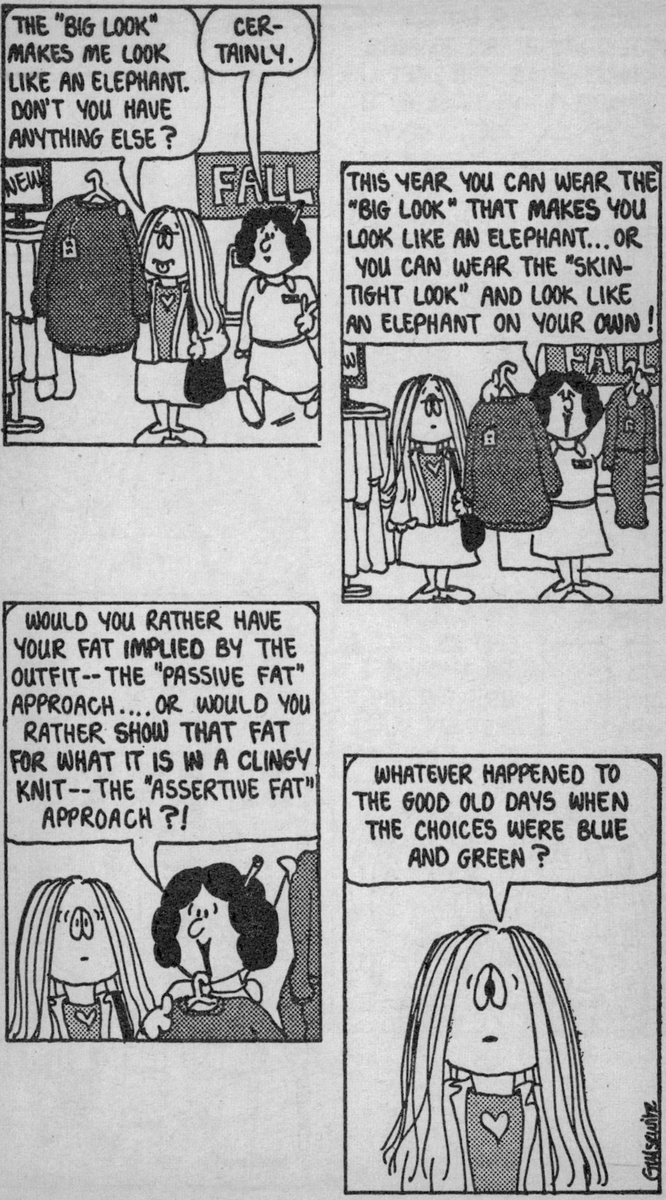
THE "BIG LOOK" MAKES ME LOOK LIKE AN ELEPHANT. DON'T YOU HAVE ANYTHING ELSE?
CER-TAINLY.
NEW
FALL
THIS YEAR YOU CAN WEAR THE "BIG LOOK" THAT MAKES YOU LOOK LIKE AN ELEPHANT... OR YOU CAN WEAR THE "SKIN-TIGHT LOOK" AND LOOK LIKE AN ELEPHANT ON YOUR OWN!
WOULD YOU RATHER HAVE YOUR FAT IMPLIED BY THE OUTFIT-- THE "PASSIVE FAT" APPROACH.... OR WOULD YOU RATHER SHOW THAT FAT FOR WHAT IT IS IN A CLINGY KNIT-- THE "ASSERTIVE FAT" APPROACH?!
WHATEVER HAPPENED TO THE GOOD OLD DAYS WHEN THE CHOICES WERE BLUE AND GREEN?

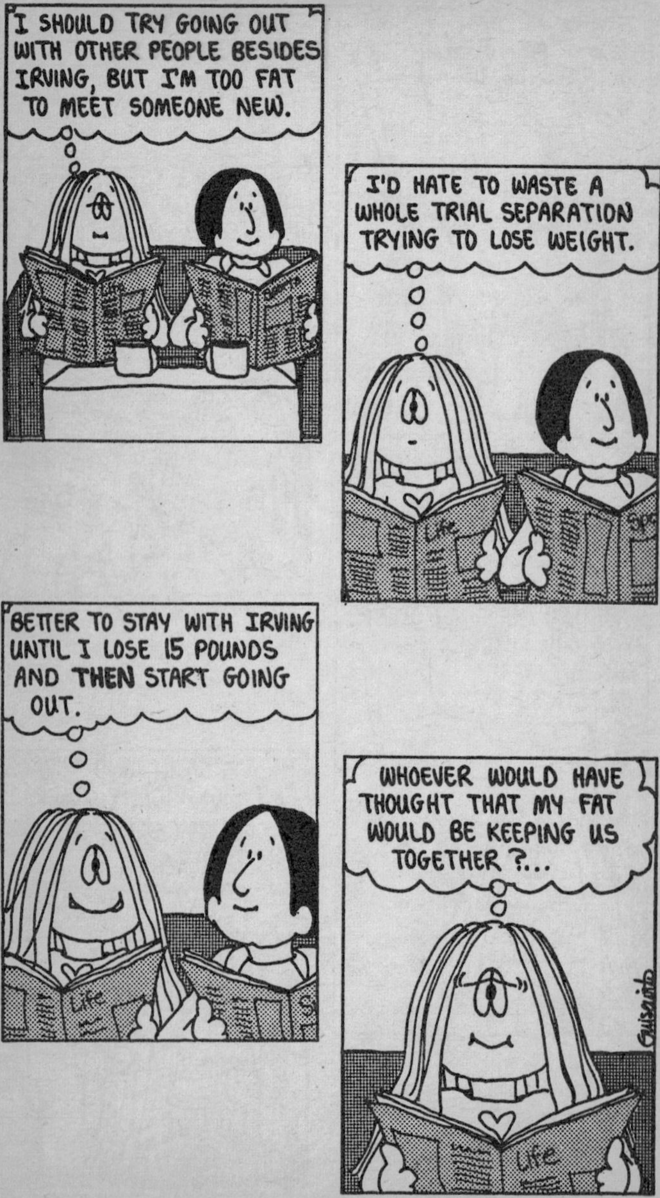
I SHOULD TRY GOING OUT WITH OTHER PEOPLE BESIDES IRVING, BUT I'M TOO FAT TO MEET SOMEONE NEW.
I'D HATE TO WASTE A WHOLE TRIAL SEPARATION TRYING TO LOSE WEIGHT.
BETTER TO STAY WITH IRVING UNTIL I LOSE 15 POUNDS AND THEN START GOING OUT.
WHOEVER WOULD HAVE THOUGHT THAT MY FAT WOULD BE KEEPING US TOGETHER?...

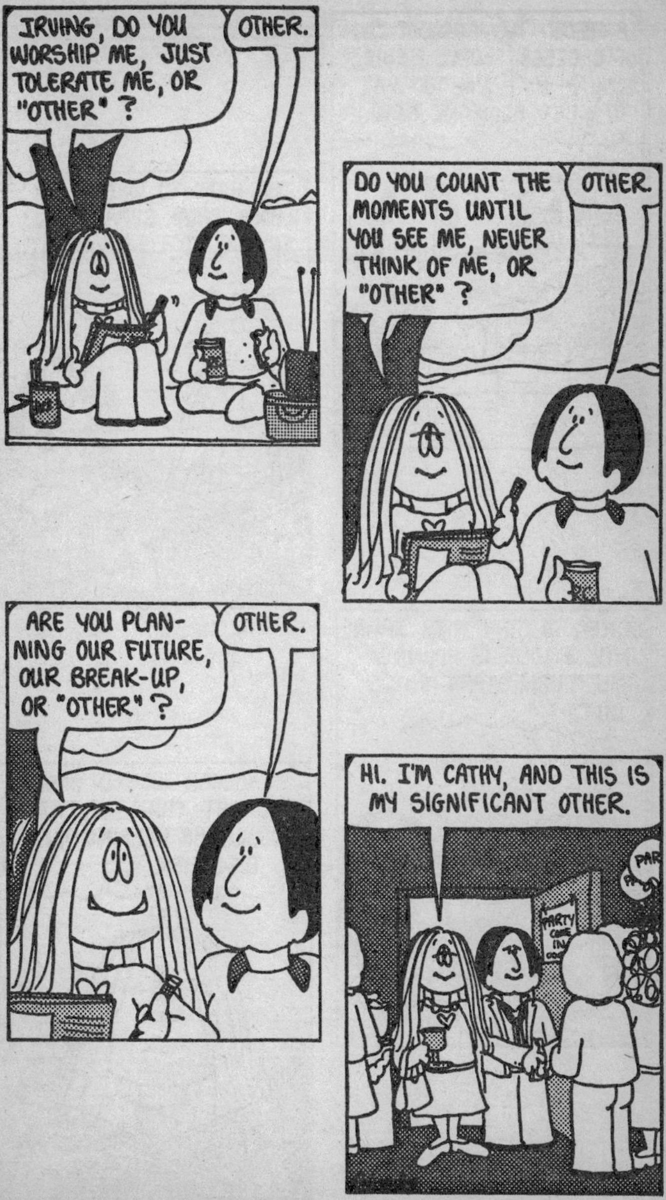
IRVING, DO YOU WORSHIP ME, JUST TOLERATE ME, OR "OTHER"?
OTHER.
DO YOU COUNT THE MOMENTS UNTIL YOU SEE ME, NEVER THINK OF ME, OR "OTHER"?
OTHER.
ARE YOU PLANNING OUR FUTURE, OUR BREAK-UP, OR "OTHER"?
OTHER.
HI. I'M CATHY, AND THIS IS MY SIGNIFICANT OTHER.
PARTY

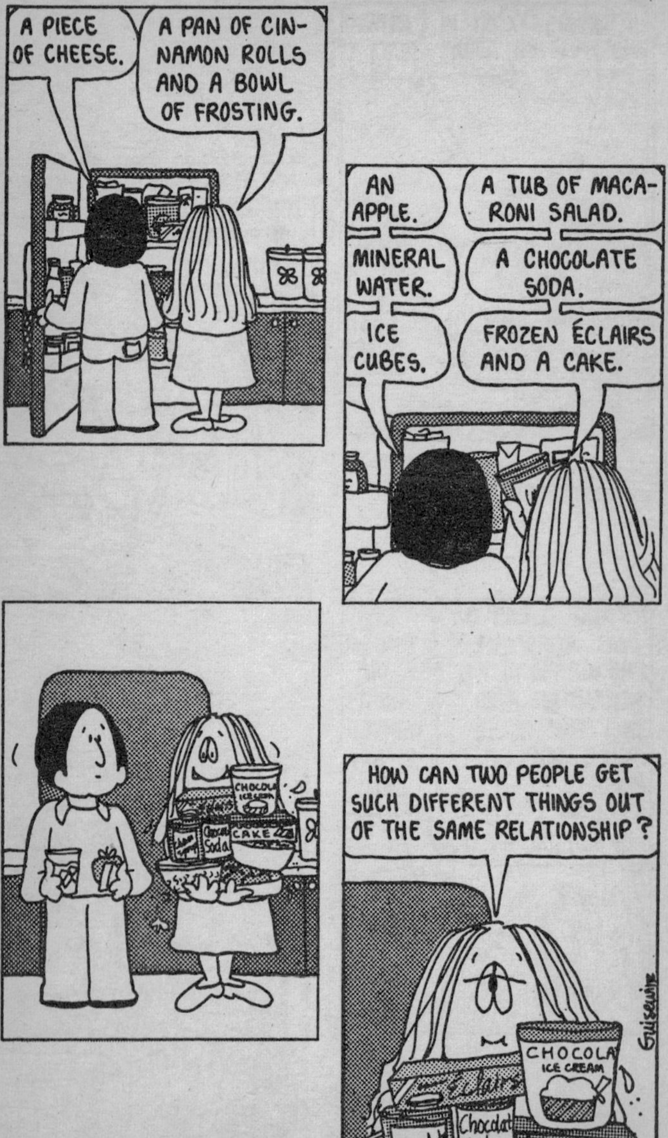
A PIECE OF CHEESE.
A PAN OF CIN-NAMON ROLLS AND A BOWL OF FROSTING.
AN APPLE.
A TUB OF MACA-RONI SALAD.
MINERAL WATER.
A CHOCOLATE SODA.
ICE CUBES.
FROZEN ÉCLAIRS AND A CAKE.
CAKE
HOW CAN TWO PEOPLE GET SUCH DIFFERENT THINGS OUT OF THE SAME RELATIONSHIP?
CHOCOLA
ICE CREAM
Chocolate Syrup
Chocolate Soda
CAKE
GUISEWITE

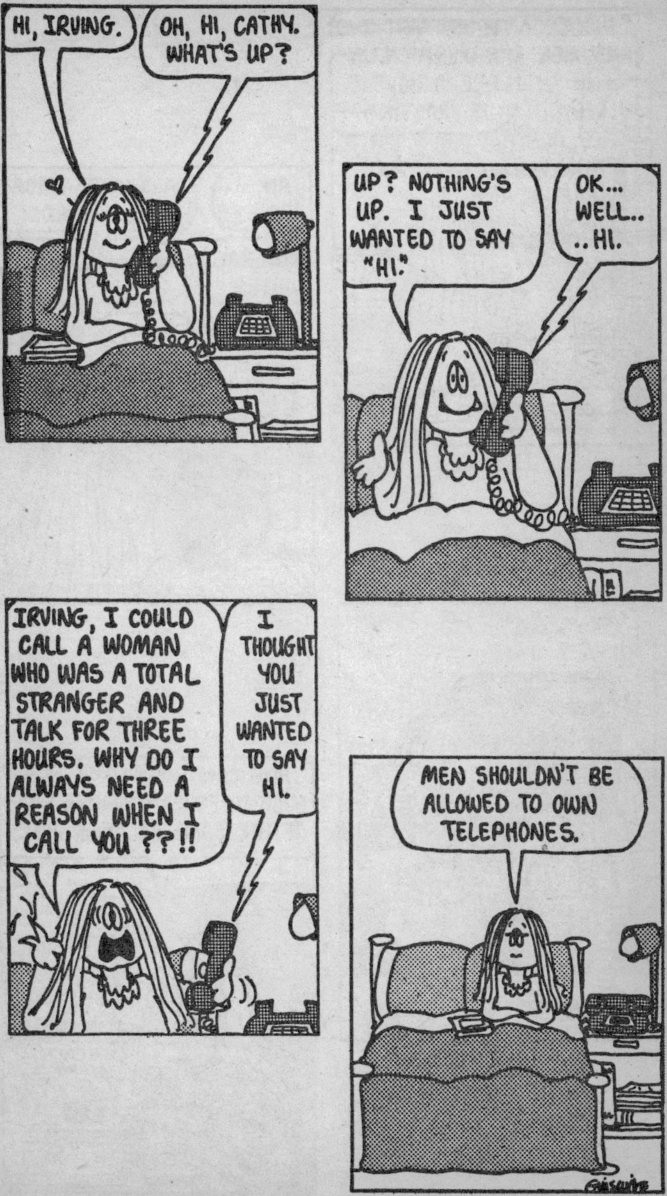
HI, IRVING.
OH, HI, CATHY. WHAT'S UP?
UP? NOTHING'S UP. I JUST WANTED TO SAY "HI."
OK... WELL.. ..HI.
IRVING, I COULD CALL A WOMAN WHO WAS A TOTAL STRANGER AND TALK FOR THREE HOURS. WHY DO I ALWAYS NEED A REASON WHEN I CALL YOU ??!!
I THOUGHT YOU JUST WANTED TO SAY HI.
MEN SHOULDN'T BE ALLOWED TO OWN TELEPHONES.

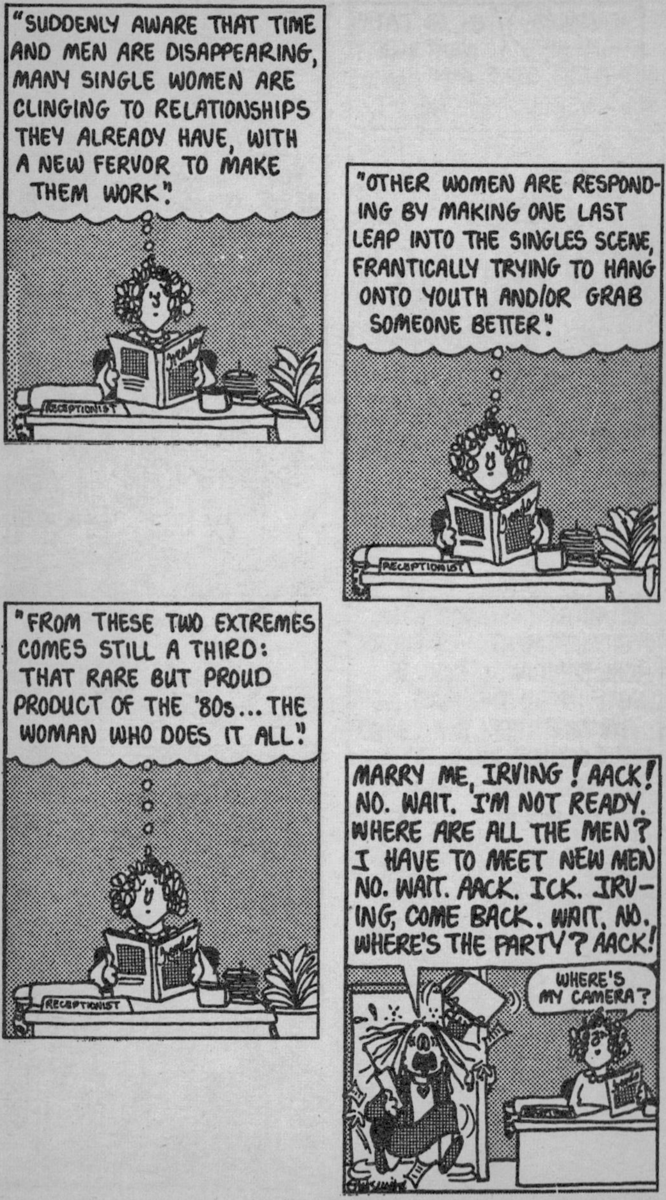
"SUDDENLY AWARE THAT TIME AND MEN ARE DISAPPEARING, MANY SINGLE WOMEN ARE CLINGING TO RELATIONSHIPS THEY ALREADY HAVE, WITH A NEW FERVOR TO MAKE THEM WORK."
RECEPTIONIST
"OTHER WOMEN ARE RESPONDING BY MAKING ONE LAST LEAP INTO THE SINGLES SCENE, FRANTICALLY TRYING TO HANG ONTO YOUTH AND/OR GRAB SOMEONE BETTER."
RECEPTIONIST
"FROM THESE TWO EXTREMES COMES STILL A THIRD: THAT RARE BUT PROUD PRODUCT OF THE '80s... THE WOMAN WHO DOES IT ALL."
RECEPTIONIST
MARRY ME, IRVING! AACK! NO. WAIT. I'M NOT READY. WHERE ARE ALL THE MEN? I HAVE TO MEET NEW MEN NO. WAIT. AACK. ICK. IRVING, COME BACK. WAIT. NO. WHERE'S THE PARTY? AACK!
WHERE'S MY CAMERA?

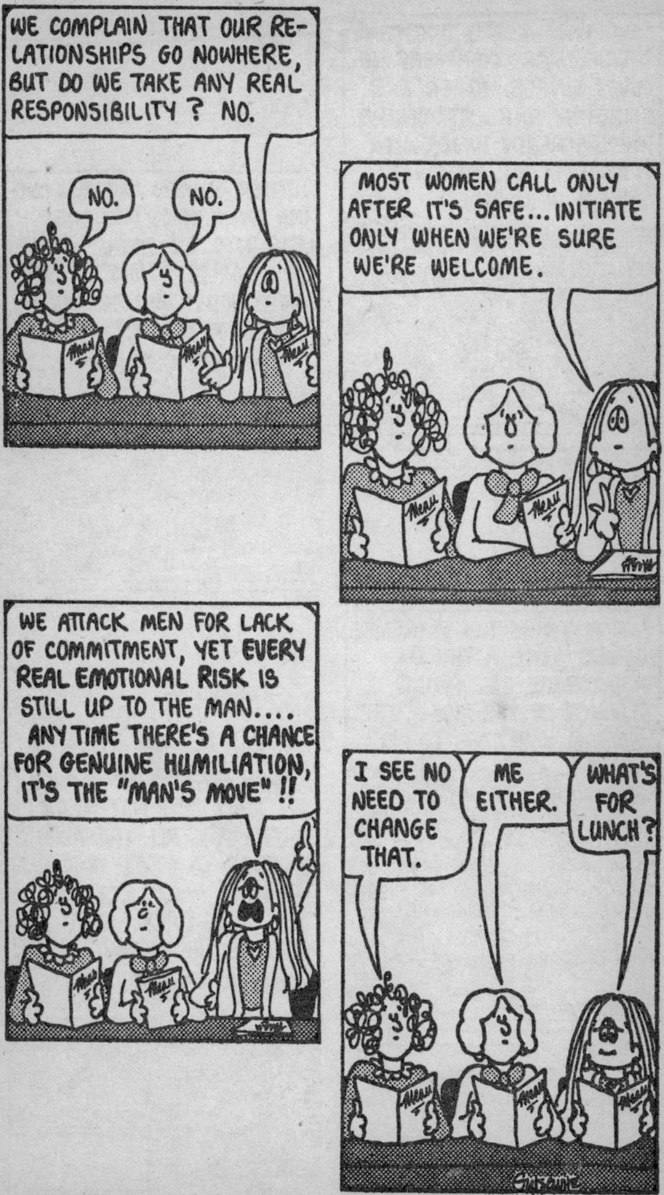
WE COMPLAIN THAT OUR RELATIONSHIPS GO NOWHERE, BUT DO WE TAKE ANY REAL RESPONSIBILITY? NO.
NO.
NO.
MOST WOMEN CALL ONLY AFTER IT'S SAFE... INITIATE ONLY WHEN WE'RE SURE WE'RE WELCOME.
WE ATTACK MEN FOR LACK OF COMMITMENT, YET EVERY REAL EMOTIONAL RISK IS STILL UP TO THE MAN.... ANY TIME THERE'S A CHANCE FOR GENUINE HUMILIATION, IT'S THE "MAN'S MOVE"!!
I SEE NO NEED TO CHANGE THAT.
ME EITHER.
WHAT'S FOR LUNCH?
Guisewite